Genders and Sexualitie

Series Editors
John Arnold
King's College
University of Cambridge
Cambridge, UK

Sean Brady
Birkbeck College
University of London
London, UK

Joanna Bourke
Birkbeck College
University of London
London, UK

Palgrave Macmillan's series, Genders and Sexualities in History, accommodates and fosters new approaches to historical research in the fields of genders and sexualities. The series promotes world-class scholarship, which concentrates upon the interconnected themes of genders, sexualities, religions/religiosity, civil society, politics and war.

Historical studies of gender and sexuality have, until recently, been more or less disconnected fields. In recent years, historical analyses of genders and sexualities have synthesised, creating new departures in historiography. The additional connectedness of genders and sexualities with questions of religion, religiosity, development of civil societies, politics and the contexts of war and conflict is reflective of the movements in scholarship away from narrow history of science and scientific thought, and history of legal processes approaches, that have dominated these paradigms until recently. The series brings together scholarship from Contemporary, Modern, Early Modern, Medieval, Classical and Non-Western History. The series provides a diachronic forum for scholarship that incorporates new approaches to genders and sexualities in history.

More information about this series at
http://www.springer.com/series/15000

Linsey Robb · Juliette Pattinson
Editors

Men, Masculinities and Male Culture in the Second World War

Editors
Linsey Robb
Northumbria University
Newcastle Upon Tyne, UK

Juliette Pattinson
University of Kent
Canterbury, UK

Genders and Sexualities in History
ISBN 978-1-349-95787-3   ISBN 978-1-349-95290-8   (eBook)
https://doi.org/10.1057/978-1-349-95290-8

This Palgrave Macmillan imprint is published by Springer Nature
The registered company is Macmillan Publishers Ltd.
The registered company address is: The Campus, 4 Crinan Street, London, N1 9XW,
United Kingdom

FOREWORD

I have always been fascinated by the experience of the Second World War in Britain. Born in 1956, my earliest memories are imbued with fragmented traces of the war—the Doncaster bombsite a block away from our new-build council house; the otherness of my mother's German dress-maker, blonde-haired where my mother's was black—and a sense of unsettling proximity to something vaguely threatening. Growing up, there were the war stories of boyhood culture: the heroic films of land, sea and air war on TV, and my weekly comic, *The Victor*, whose staple ingredient was Second World War combat stories celebrating manly deeds of British military prowess.

I also grew up with a different kind of war story: that of my parents, who lived through the war as teenagers. In 1982, I recorded their memories of this decisive epoch in their lives. As a boy himself, my father, Frank Dawson, was enthralled by the romantic cult of the aeroplane. On reaching 18 in March 1944, he passed the RAF's aptitude tests and was accepted for training as a pilot. 'From fourteen [...] I'd been four and a half years preparing for this [...] It was the joy of my life, I couldn't get there quick enough to become a pilot. The thought of being killed, or the fighting, it just didn't [...] It was so childish, really, the whole thing was [...] just the opportunity to be able to fly and pilot an aeroplane, a Spitfire, it didn't matter what [...] And then the horror of the Army!' The disappointment when he ended up in the 'bloody infantry' was a 'shattering blow', but: 'You don't know, it may have turned out for the good. At least I finished up here.' In the Army, his draft for active service overseas kept being deferred, and meanwhile he was able to wangle himself a desk-job: 'I never did go. I finished up working my way out of the draft system into the office, where I was posting clerk, putting other people on draft. [...] When I realized that the number was catching up on me, and I was going to get clobbered myself, I posted myself to a Civil Resettlement Unit for returning soldiers.' For my father, being a desk-bound clerk was the next best thing to being a pilot, given the tangible dangers known to await an infantry soldier posted overseas, evoked especially in news from Burma. Tracing a winding trajectory that takes him from heedless pilot fantasies to the first steps towards his future teaching career in the Army Education Corps, interwoven with courtship and marriage (he was handsome in Army uniform) as a 20-year-old in 1946, my father told his singularly unheroic story with satisfaction and some pride at his youthful working-class resourcefulness in the face of what 'they' want to do with you.

Until the early 1980s, stories like my father's about everyday lives in wartime were largely invisible in British public memory, which focused on celebrating the mythic fighting nation with its Blitz spirit, united behind its totemic leader, Churchill. Pete Grafton's oral history, *You, You and You! The People Out of Step with World War Two* (1981), was one early intervention that challenged this narrowly patriotic frame and created space for experiential stories of lives lived in more complex relations to the war effort. The interview that I did with my parents in April 1982 as a budding oral historian motivated by my Ph.D. research, which began as an investigation into the popular memory of the Second World War in Britain, its current politics and relationship to the conflicting frameworks of meanings generated during the war itself. Very little work existed at that time on the everyday social history and popular culture of wartime Britain, and Angus Calder's *The People's War* (1969) remained the only major study and principal reference point. I planned and researched case studies on Spitfire pilot biographies, Mass-Observation's directives, the radical politics of 'the war to win the war', the history, memory and commemoration of Dunkirk and the Blitz, and asked questions such as 'What does Britain mean to you?'.

However, in the new political context created by the Falklands–Malvinas War of April to June 1982—for which popular support was secured in a language permeated by rhetoric and slogans from the invasion scare of 1940 that cast Prime Minister Thatcher as a Churchillian leader of democratic Britain standing firm against the fascists—most of this research was never finished or written up. Instead, my Ph.D. research became reoriented to trace a longer cultural history of the intersection between war, masculinity and British popular national identity, and the continuities and shifts in a hegemonic formation connecting the moment of 1982 not only with the 1940s but with Victorian popular imperialism. This thesis, submitted in the context of another British 'post-colonial' war in 1991, developed into my monograph *Soldier Heroes: British Adventure, Empire and the Imagining of Masculinities* (1994).

Soldier Heroes was shaped by my anti-war activism of the 1980s and 1990s, but was also rooted in my boyhood experience growing up in the cultural aftermath of the Second World War. In an autobiographical case study it reflects explicitly on these two moments and the relation between them. This study uses personal memory to investigate how stories about the soldier as hero, constructed and circulated by a historically specific 'popular masculine pleasure-culture of war', are taken into the imaginative world of boys, where they provide a basis for gendered self-identification and a means of securing social recognition as properly masculine. Soldiers' stories from the Second World War are seen to furnish transgenerational imaginative forms of masculinity that inform gender identifications made by post-war children. In other respects, the Second World War is an absent centre in a book that traces a history of these imaginative forms back to the hero-making narratives of the Victorian Empire in India and colonial adventures of the First World War in the Middle East. It finds in the telling and retelling of stories about Sir Henry Havelock and Lawrence of Arabia a reproduction of triumphalist imaginings of a British masculinity that is characterised by military virtues and felt to be ideally powerful, superior to others, and free from the domestic attachments and responsibilities which are associated with 'unmanliness' and the risk of denigration as 'sissy' or 'pansy'. Secured through modern forms of adventure narrative predicated on imaginative escape from 'home' into a landscape where quest, encounter and victorious combat may be enacted, imperial soldier heroes of this kind, I argued, were adopted as templates for subsequent imaginings in the context of the 1930s and the Second World War Moreover, their own stories survived in popular cultural production—albeit transformed by engagement with post-colonial realities—well into the 1960s. *Soldier Heroes* proposes that, through this process, the nineteenth-century 'splitting' of masculinities, along a fault-line between the public sphere of adventure and the private sphere of domesticity, is carried into dominant imaginings of masculinity in the later twentieth century, and structures a conflict between contradictory and competing identifications that men and boys must negotiate in their lived experience.

Like the social and cultural history of wartime Britain, the history of masculinity was a largely unexplored terrain in the 1980s. While working on *Soldier Heroes* in 1988–89, I benefited from participation in a reading group (HOMME—the History of Men, Masculinity Etc.) of interdisciplinary scholars in social history, sociology, literature and cultural studies brought together by John Tosh and Michael Roper to begin the task—articulated in the introduction to their ensuing collection, *Manful Assertions: Masculinities in Britain since 1800* (1991)—of 'making men visible as gendered subjects'. In refuting essentialist and homogeneous conceptions of a singular masculinity, and advocating focus instead on the plural and changeable forms of masculinities as these intersect with class and 'race', *Manful Assertions* helped to open up a new kind of gender history centred on the historically variable relations established between masculine and feminine, women and men. Itself the product of a specific historical culture of masculinity that was at once open to being problematised politically by feminist critique but also sought out the space for alternative or transformative practice, the book moved beyond a 'social roles' approach to consider the relations between patriarchal structures of power and men's experiences, to investigate contradictions between the institutional realities of men's lives and their desires and expectations, and to explore how cultural representations of dominant and subordinate masculinity are negotiated subjectively. My own contribution introduced a distinction between 'the representation of masculinities in images and narratives' and 'the complexities of any such identity as it is lived out amidst the contradictory demands and recognitions [... in] actual social relations.' I argued that representations of the soldier as hero construct an idealised form of masculinity, powerful because free of such lived contradictions and conflicts, that men inhabit subjectively and strive to emulate in reality by becoming the man they wish to be. This relation between 'imagined' and 'lived' gender identities is encapsulated in the first, and most widely quoted, sentence in *Soldier Heroes*: 'Masculinities are lived out in the flesh, but fashioned in the imagination.'

I have been honoured by the invitation from Linsey Robb and Juliette Pattinson to write this Foreword to their excellent edited collection, and by finding that my own work is still proving to be a useful reference point in new history-writing about masculinities in wartime. *Men, Masculinities and Male Culture in the Second World War* is a long over-due book but in many ways is the stronger for it, as a product of the cultural and social history of gender which has blossomed since the 1990s. Not only in the editors' fine Introduction, but throughout the book, the fresh thinking developed in these new studies is rooted firmly and critically within the histories and traditions of scholarship from which it has emerged, whilst extending the reach and depth of the field. The editors and contributors situate themselves in relation to, and build on, what is now an accumulating literature exploring the significance of the two world wars for the history of masculinities in the twentieth century. The collection offers a wide-ranging account of the multiple ways of being a man in Britain during the Second World War, embracing civilian as well as military masculinities in their co-existence within and across theatres of combat and the Home Front. Whilst recognising the particular imaginative grip exerted by the hegemonic masculinity of soldier heroes during wartime, the book paints a highly nuanced picture of, and enables usefully comparative reflection about, the variety of ways in which men experienced, lived with, and—like my father—found ways of contesting or at least negotiating its pressures.

This book also benefits from the rich array of critical tools now available to explore the power relations and practices that constitute different forms of masculinity, through subjection to regulatory institutional structures and their mediating discourses but also by the exercise of agency, including resistance to the dominant. One notable advance is its emphasis on embodiment, informed by disability history, the history of emotions and queer thinking about performativity, to explore the wounded or malfunctioning body and expose assumptions about 'normal' manliness. (It has been said that, for all its insistence on masculinities being 'lived out in the flesh', there are no bodies in *Soldier Heroes*.) One resonant phrase echoing throughout this book is 'emasculation', a concept that identifies the exclusionary and demoralising effects of hegemonic masculine identities which are not attainable by all men but establish the measure of their subordination. Yet *Men, Masculinities and Male Culture in the Second World War* is also permeated by questions of subversion, unsettlement, challenge, contestation, the seeking of control and the assertion of alternatives. The use of oral history and life writing to populate the book with the voices of men from the Second World War or who remember their wartime lives subsequently, is especially striking.

This is a book engaged with questions of cultural memory as well as history. It emerges at a poignant time, as the generation of men who lived through the Second World War begins to pass away, taking with it the living memory of wartime experience. As we've seen in the case of the First World War, such a transition may also generate new kinds of interest in the lives and experiences of our antecedents within a gendered world that is in some ways familiar but also challengingly different. In 2017, the end of the Second World War is twice as distant in historical time as it was in 1982 when I interviewed my father. Yet through inter- and transgenerational relationships, enacted in families but also in many other arenas, new temporal connections, legacies, and links are continually being made and remade. Through the multiple ways it engages with and speaks to the unfinished history of men, masculinities and male culture, this book provides a valuable resource for future conversations not only about gender and the Second World War, but also about the complex temporal existence of this significant 'past'.

Graham Dawson

Series Editors' Preface

The history of masculinity and military conflict is one of the most dynamic fields in war studies. Juliette Pattinson and Linsey Robb's volume entitled *Masculinities at War: Men and Male Culture in the Second World War* is a particularly exciting contribution to this literature because it integrates analyses of civilian masculinities with front-line ones. Focusing on the British experience of the Second World War, contributors to this volume explore combat masculinities, fantasies of heroism and resistance, fear of mutilation and death, male bonding, prisoners of war, civilian bodies, scientific masculinities at Bletchley Park, and commemorative practices involving civilian men. All the chapters are grounded in recent theoretical insights into masculinity. They provide the most convincing evidence of the power of masculine ideals in shaping men's sense of self. In common with all the volumes in the 'Gender and Sexualities in History' series, *Masculinities at War* is a multifaceted and meticulously researched scholarly study. It is an exciting contribution to our understanding of gender and sexuality in the past.

John Arnold, Joanna Bourke, Sean Brady

ACKNOWLEDGEMENTS

This collection emerged from a symposium, 'Masculinities at War', held at the Scottish Oral History Centre at the University of Strathclyde in January 2015. This vibrant and engaging symposium produced many stimulating conversations and debates which have undoubtedly under-pinned the chapters produced here. Accordingly, we would like to thank all the speakers and attendees. For Linsey Robb, Juliette Pattinson and fellow contributor Arthur McIvor, the symposium also marked the end of an Arts and Humanities Research Council (AHRC)-funded project entitled 'Masculinities Challenged?', a large-scale oral history study capturing the memories of men in reserved occupations during the Second World War. The research undertaken for the co-authored book forms the basis of both McIvor's and Robb's chapters in this collection. Moreover, the grant funded the symposium. We would therefore like to express our gratitude to the AHRC for their generosity. We would also like to thank the contributors to this volume who have produced insightful chapters. It has been a pleasure to work with them. Finally, we would like to thank Emily Russell and Carmel Kennedy of Palgrave Macmillan for their hard work in helping us assemble this collection.

Contents

Editors and Contributors

About the Editors

Linsey Robb is Lecturer in History at Northumbria University, UK, and a social and cultural historian specialising in the study of gender in the Second World War. Key publications include *Men at Work* (Palgrave, 2015), and *Men in Reserve* (2017), co-authored with Juliette Pattinson and Arthur McIvor. She is currently researching British conscientious objection during the Second World War.

Juliette Pattinson is Reader at the University of Kent, UK, and a gender historian specialising in the Second World War. Key publications include *Behind Enemy Lines* (2007), *Men in Reserve* (2017) and three co-edited collections: *Fighting for Britain?* (2015), *British Cultural Memory and the Second World War* (2014) and *War in a Twilight World* (2010).

Contributors

Frances Houghton specialises in the military, war, memory, and personal testimony during the twentieth century. She is currently working as Lecturer in Modern British History at the University of Manchester, and is writing a monograph that addresses British veteran memoirs of the Second World War.

Arthur McIvor is Professor of Social History and Director of the Scottish Oral History Centre at the University of Strathclyde. His publications include *Working Lives* (2013) and, with Juliette Pattinson and Linsey Robb, *Men in Reserve* (2017). He is currently working on a book on occupational health and safety during the Second World War.

Clare Makepeace is an Honorary Research Fellow at Birkbeck College, University of London. Her research on British servicemen's experiences in the two world wars appears in numerous academic publications, as well as *History Today*, the *Daily Mail* and *BBC News Online*. She is the author of *Captives of War: British Prisoners of War in Europe in the Second World War* (2017).

Emma Newlands is a Lecturer in History at the University of Strathclyde. Her first monograph, *Civilians into Soldiers: War the Body and British Army Recruits, 1939–45* (2013).

Corinna Peniston-Bird is a Senior Lecturer in Cultural History in the Department of History at Lancaster University. Since 1998 her research and teaching has centred on gender dynamics in Britain in the world wars, with an emphasis on the relationship between memories and cultural representations. Previous publications on commemoration include 'The People's War in Personal Testimony and Bronze: Sorority and the Memorial to The Women of World War II', in Lucy Noakes and Juliette Pattinson (eds), *British Cultural Memory and the Second World War* (2013); 'All in it Together and Backs to the wall': Relating Patriotism and the People's War in the 21st Century' in the journal *Oral History*, (2012); and the co-edited special issue, with Wendy Ugolini, of *Journal of War and Culture Studies* 'Silenced Mourning' (2014). She has recently co-edited, with Emma Vickers, *Gender and the Second World War: Lessons of War* (2017).

Chris Smith who is a Lecturer in History at Coventry University, is a social and cultural historian with particular interest in Britain's intelligence services. His first monograph, *The Hidden History of Bletchley Park*, was published in 2015. He is currently writing a biography of the Soviet mole John Cairncross.

ABBREVIATIONS

AHRC   Arts and Humanities Research Council
ATS   Auxiliary Territorial Service
AWOL   Absent Without Leave
BCRA   Bureau Central de Renseignements et d'Action
CIA   Central Intelligence Agency
CO   conscientious objector
GC&CS   Government Code and Cypher School
IRA   Irish Republican Army
IWM   Imperial War Museum
NCO   non-commissioned officer
OSS   Office of Strategic Services
POW   prisoner of war
RAF   Royal Air Force
RFC   Royal Flying Corps
RoSPA   Royal Society for the Prevention of Accidents
SAB   Student Assessment Board
SOE   Special Operations Executive
SIS   Secret Intelligence Service
VC   Victoria Cross
WAAF   Women's Auxiliary Air Force
YMCA   Young Men's Christian Association

LIST OF FIGURES

CHAPTER 1

Becoming Visible: Gendering the Study of Men at War

Linsey Robb and Juliette Pattinson

The Way Ahead (Carol Reed, 1944), released in cinemas in June 1944 with an all-star cast, followed a group of British conscript soldiers as they navigated training and experienced torpedo fire, and subsequent sinking, at sea before culminating in battle in North Africa. The recruits grumble and grouse throughout their training and wilfully allow themselves to be captured while on an exercise scheme in order to return prematurely to the barracks where beds and hot food awaited them. However, in the face of danger the men are proven to be competent and brave soldiers. In the closing minutes of the film Lieutenant Jim Perry, played by real-life soldier David Niven, defiantly tells German soldiers, who are offering them the opportunity to surrender during a respite from attack, to 'go to hell' before leading his men forward to battle. As the men fix

L. Robb (✉)
Northumbria University, Newcastle Upon Tyne, UK
e-mail: linsey.robb@northumbria.ac.uk

J. Pattinson
University of Kent, Canterbury, Kent, UK
e-mail: J.Pattinson@kent.ac.uk

© The Author(s) 2018
L. Robb and J. Pattinson (eds.), *Men, Masculinities and Male Culture in the Second World War*, Genders and Sexualities in History,
https://doi.org/ 10.1057/978-1-349-95290-8_1

1

bayonets and ready themselves for action they mock both the situation and each other, asking if they 'have enough to grumble about' and complaining of being hungry. Before they move from their sheltered position Sergeant Fletcher, played by William Hartnell, rallies them by jesting 'come on lads. Once more for the day you missed on the exercise.' The men walk resolutely towards the enemy to the sound of a military brass band playing an upbeat tune. Their fate is left unknown as they disappear one by one into the smoke-strewn battlefield, but while this is the last scene of the film, the audience are informed by a title card that this is 'The Beginning'.

In many respects, *The Way Ahead* is typical of the British war film. The men are a cross-section of British society: an older ill-tempered cockney working as a boiler stoker in the House of Commons, who has a grown-up assertive daughter; a young malingerer and complainer; a Scottish farmer; a conceited youthful man who drinks too much; an enthusiastic travel agent; a middle-class store manager and his younger and deferential colleague; a tough working-class sergeant; and a married upper middle-class officer with a received pronunciation accent. This was a common trope in war films, such as *In Which We Serve* (Noel Coward, 1942), *San Demetrio, London* (Charles Frend, 1943), *The Gentle Sex* (Leslie Howard, 1943) and *Millions Like Us* (Sidney Gilliat and Frank Launder, 1943), which all brought together disparate characters from a range of class backgrounds, ages and regions across Britain, albeit never Northern Ireland, and charted over the course of the film their emergence as a functioning cohesive group. This narrative premise was crucial in emphasising the unity of the country in fighting a 'People's War'. Also in common with other war films, notably *We Dive at Dawn* (Anthony Asquith, 1943), the men in *The Way Ahead* overcome initial animosity and competing tensions to become comrades and 'pull together' effectively in the face of battle. The emphasis on the homosocial aspect of the military was common throughout wartime society. Indeed, a 1940 guide entitled *Joining Up* instructed its readers, 'whatever branch of the Service you eventually find yourself in is an honourable one and you'll find good pals there'. And this sentiment even extended to uniformed quasi-military civilian organisations, with Sir James Grigg, the Under-Secretary of State for War, calling the Home Guard a 'brotherhood'.[1] Another persistent trope of British masculinity documented in *The Way Ahead*, and many other wartime films such as *San Demetrio, London*, was the ability to 'keep smiling through' and joke in the face of danger.

Wartime films, like *The Way Ahead*, are in many ways formulaic, with common themes repeated frequently. These ideas, in turn, have come to shape the popular memory of the war. Indeed, the narrative of Britain as a nation of plucky underdogs who stood united together, laughing in the face of the much more powerful Nazi war machine, has gained huge traction in modern Britain. These repeated patterns of representation, regardless of the branch of the armed forces, suggest that military service was a very homogeneous experience. However, war is inevitably a point of rupture. The Second World War was no different: men were allowed, and even encouraged, to kill; women took on previously inconceivable roles in the military and civilian sphere; even children were taken from their parents to be raised by others in areas far from home. Such acts shifted seemingly inviolable social codes. Inevitably, then, there were also shifts in idealised conceptions of malehood. Moreover, as the military expanded massively and rapidly, many men found themselves in new overwhelmingly male environs. In many ways this makes war an ideal moment to examine male cultural practices as the epitome of manly duty and masculinity became singularly focused on the military. Indeed, as Corinna Peniston-Bird argues, 'opportunities for contradiction, transformation and resistance were limited. Men did not have a choice whether to conform or reject hegemonic [military] masculinity: they positioned themselves in relation to it.'[2] However, as this collection shows, the male wartime experience was far from singular: the war was experienced differently by the spitfire ace based in Britain, the army serviceman stationed on the home front, the skilled worker retained in his civilian employment, the soldier who engaged in land combat overseas, the paramilitary fighter who undertook guerrilla operations, the combatant who was made a prisoner of war and the man who sustained disabling injuries. Moreover, these diverse experiences shaped not only men's retrospective memories of their wartime lives, produced in oral history interviews and memoirs, but also the ways in which they have been remembered in post-war society, commemorated and immortalised in print, film and stone. Clearly, therefore, despite the enduring popularity of the war film with its rigid one-dimensional representation of masculinity, being a British man during the Second World War could involve a broad range of roles, challenges and activities which had diverse effects on men's sense of self. As such, this collection explores the myriad ways war impacted on British men, masculinity and male culture. It reveals that masculine desires for war service were complex and challenging; that manliness could be forged in the workplace and in the field of battle but that emasculation nearly always haunted wartime performances of masculinity; that all-male groups fostered their own renderings of masculinity that were specific to a given context and could be looked on as perplexing by outsiders; and that many post-war representations of wartime service, in contrast to lived experiences, often became simplified and lacked nuance. All of the chapters exploring men's wartime experiences engage with highly personal subjective accounts: oral testimonies and written memoirs enable the authors to reconstruct in very rich detail the lived experiences of British men during the Second World War. This introduction chapter surveys some of the key developments in the field of gender history over the last forty years in order to locate this collection in the wider context of the project to make visible men's gendered lives.

TOWARDS A GENDERED STUDY OF MEN: MAKING MASCULINITIES VISIBLE

Histories of men dominate bookshelves: thousands of studies have been published about kings, politicians, imperial adventurers, revolutionaries, inventors, warriors and sportsmen. Yet analysing men's experiences through the adoption of a gendered perspective is very much a late twentieth-century phenomenon. The history of masculinity was preceded by, and developed out of, the field of women's history. It was in the late 1960s and early 1970s that the discipline of women's history bloomed alongside the new social history and as a direct consequence of a growing mass 'second-wave' feminist movement. A key focus of such enquiry was to recover a 'herstory', providing a corrective to centuries of androcentric scholarship, or *his*tories, which erased women as historical agents. This was 'Men's Studies Modified', in which women, the ahistorical 'Other' positioned on the margins outside of history, were placed centre stage.[3] The titles of texts such as Sheila Rowbotham's *Hidden From History* (1973) and Renate Bridenthal and Claudia Koonz's *Becoming Visible* (1977), were explicit affirmations of the endeavour of restoring women to the historical record.[4] The ideology of 'separate spheres', which located women in the domestic arena and men in the public realm of work, politics and war, was a useful, although later critiqued, discourse for those researching women's lives since the 1750s.[5] It enabled historians of women to move beyond the recovery phase towards a proclamation of the significance of gender as an organising principle within a class society.

While the primary focus of most historians of women was, quite obviously and unapologetically, women, some advocated a relational view of gender, noting that women ought not be studied in isolation. Natalie Zemon Davis, for example, argued in 1976 that 'we should now be interested in the history of both women and men. We should not be working on the subjected sex any more than a historian of class can focus exclusively on peasants.'[6] The discipline of women's history developed into, but was not eradicated by, the emergent field of gender history which foregrounded the social constructedness of femininity and masculinity, which were defined in relation to each other. Joan Wallach Scott, who argued in 1986 that the focus on *herstory* actively ghettoised women's history, urged a new way of writing about historical women. She asserted that gender was a more 'useful category of historical analysis' and in so doing, shifted the paradigm.[7] Noting that historians have too often conflated sex, the fixed biological assignation, and gender, a fluid and socially constructed set of behaviours, Scott deconstructed the term 'woman', focusing on the differences, rather than commonalities, between women. She advocated an examination of language and discourse in which gender takes shape so as to acknowledge a multiplicity of ideas and change over time. Within a couple of years of Scott's landmark article being published, the journal *Gender and History* was founded, its first issue produced in 1989.

Central to gender history has been an examination of the workings of femininity and masculinity using theoretical concepts from post-structuralism, post-modernism and queer theory, all of which have pushed the discipline in exciting new directions.[8] Gender historians have reinvigorated labour history, have embraced the linguistic turn and also the cultural turn, and have utilised a range of methodologies including oral history, film analysis and census data as well as traditional archived material.

Gender is not something that only women and girls inhabit and there was a growing recognition that, in many ways, it was men that had no (gendered) history and were barely visible in historical accounts. In 1987, Harry Brod made the 'case for Men's Studies', one that was to be informed by the critical theories that had underpinned Women's Studies and rooted in feminist scholarship.[9] This was because, as Michael Kimmel noted:

[V]irtually every history book is a history of men ... But these books feel strangely empty at their centers, where the discussion of men should be. Books about men are not about men as men. These books do not explore how the experience of being a man structured the men's lives, or the organizations and institutions they created, the events in which they participated. American men have no history as gendered selves; no work describes historical events in terms of what these events meant to the men who participated in them as men.[10]

Kimmel argued that to write a history of men *as men* required an assessment of the ways in which the construction and experience of manhood shaped the meanings of men's actions across time and different classes. In Britain, masculinity had begun to emerge as a 'useful category of historical analysis' in the early 1980s. The first books to adopt a gender lens to examine men's lives paralleled the early women's histories in that many focused on single-sex institutions. These homosocial domains were bastions of male culture and expressly excluded women. Studies examined how public schools and youth groups (including the Scouts and Boys' Brigade) understood manliness and the ways in which they socialised boys into adopting appropriate manly codes of behaviour.[11] Indeed, the overt focus of such works was 'manliness', as made evident in the title of J.A. Mangan and James Walvin's edited collection *Manliness and Morality*.[12] However, as Mark C. Carnes and Clyde Griffen note, these studies were often 'top downward' and assumed that men, regardless of class, possess a shared notion of what constitutes 'manliness'.[13] In examining the lives of boys and men in the public domain, these works unconsciously employed the discourse of separate spheres ideology that pioneer women's historians had found so persuasive. In doing so, they placed men outside of the domestic arena and entirely ignored men's interactions with women in the home. John Tosh was one historian who sought to move beyond homosocial locales and site men in the private sphere. He produced a number of articles recovering men's domestic lives, revealing supportive husbands and emotionally engaged fathers.[14]

Early historical works explicitly exploring masculinities sought to problematise the male experience, to show that in all regards men's lives were also historically shaped by gender. As Michael Roper and John Tosh asserted in 1991 in their introduction to *Manful Assertions*, 'Our aim is to demonstrate that masculinity has a history; that is subject to change and varied in its forms.'[15] They laid the foundation for historicising masculinity, calling for it to be examined not just as a cultural construction, but also as a subjective identity. Indeed, their ground-breaking collection examined a broad range of male experiences, including domestic life, religious beliefs, warfare and the purchase of consumer goods, all through the lens of masculinity. Histories began to be produced in which masculinity was understood to intersect with other aspects of identity, to be constituted by, as well as constitutive of, a broad range of social relations, including ethnicity, race, class, religion, sexuality, (dis)ability, nation and region. Indeed, there is now a booming research field examining historical masculinities through a broad range of lenses. The field has moved on from its origins of uncovering idealised codes of manliness and has achieved a fuller articulation of what it meant to be a man by providing nuanced examinations of masculinity as a lived experience and the fashioning of masculine subjectivities. There has been a remarkably rich abundance of texts on masculinity.[16] Perhaps the most influential theorist in this field has been R.W. Connell Drawing on the works of Italian Marxist theorist Antonio Gramsci, Connell uses the term 'hegemonic' to explain how a particular group claims and maintains a dominant social position. Connell asserts that in any culture, one mode of masculinity is more highly esteemed than other marginalised and subordinated forms. Masculinity, Connell argues, is not singular: we should then talk in term of masculin*ies*. Moreover, masculine ideals are shaped by factors including, but not limited to, race, class, sexuality, nationality and occupation. And despite some criticisms to the contrary, Connell highlights that masculine ideals are temporally, as well as culturally, specific, fluid and subject to change. While there is a singular cultural masculine ideal at any specific moment, other forms of masculinity exist in relation to it. Connell delineates three key forms of non-idealised masculinity: 'subordinate masculinity', which in the late twentieth century could be epitomised by homosexuality; 'complicit masculinity', which denotes the majority of men who do not necessarily embody the idealised form, as few men do, but who subscribe to the ideals and reap the rewards of patriarchy; and 'marginalised masculinity', such as non-white masculinity.[17] While not universally accepted,[18] Connell's notion of masculinities as plural and relational have been deeply influential, especially to historians of the Second World War.

This has not always been the case, however. In a review of the state of masculinity studies in 2002, Martin Francis asserted that few scholars of masculinity had written about the two world wars: 'It is hoped that historians will be more eager in future to explore this critical period for the mapping of the changing configurations of twentieth-century British masculinity.'[19] Similarly, in 2008, he noted 'a critical lacuna in the historiography of modern British masculinity' regarding the Second World War.[20] Francis's wish for more studies to address the omission proved to be highly prescient.

MAPPING SECOND WORLD WAR MASCULINITIES

While Francis called for more studies to be undertaken foregrounding masculine identities during the Second World War, this conflict is not without scholarly attention: over the previous seven decades, millions of words of analysis and debate had been produced. In one sense, as with history writing in general, men had been implicitly at the heart of such discussions. Early accounts were mainly military in focus, examining strategy, battles and specific combat units.[21] Such histories, by their very nature, excluded women. And by regarding men solely as fighting units, they presented only a partial view of the male experience. Men's emotional reactions to battle and their familial roles as husbands, fathers and sons were omitted. Such military-focused histories also, quite obviously, excluded the men who remained on the home front, regardless of their centrality to the war effort.

More recent studies have taken a 'cultural turn', shifting the focus towards wartime experiences and representations, influenced in particular by feminism and social history. Acknowledging that war is a domain in which meanings about gender are produced, negotiated and circulated, historians have confronted head on the complexities of analysing the instability, fluidity and uncertainty of wartime gender constructions.[22] Many of these new histories centred on women, considering the effects of warfare on the female war worker, the auxiliary service member and the housewife.[23] The gendered male experience of the Second World War has only recently begun to be explored. Perhaps, the most influential text to date regarding masculinities during the Second World War is Sonya Rose's *Which People's War?*[24] This was made evident at the symposium, from which this collection developed, as nearly all speakers engaged with Rose's arguments. She asserts that during the Second World War for any man to embody the idealised form of masculinity, and hence become the model citizen, he had to be under military control.

Moreover, he had to display traditional martial traits such as bravery, strength and heroism. However, in direct comparison to the notion of the cold-blooded Nazi killer, he was also a kind, considerate 'ordinary' British man. Rose synthesises these two distinct ideals into, what she terms, the 'temperate hero':

> In World War II Britain, the nation-at-war was a masculine subject, but this was a temperate masculinity. Combining good humour and kind-liness with heroism and bravery was an unstable mix. Pushed too far in one direction, it could uncomfortably resemble the hyper masculine Nazi enemy. Pushed too far in the other direction, it could slide into effeminacy. In order for men to be judged as good citizens, they needed to demon-strate their virtue by being visibly in the military. It was only then that the components of hegemonic masculinity could cohere.[25]

Rose asserts that those who could not embody this idealised form of masculinity were not considered 'real men'. Such emasculation, and the potential for it, is a central theme in the collection. A number of the chapters deal with the dissonance between idealised forms of male-ness and warfare and the reality of fighting, or indeed not fighting, in a bloody, protracted total war. Moreover, Rose also makes plain this was a very British notion of masculinity, drawn in direct opposition to the hor-rors and violence associated with Nazism.

Indeed, Britishness is a central theme of this edited collection, and the ways national identity interacted with other categories of analysis, specifi-cally gender and class, are paramount.[26] The British men under examina-tion here, those that served in the Jedburghs, the army and the Royal Air Force (RAF), that worked for the Government Code and Cipher School and those that were incarcerated in prisoner of war camps, came from varied class and regional backgrounds. Men were brought together from the four constituent nations of the British Isles and from across the class spectrum to work and live in close proximity. The exception to this among the men in this collection were those in reserved occupations who remained in their own communities and continued to work along-side colleagues who were largely men of their own class and locale. These men were exceptional in other ways too: as Lucy Noakes makes evident, during the Second World War men and women were 'encouraged to identify themselves as members of the nation in very gendered ways: man as soldier and woman as ... war-worker'.[27] But what of the man who was not able to visualise himself in a military uniform? How did he identify himself as part of the nation at war? Perhaps it was through a sense of togetherness and a shared culture, which was considered to be heightened during the war. Thomas Hajkowski terms this the '"we feeling" of belonging to a particular nation'.[28] 1940, more than any other year, was arguably 'the high-water mark of Britishness' in that the evacuation of the British Expeditionary Force from Dunkirk, the Battle of Britain and the Blitz, as well as the formation of the Local Defence Volunteers, later renamed the Home Guard, were thought to override class and regional tensions. Nevertheless, this notion of what it meant to be British was resilient, enduring steadfastly throughout the war.[29]

Since the publication of *Which People's War?* the study of masculinities and male behaviours has mushroomed, often challenging and nuancing the broad overview of wartime masculinity outlined by Rose. These works, many of which focus on a particular group of wartime men, have continued to deepen our understanding of the male experience in the Second World War. It is now widely accepted that a multiplicity of masculinities worked alongside each other on the battlefield and the home front, with no singularly accepted way of 'being a man'. Indeed, even Britain's most prominent politicians varied in this regard, evidenced by the understated style of Clement Attlee in opposition to the bombastic personality of aristocratic Winston Churchill with his 'exaggeratedly epic rhetoric'.[30] *The Flyer*, Martin Francis's landmark study of the RAF, is a case in point. Alongside his discussion of hierarchies, uniforms and technologies, conventional topics to be expected in a military history, Francis devotes two chapters to love and domestic life, not only presenting a fully rounded view of male life in the wartime RAF but also adding to the growing literature examining masculinity and the domestic.[31] Similarly, Emma Vickers' *Queen and Country*, on homosexuality in the British armed forces, and Emma Newlands' *Civilians into Soldiers*, on the male body in the British Army, have further expanded understandings of the gendered experience of military service in this period.[32] In addition, Juliette Pattinson's *Behind Enemy Lines* adopts Judith Butler's theorisation of 'performativity' to explore how masculinities were consciously enacted by male secret agents of the Special Operations Executive.[33] There has also been an overt focus on the damage to bodies and minds that warfare can effect. Julie Anderson's *War, Disability and Rehabilitation in Britain* explores the ways injured men were treated and rehabilitated after the Second World War.[34] These works have fruitfully built on, and engage with, some seminal texts that examine the military man in broader context. Graham Dawson's partially autobiographical *Soldier Heroes* (1994), discussed in his foreword to this collection, was a ground-breaking exploration of the enduring link between idealised masculinity and military service. He asserts:

> The soldier hero has proved to be one of the most durable and powerful forms of idealised masculinity within Western cultural tradition since the time of the Ancient Greeks ... Celebrated as a hero in adventure stories telling of his dangerous and daring exploits, the soldier has become a quintessential figure of masculinity.[35]

Another pioneering study, Joanna Bourke's *Dismembering the Male* (1996), examined how masculinities shifted during the First World War using the prism of the male body: 'those experiences still fundamentally affected not only the shape and texture of the male body, but also the values ascribed to the body and the disciplines applied to masculinity.'[36] Male corporeality is examined here with regards to the fear of disfigurement, disablement and death. Indeed, as Bourke's work highlights, the study of masculinities and warfare is equally vibrant with regards to the First World War. For example, Jessica Meyer's *Men of War* uses servicemen's letters and diaries to examine personal constructions of masculinity both during the war and after.[37] Moreover, Mike Roper's *The Secret Battle* is a pioneering work of emotional history, examining the soldier's relationship with home during the First World War.[38]

A 'privileged space' has been preserved in popular memory for the male soldier, as Lucy Noakes has noted.[39] However, sociocultural historians have also started to look beyond the military man, acknowledging the multiplicity of roles played by men on the home front. The Home Guard, the voluntary defence force that was established at the height of the invasion scare, is the focus of Penny Summerfield and Corinna Peniston-Bird's *Contesting Home Defence* (2007). They challenge the dominant *Dad's Army* view of this organisation as an elderly band of ineffectual soldiers and examine how and why such an image became cemented in British culture.[40] Another organisation that civilian men might volunteer for was Civil Defence. Lucy Noakes highlights that recruitment propaganda attempted to combat the emasculating notion that it was 'women's work' by emphasising idealised masculinity.[41] Men of conscription age who volunteered for home guard duties, civil defence, air raid precaution, firewatching or ambulance work were employed in the reserved occupations, prevented by the state from going into the forces. This vast army of male labour required to sustain a total war has also been the focus of recent scholarly enquiry. The Merchant Navy, firefighters, agricultural workers and industrial workers are the subject of Linsey Robb's *Men at Work* (2015). She argues that there was a clear cultural hierarchy of civilian roles in British culture during the Second World War, with proximity to the dangers of warfare the key to being considered a truly masculine civilian.[42] While Robb utilises cultural representations, including radio broadcasts, films and posters, Juliette Pattinson, Arthur McIvor and Linsey Robb's study of working-class men who were concentrated in heavy industry uses primarily oral histories. *Men in Reserve* (2017) argues that not all men were frustrated by their civilian status despite the prominent focus on the 'soldier hero' in popular culture. While many men tried to evade their reserved status, engineering routes out of their reserved occupations and into the services, many were comfortable with their contributions to the war effort and were buoyed by guaranteed work, prestige and high wages. This was especially true of men who lived in areas worst hit by the depression. The war could, then, be both an emasculating and a masculinising force for the working civilian male.[43] Class, then, has also emerged as a key lens through which to examine the male experience of war. Despite the enduring image of Britain being 'all in it together', a central ideal of this 'People's War', class remained a significant focus of public debate. Sonya Rose argues that:

> The war years were indelibly etched by the interplay of two seemingly opposite tendencies. There was, on the one hand, the dynamic unleashed by a powerful fantasy of national cross-class unity, coupled with the belief that the war was or would be a levelling influence. And, on the other, there were persistent expressions of class antagonisms.[44]

Indeed, the number of industrial strikes rose sharply as the war progressed and there were persistent class-based tensions regarding inequalities engendered or exposed by rationing, evacuation and air raids. As such, class clearly remained an important determinant of wartime experiences, something which is explored further in several of the chapters here.

Building on this growing body of scholarship on military and civilian masculinities this edited collection brings together cutting-edge research on the myriad ways British men experienced, understood and remembered their wartime exploits during the Second World War, as (non-) active combatants, prisoners and as civilian workers.

THE COLLECTION

This edited collection developed out of a symposium held at the Scottish Oral History Centre (University of Strathclyde) in 2015, entitled 'Masculinities at War'. It brought together established academics, early career researchers and doctoral students who were researching male identities, roles and representations on the home front and in the armed forces during the Second World War, as well as the ways such roles have been remembered subsequently. The symposium, and this edited collection, quite emphatically demonstrate that the lacuna Martin Francis identified has largely been filled. *Men, Masculinities and Male Culture in the Second World War* presents a broad cross-section of the important and exciting work being undertaken in this area today and we hope that this analysis of previously underexplored male experiences makes a vital contribution to the historiography of Britain in the Second World War, as well as to understandings of historical masculinities more generally. The collection is firmly grounded in current historical research and theoretical work on masculinity. All the contributors are historians who take a critical approach to masculinity, seeing it as something culturally produced and embodied, rather than as an innate fixed quality. The collection is split into two broad sections which examine the experiences of men in the armed services and those on the home front. Both consider not only wartime experiences but also the ways these wartime roles were remembered or, indeed, forgotten once the war had ceased. This separation of military and civilian identities is not to assert, however, that they were necessarily always distinct: the mobilisation of male civilians into the armed forces, many of whom were stationed on the home front either for the duration or before deployment overseas, and the donning of military-style uniforms by civilian men who undertook a range of Home Defence roles is evidence of the blurred boundary. That fuzziness is engaged with in several chapters in this collection, most notably Chris Smith's on the Government Code and Cipher School and Corinna Peniston-Bird's on the post-war memorialisation of the civilian worker.

Part I of the edited collection explores the wartime experiences and post-war representations of men who served in the forces. Five million

British men donned military uniform and were conscripted into the armed services during the Second World War.[45] The heroic status of service personnel was largely secure. Perhaps the most heroic and glamourous of all service roles, at least in the early part of the war, was the chivalric knight of the air, 'the Few' to whom so much was owed by so many. The RAF pilot might be regarded as being at the pinnacle of the hierarchy of wartime masculinities. This is evidenced in Jonathan Foss' posters depicting an airman with the RAF rondel placed like a halo.[46] But while the Battle of Britain pilot was celebrated as the epitome of masculinity, some servicemen stationed on the home front felt that they were not sufficiently contributing and sought to negotiate their way into a more active combatant role where they would directly engage the enemy. Juliette Pattinson explores in her chapter the army men who volunteered for especially hazardous duties in the Jedburghs, three-man inter-allied teams which parachuted into occupied France in uniform after D-Day to foment resistance. She utilises oral testimonies, memoirs and official Jedburgh team reports to expose the gap between boyhood fantasies of soldierly action and the more mundane reality of frustrated wartime experiences in order to illuminate the fragility of masculine subjectivities.

While Pattinson's chapter focuses on those keen to experience the most extreme dangers of warfare these men were not representative of all men serving in the British Army. Indeed, a key way in which army personnel may have struggled to embody the 'soldier hero' ideal is through experiencing debilitating fear. This is the focus of Emma Newlands' chapter. She uses personal testimonies of front-line troops, predominantly soldiers conscripted to service rather than volunteers, archived at the Imperial War Museum to examine the ways that men expressed fear. The loss of body parts signifying masculinity, such as genitalia, were a special cause for concern. Both Newlands' and Pattinson's chapters highlight how lack of control led to varying degrees of emasculation, a phenomenon which reaches its extreme in Clare Makepeace's chapter examining experiences of British prisoners of war in Germany. No longer able to fulfil their part of the gender contract, prisoners of war may have felt emasculated, or feminised even. Indeed, some men played around with their gender identities, performing femininity publicly. By assessing other prisoners' reactions and relationships to female impersonators, Makepeace reveals the complexity of both gender hierarchies and male desire in this period. The final chapter in this first section examines 'the Few' in post-war memory and remembrance, again highlighting the internal discomposure which could arise when ideals of warfare were displaced by combat experience. Frances Houghton's chapter examines the memoirs of the fighter pilots who fought in the Battle of Britain in order to consider how they have sought to portray their war. She argues that ultimately these memoirists, despite emphasising their wartime experiences as formative, portrayed their lived experiences of battle as fundamentally at odds with the gentlemanly and chivalric ideas of war which they had been exposed to in their youth. In so doing, Houghton, like Pattinson, flags the impediments to embodying that masculine ideals that had been inculcated during their boyhoods.

Part II of the book examines the men less valorised by wartime culture but no less valuable to the war effort: the home front man. Contrary to the perception propelled by 'separate spheres' ideology that 'the home' was women's domain, the '*home* front' during the Second World War, and indeed the First, was also populated by large numbers of men. In addition to underage boys and older males, there were millions of men of conscription age who remained in their civilian occupations during the war. Two–thirds of the 15 million men who were aged within the call-up range remained in Britain working in a variety of skilled occupations, both blue-collar trades and white-collar professions. In June 1940, for example, six times as many men were working in industry than were in the services.[47] And they continued to far outnumber the female workforce despite the influx of women into the labour market: 61% of wartime workers were male and many workplaces, such as docks, shipyards and railways, remained masculine spaces. In a protracted total war, not only were men required in large numbers to fight the enemy, but also workers were needed who could equip them as well as maintain essential services at home. As Sir John Anderson, the Lord Privy Seal, noted in December 1938, civilian male workers 'can best serve the State by remaining at the work for which they have been trained'.[48] Not all men concurred, however: Ron Spedding, a Durham railway worker, asserted: 'I remember feeling peeved and also a little guilty when some of my friends joyously told me they had been released and were off to join the Air Force.'[49] While Spedding notes that these men were liberated from their civilian jobs and permitted to enlist in the services, others who were not successful in securing their discharge have spoken of 'feeling stuck' and 'fastened down'.[50] As such, they felt diminished as men, subordinate to the 'soldier hero' and unable to fulfil their side of the gender contract.

The masculinities of non-uniformed civilian men are explored in Arthur McIvor's chapter. He utilises oral testimony to highlight that far from being emasculated, the war could prove to be a remasculinising force, providing almost unlimited work and the subsequent large wage packet. This was especially the case for working-class men in areas previously worst hit by the privations of the 1930s Depression. By focusing his analysis on the male body, McIvor persuasively argues that physical labour and risk-taking behaviours allowed these working-class men to build a narrative of sacrifice and graft for the war effort.

Muscularity and skill have long been seen as qualities associated with masculinity. Yet, especially for the middle and upper classes, so too have logic and intelligence. These are central to Chris Smith's chapter, which explores a masculine identity built entirely on mental alacrity rather than physical brawn. His chapter works alongside McIvor's as both clearly highlight the ways specific classed notions of masculinity shaped war experiences. Smith's exploration of the Government Code and Cipher School, the infamous codebreakers of Bletchley Park, underlines our earlier discussion of the unclear boundaries between military and civilian experience. While these men donned service uniform, they were never expected to hold a weapon. Smith shows that GC&CS explicitly sought men from middle- and upper-class backgrounds believing them to be ideally suited to the job. Yet the specific scholarly, as well as classed, qualities required would, as Smith's chapter demonstrates, create tension with regular army personnel.

This section then moves on to post-war representations and commemorations. Linsey Robb's chapter explores the depiction of the civilian man in film and television. During the war, as McIvor's chapter highlights, these men were not shunned, nor considered shirkers and cowards. Moreover, the wartime civilian worker was very rarely portrayed in film as the focus of open hostility.[51] However, Robb argues that this image is very different in the post-war period. At best the civilian was missing entirely but at worst he was presented as morally suspect: the shirker, the coward, the spiv or the philanderer, all attributes which compared poorly to the increasingly valorised wartime fighting man.

The cultural amnesia regarding the male civilian worker is further explored in Corinna Peniston-Bird's chapter on memorialisation of reserved workers. She highlights that civilian men are inconsistently commemorated in stone despite a recent memory boom which has seen a rash of memorial building. Moreover, those that are depicted closely ape the experiences of military service, underscoring the fuzzy line between civilian and military, and leading Peniston-Bird to suggest a 'third way' of conceptualising wartime roles.

While the studies included here are wide-ranging, it is impossible to cover every aspect of what it meant to be a man during the Second World War. Culturally, masculine ideas narrowed; yet in reality masculine identities became increasingly pluralised and fragmented during the war. What is missing in this collection is a discussion of how homosexual, black, disabled, Irish, Jewish and enemy alien men experienced the war, either on the home front or in the forces, the ways in which masculinity intersected with Scottishness or Welshness, for example, or how men who served in the Royal Navy recollected their wartime activities. Some of these experiences have been addressed elsewhere, most notably in Wendy Ugolini and Juliette Pattinson's *Fighting for Britain?*, Ugolini's *Experiencing the War as the 'Enemy Other'* and Rose's *Which People's War?*[52] Nevertheless, there remains a gap in the historiography to explore these lived experiences through an explicit gendered lens. As such, while this collection highlights the strength and vibrancy of the field, the editors also present something of a call to arms to further diversify and strengthen the research being carried out in this area.

Some Second World War veterans have reported that 'the question of gender did not arise as the organisations were all male', that gender had 'simply *nothing* to do with it' and that it 'didn't exist' and was 'invented' by the present generation.[53] However, it is our contention that not only did gender exist during the Second World War, but that male experiences and sense of self were fundamentally shaped by masculine ideals. This collection, then, endeavours to show that masculinities, had *everything* to do with the experience of serving in the military and being stationed on the home front during the Second World War.

NOTES

1. Anon. (1940), *Joining Up: A Complete Guide to Those Joining the Army, Navy or Air Force, Etc* (London: War Facts Press), pp. 7–8; P.J. Grigg (1944), 'Foreword', in J. Brophy (1945), *Britain's Home Guard: A Character Study* (London: George G. Harrup and Co).
2. C.M. Peniston-Bird (2003), 'Classifying the Body in the Second World War: British Men In and Out of Uniform', *Body and Society*, 9:4, pp. 31–48.

3. D. Spender (ed.) (1981), *Men's Studies Modified: The Impact of Feminism on the Academic Disciplines* (Oxford: Pergamon).

4. S. Rowbotham (1973), *Hidden from History: 300 years of Women's Oppression and the Fight Against It* (London: Pluto Press); R. Bridenthal and C. Koonz (eds.) *Becoming Visible: Women in European History* (Boston: Houghton Mifflin); B.A. Carroll (1976), *Liberating Women's History: Theoretical and Critical Essays* (London: Illinois University Press).

5. A. Vickery (1993), 'Golden Age to Separate Spheres? A Review of the Categories and Chronology of English Women's History', *The Historical Journal*, 36:2, pp. 383–414, here p. 413.

6. N. Zemon Davis (1976), 'Women's History in Transition: The European Case' *Feminist Studies*, 3.

7. J.W. Scott (1986), 'Gender: A Useful Category of Historical Analysis', *The American Historical Review*, 91, pp. 1053–1075.

8. B. Smith (2000), *The Gender of History: Men, Women, and Historical Practice (London:* Harvard University Press); K. Canning (2006), *Gender History in Practice: Historical Perspectives on Bodies, Class and Citizenship* (Ithaca, NY: Cornell University Press). Not all agree, however. Joan Hoff, for example, argued that gender, rather than being a useful category of analysis, is in fact, a 'Postmodern Category of Paralysis'. J. Hoff (1994), 'Gender as a Postmodern Category of Paralysis', *Women's Studies International Forum*, 17:4, pp. 442–447.

9. H. Brod (1987), 'The Case for Men's Studies', in H. Brod, *The Making of Masculinities: The New Men's Studies* (Boston: Allen and Unwin), pp. 39–62.

10. M. Kimmel (1993), 'Invisible Masculinity: Examining Masculinity in Relation to History and the Social Sciences', *Society*, 30, pp. 28–35.

11. See, for example, N. Vance (1985), *The Sinews of the Spirit: The Ideal of Christian Manliness in Victorian Literature and Religious Thought* (Cambridge: Cambridge University Press); J.A. Mangan (1981), *Athleticism in the Victorian and Edwardian Public School: The emergence and consolidation of an Educational Ideology* (Cambridge: Cambridge University Press).

12. J.A. Mangan and J. Walvin (eds.) (1987), *Manliness and Morality: Middle-Class Masculinity in Britain and America, 1800–1940* (Manchester, Manchester University Press).

13. M.C. Carnes and C. Griffen (1990), 'Introduction', in M.C. Carnes and C. Griffen (eds.) *Meanings for Manhood: Constructions of Masculinity in Victorian America* (Chicago, University of Chicago Press), p. 2.

14. J. Tosh (1991), 'Domesticity and Manliness in the Victorian Middle-Class: the Family of Edward White Benson', in M. Roper and J. Tosh (eds.), *Manful*

Assertions: Masculinities in Britain since 1800 (London: Routledge), pp. 44–73; J. Tosh (1994), 'What Should Historians Do with Masculinity? Reflections on Nineteenth-Century Britain', *History Workshop Journal*, 38:1, pp. 179–202; J. Tosh (1999), *A Man's Place: Masculinity and the Middle-Class Home in Victorian England* (London: Yale University Press).

15. M. Roper and J. Tosh, 'Introduction: Historians and the Politics of Masculinity', in Roper and Tosh (eds.), *Manful Assertions*, p. 1.

16. M. McCormack (2015), *Embodying the Militia in Georgian England* (Oxford: Oxford University Press); C. Kennedy and M. McCormack (2013), *Soldiering in Britain and Ireland, 1750–1850: Men of Arms* (New York: Palgrave Macmillan); E. Mackie (2009), *Rakes, Highwaymen and Pirates: the Making of the Modern Gentleman in the Eighteenth Century* (Baltimore: Johns Hopkins University Press); B. Murphy (2013), *British Queer History: New Approaches and Perspectives* (Manchester: Manchester University Press); B. Beavan (2005), *Leisure, Citizenship and Working-Class Men in Britain, 1850–1945* (Manchester: Manchester University Press); L. King (2015), *Family Men: Fatherhood and Masculinity in Britain, c.1914–1960* (Oxford: Oxford University Press).

17. R.W. Connell (1995), *Masculinities* (Cambridge: Polity), pp. 78–81.

18. The concept has been criticised for ignoring the range of ideal masculinities in any given culture by emphasising just one culturally exalted form. M. Donaldson (1993), 'What is Hegemonic Masculinity?', *Theory and Society*, 22:5, pp. 643–657.

19. M. Francis (2002), 'The Domestication of the Male? Recent Research on Nineteenth- and Twentieth-Century British Masculinity', *The Historical Journal*, 45:3, pp. 637–652, here p. 648. See review essays by J. Hearn (1987), 'Review: Men and Masculinity or Mostly Boys' Own Papers', *Theory, Culture and Society*, 6, pp. 665–689; M. Roper (1990), 'Recent Books on Masculinity', *History Workshop Journal*, 29, pp. 184–192; L. Cody (1995), 'This Sex Which Seems to Have Won: The Emergence of Masculinity as a Category of Historical Analysis', *Radical History Review*, 61, pp. 175–183.

20. M. Francis (2008), *The Flyer: British Culture and the Royal Air Force, 1939–1945* (Oxford: Oxford University Press), p. 4.

21. See, for example, C.L. Verney (1954), *The Desert Rats: The 7th Armoured Division in World War II* (London: Hutchison); W. Kirby (1961), *The War Against Japan* (London: HMSO); B. Bond (1975) *France and Belgium, 1939–1940* (London: Davis Poynter).

22. A number of edited collections have brought scholars into conversation in which they are 'gendering war talk' across geographic, temporal and disciplinary borders. Ana Carden-Coyne's *Gender and Conflict Since 1914* adopts an interdisciplinary approach, incorporating chapters

by sociologists, art historians, literature specialists, legal scholars and sociocultural historians, who examine how gendered meanings change over time. Gerry DeGroot and Corinna Peniston-Bird's *A Soldier and a Woman* provides case studies ranging from the early modern period to the late twentieth century and moving across the globe to take in China, Russia/Soviet Union, Algeria, Vietnam, Israel, France and Britain to illustrate women's attempts to contest the masculine nature of conflict. Corinna Peniston-Bird and Emma Vickers' *Gender and the Second World War* uses a transnational perspective to examine masculinities and femininities in the forces and on the home front. A. Carden-Coyne (ed.) (2012), *Gender and Conflict Since 1914* (Basingstoke: Palgrave); G. DeGroot and C. Peniston-Bird (2000), *A Soldier and a Woman: Sexual Integration in the Military* (Harlow: Pearson); C. Peniston-Bird and E. Vickers (eds.) (2017), *Gender and the Second World War: Lessons of War* (London: Palgrave).

23. A pioneer in this field was Arthur Marwick who saw both the First and Second World Wars as emancipatory, transforming women's lives socially, politically and economically. A. Marwick (1965), *The Deluge: British Society and the First World War* (London: Bodley Head); A. Marwick (1988), *Total War and Social Change* (Basingstoke: Macmillan). Harold Smith and Penny Summerfield have persuasively argued against Marwick's thesis, asserting that the Second World War strengthened rather than challenged traditional gender roles. H.L. Smith (1986), 'The Effect of the War on the Status of Women' in H.L. Smith, *War and Social Change: British Society in the Second World War* (Manchester: Manchester University Press), p. 225; P. Summerfield (1989) *Women Workers in the Second World War: Production and Patriarchy in Conflict* (London: Routledge); P. Summerfield (1998), *Reconstructing Women's Wartime Lives* (Manchester: Manchester University Press).

24. S.O. Rose (2003), *Which Peoples War? National Identity and Citizenship in Wartime Britain, 1939–1945* (Oxford: Oxford University Press), p. 196.

25. Rose, *Which People's War?*, p. 196.

26. P. Ward (2004), *Britishness Since 1870* (London: Routledge).

27. L. Noakes (1997), *War and the British: Gender, Memory and National Identity, 1939–1991* (London: I.B.Tauris), p. 52.

28. T. Hajkowski (2002), 'The BBC, the Empire and the Second World War, 1939–1945', *Historical Journal of Film, Radio and Television*, 22:2, pp. 135–155, here p. 141.

29. P. Addison (2002), 'National Identity and the Battle of Britain', in B. Korte and R. Schneider (eds.), *War and the Cultural Construction of Identities in Britain* (Amsterdam: Rodopi), pp. 225–240, here p. 235.

30. Francis, 'Domestication of the Male?', p. 649.

31. Francis, *The Flyer.*

32. E. Vickers (2013), *Queen and Country: Same-sex desire in the British Armed Forces, 1939–45* (Manchester: Manchester University Press); E. Newlands (2014), *Civilians into Soldiers: War, the Body and British Army Recruits, 1939–45* (Manchester: Manchester University Press).

33. J. Pattinson (2007), *Behind Enemy Lines: Gender, Passing and the Special Operations Executive in the Second World War* (Manchester, Manchester University Press).

34. J. Anderson (2011) *War, Disability and Rehabilitation in Britain: 'Soul of a Nation'*, (Manchester: Manchester University Press); A. Carden-Coyne (2014), *The Politics of Wounds: Military Patients and Medical Power in the First World War* (Oxford: Oxford University Press).

35. G. Dawson (1994), *Soldier Heroes: British Adventure, Empire and the Imagining of Masculinities* (London: Routledge), p. 1.

36. J. Bourke (1996), *Dismembering the Male: Men's Bodies, Britain, and the Great War* (Chicago: University of Chicago Press), p. 40.

37. J. Meyer (2009), *Men of War: Masculinity and the First World War in Britain* (Basingstoke: Palgrave Macmillan).

38. M. Roper (2010), *The Secret Battle: Emotional Survival in the Great War* (Manchester: Manchester University Press).

39. Noakes, *War and the* British, p. 164.

40. P. Summerfield and C. Peniston-Bird (2007), *Contesting Home Defence: Men, Women and the Home Guard in the Second World War* (Manchester, Manchester University Press).

41. L. Noakes (2012), '"Serve to Save": Gender, Citizenship and Civil Defence in Britain 1937–41', *Journal of Contemporary History*, 47:4, pp. 634–753.

42. L. Robb (2015), *Men at Work: The Working Man in British Culture, 1939–1945* (Basingstoke: Palgrave Macmillan).

43. J. Pattinson, A. McIvor and L. Robb (2017), *Men in Reserve: British Civilian Masculinities during the Second World War* (Manchester: Manchester University Press).

44. Rose, *Which People's War?*, p. 29.

45. P. Howlett (1995), *Fighting with Figures: A Statistical Digest of the Second World War* (London: HMSO), p. 38.

46. The Imperial War Museum, London, Art.IWM PST 3774; Art.IWM PST 3096.

47. Howlett, *Fighting with Figures*, p. 38.

48. 1 December 1938, House of Commons Debate, Vol. 342 cols. 597–604.

49. R. Spedding (1988), *Shildon Wagon Works: A Working Man's Life* (Durham: Durham County Library), pp. vi–vii.

50. Pattinson et al., *Men in Reserve*, p. 105.

51. Robb, *Men at Work*.

52. W. Ugolini and J. Pattinson (eds.) (2015), *Fighting for Britain? Negotiating Identities in Britain During the Second World War* (Bern: Peter Lang); Rose, *Which People's War?*; W. Ugolini (2011), *Experiencing War as the 'Enemy Other': Italian Scottish Experience in World War II* (Manchester: Manchester University Press).

53. Correspondence with combatants in Greece and the Middle East to J. Pattinson, 3 November 1999; 28 March 2000; 14 October 1999.

The 'Soldier Hero'

CHAPTER 2

Fantasies of the 'Soldier Hero', Frustrations of the Jedburghs

Juliette Pattinson

The irregular soldier, a maverick individual who operated outside of conventional military authority, has held a particular fascination for the British public since the late nineteenth century. As John Mackenzie has demonstrated, the colonial adventures of General Gordon were rich fodder for the press, while T.E. Lawrence's exploits during the First World War further nourished that interest.[1] The Second World War witnessed the unleashing of unconventional 'ungentlemanly' warfare on a larger scale; against a merciless enemy in an all-out total war, there was no room for gentlemanliness. Stirred by his own experiences in the Second Boer War, Churchill embraced the notion of deploying small select groups of well-trained and highly motivated men to undertake 'hit and run' 'pinprick' attacks against much larger, more conventional ground troops. Consequently, Special Forces were utilised in British Army operations in every major theatre of war. This notion of 'the Few' against the many fitted with the British discourse of calm self-assurance, individualism and 'being alone' following the fall of France. Despite themes

J. Pattinson (✉)
University of Kent, Canterbury, Kent, UK
e-mail: J.Pattinson@kent.ac.uk

L. Robb and J. Pattinson (eds.), *Men, Masculinities and Male Culture in the Second World War*, Genders and Sexualities in History, https://doi.org/ 10.1057/978-1-349-95290-8_2

25

of communality, unity and 'all pulling together' being disseminated in myriad propaganda forms during the 'people's war' as Corinna Peniston-Bird has shown,[2] it was still the lone individual that featured as the ideal heroic role model: the solo pilot, tank crew member, submariner and, central to this discussion, commando.

In their examination of representations of the Commandos, an elite organisation formed in June 1940 after the withdrawal at Dunkirk, Mark Connelly and David Willcox assert that they fulfilled a 'dual function', conforming to stereotypical notions of the gentleman adventurer, audacious and adept at improvisation, while simultaneously personifying the spirit of the 'people's war', in that they were ordinary men trained to achieve the remarkable. Quoting a 1942 Pathé newsreel, they note that 'Commandos were the "Big Men" of the people'.[3] Stories began featuring commandos from 1942 onwards; the popular boys' paper *Hotspur* included a serial entitled 'the Black Flash Commandos' who cooperated with Norwegian resisters and a novel by W.E. Johns, *King of the Commandos* (1943), was set in northern France.

The celebration of the irregular soldier continued after the Second World War in post-war adventure films and boys' comics, fuelled by heroic stories about secret agents, commandos, guerrillas and partisans in this less orthodox warfare. In his ground-breaking book on iconic imperial adventurers, Graham Dawson charts the impact that cultural narratives of the 'soldier hero' had on him and his generation growing up in the 1950s. He reveals the ways in which boys and men internalise this idealised form of manliness, 'fashioning in the imagination' masculinities that are 'lived out in the flesh'.[4] In its imperial manifestations, masculinity is inextricably bound up with an 'external code of conduct' as John Tosh has examined.[5] Yet a consideration of masculinity that is something more than simply 'a set of abstract codes' recognisable in the performances undertaken by men needs to acknowledge the role of the inner mind. Mike Roper's work on the unconscious is revealing here. In his analysis of subjectivity in memoirs about First World War experience, he notes that scholars of masculinity need to take account of emotional experience, as well as cultural constructions and social relations, without collapsing the distinctions.[6] These conceptualisations of masculinity point to the hierarchy that exists; as R.W. Connell asserts, in any given culture some modes of manliness are celebrated and are positioned above others which are marginalised.[7] The 'hegemonic' form of masculinity is never numerically dominant, however, which augments its elite status.

During the Second World War, some men who served in the British Army regarded their contribution as insufficiently active and, aspiring to undertake a more dynamic role which brought them into closer contact with the enemy, volunteered for 'special duties' that were considered especially hazardous. One such unit was the Jedburghs: three-man teams of mixed Allied nationality that parachuted in uniform into occupied France and the Netherlands as a post-D-Day operational reserve, tasked with stimulating and sustaining guerrilla warfare and coordinating resistance forces. The formation of Jedburgh teams was the idea of Peter Wilkinson, an officer in the British clandestine organisation the Special Operations Executive (henceforth SOE) who, observing civilian attempts to support Allied forces in repelling the German airborne assault of Crete in May 1941, concluded that civilians could be harnessed by Allied agents at the time of the invasion.[8] Ninety-three three-man teams, given either men's forenames (Ivor and Guy for example) or the names of patented medicines (such as Quinine and Ammonia), comprising a leader, an officer and a non-commissioned radio operator, were parachuted in uniform into occupied France and seven teams into the Netherlands after the Allied invasion. The deployment of government-sanctioned uniformed military units undertaking irregular warfare behind enemy lines in tandem with local partisans in a coordinated strategy with conventional Allied invasion ground forces was unprecedented, as was the use of a coalition involving British, French and American Special Forces. The Jedburghs stemmed from a partnership between the SOE, its American counterpart the Office of Strategic Services (OSS) and the Free French Bureau Central de Renseignements et d'Action (BCRA). Inter-allied cooperation was at the very heart of the Jedburgh concept: it was sited in France, where the Allies planned to launch their invasion; it was equipped by the Americans, who possessed the aircraft to infiltrate personnel into occupied Europe; and it was a British scheme, utilising British training methods, organisation and planning, and was informed by the unconventional warfare conducted twenty-five years earlier by T.E. Lawrence and, perhaps surprisingly, by Michael Collins, an Irish Republican Army (IRA) activist who organised attacks against representatives of the British state in Ireland.

The Jedburghs were the first truly international military force. Yet they are a little-known unit. The handful of books that have been produced about them have been popular in tone, focusing on mission facts.[9] One exception is Benjamin F. Jones' *Eisenhower's Guerillas*, a scholarly account examining the broader political and military context.[10] The confinement of Jedburgh narratives to popular works shows the continued importance of particular types of soldier heroisation to national memory. More significantly, the lack of sustained scholarly attention is suggestive of the continued discomfort felt about their lack of operational success: the shortfall between their gendered expectations and the realities of their deployment. Indeed, this chapter takes a very different approach by adopting a gendered perspective and by foregrounding the personnel. It is based on the personal testimonies I collected with eight British Jedburghs, twenty-seven interviews archived at the Imperial War Museum, published and unpublished memoirs and over a hundred files deposited at the National Archives. While few men were explicit in talking about masculinity, the nature of volunteering for hazardous duties for an organisation that only deployed men meant that the narratives they composed were, unsurprisingly, revealing of their masculine subjectivities. This chapter explores men's desires to volunteer for dangerous work and analyses their evaluations of their wartime contributions in order to show the gap between masculine fantasies of soldierly heroism and the actuality of lived military experience. It considers the consumption of popular literature in the inter-war period, heroic posturings, the recruitment and training processes which rewarded manifestations of hyper-masculinity and the blows to manhood that undermined the ability to construct fully heroic narratives. By exploring these issues, this chapter demonstrates the impact of gendered hero discourses in shaping and influencing the military experiences and choices of men in the Second World War. Their consumption of masculinity was effective and affective, but ultimately made them a promise that operational realities could not fulfil.

'MAKE ME A SOLDIER, LORD … MAKE ME A MAN': GROWING UP IN THE SHADOW OF WAR

The men who served in the Jedburghs were part of a generation brought up in the wake of the First World War. This modern form of industrialised warfare is considered by some scholars to have had an emasculating effect: it wrought havoc on men's bodies, with bullets blasting and shrapnel shredding the long-held belief in physical perfection as a marker of ideal masculinity, and emotionally incapacitating men whose nerves were unravelled by shellshock, mental breakdown and neuroses, the latter a complaint long associated with 'hysterical' women.[11] The potency of the soldier hero discourse was diluted by the experience of the war and the dominant understanding of the inter-war period is that of an outpouring of pacifist literature, such as Henry Williamson's *A Patriot's Progress* (1930), which emphasised the horror and futility of trench warfare. Consequently, Alison Light and Sonya Rose argue that a 'significant shift in masculine identity' occurred in the inter-war period, one that was not bound up with 'hard', aggressive heroism but rather was 'softer', pacifistic, sensitive to fear and anti-heroic.[12]

That a modified masculine discourse was in circulation has, however, been challenged, by Jessica Meyer, among others.[13] While the notion of what it meant to be a man was under extreme pressure, the 'soldier hero' as a masculine ideal survived the First World War intact. Conceptualisation of the dead as the 'lost generation' and the 'finest flower of manhood' bolstered further the hegemonic status of the soldier.[14] The orthodox view of the war as futile is founded on a small number of disillusioned poets whose impact on popular memory has been disproportionate: sales of Rupert Brooke's collection of heroic poems were 214 times higher by 1929 than that of Wilfred Owen's, for example.[15] Jedburgh Glyn Loosmore, born in 1923, recalled the poems he was able to recite as a teenager: '"The Charge of the Light Brigade", "The Last Fight of the Revenge" and "How Horatius Kept the Bridge" … "The Private of the Buffs", "The Red Thread of Honour"… Grenfell's "Into Battle" and Hodgson's "Before Action". Learn those poems and you will probably want to be a soldier yourself.'[16] These poems provided Loosmore with a clear model of what a young man should aspire to be in order to become manly. 'This is what I was born for', he asserted.[17] 'Before Action', a poem written on the eve of the first day of the Battle of the Somme, includes a plea to 'Make me a soldier, Lord … Make me a man, O Lord … Help me to die, O Lord.'[18] Such poetry imbued Loosmore with a highly romanticised view of war and an undisputed notion of British superiority. His belief that it was glorious to die for King and Country was not compromised by the knowledge of what had befallen three-quarters of a million British men in the First World War; his heroic image of war was undiluted, if not encouraged and nurtured by the everyday masculine culture of the inter-war years.

Moreover, despite lamenting the 'doomed youth' who 'die like cattle', very few writers were avowedly anti-war.[19] Conflict was still presented as a heroic and ennobling opportunity in which comradeship was paramount. Perusal of a much greater variety of texts complicates the accepted view of futility. While R.C. Sherriff's play *Journey's End* (1928) has shaped later perceptions, over 400 plays and novels, many of which celebrated camaraderie and adventure, were published in the inter-war period, imbuing another generation with a highly romantic notion of war. Loosmore reflected: 'Without being in any way militaristic, I think boys read stories about the war which conditioned them to think that serving in the forces was the common lot of young men … Lots of boys soaked themselves in this.'[20]

Furthermore, cheap and readily circulated papers, such as *Modern Boy*, *Adventure* and *Rover*, were likely to be the chosen reading material of teenage boys of all classes in the inter-war period (in a time before comics had been devised and when childhood literacy levels were high). In her analysis of nearly a century of such publications, Kelly Boyd concludes that while stories about schoolboys replaced tales about soldiers and battles that had populated the papers in the pre-1914 period, there was 'more fighting, bleeding and brutality [featured] in the pages of inter-war story papers than ever before'.[21] As George Orwell noted in an essay about boys' weekly story papers, such 'blood-and-thunder stuff' exalted the 'picturesque side of the Great War', including stories that featured characters who were members of the air force and secret service, rather than the infantry, and, imbued with a tone of class snobbishness, 'gutter patriotism', xenophobia and conservatism, they promoted a set of values that were 'hopelessly out of date'.[22] War was depicted as offering adventure that was attainable; schoolboys could become heroes too, guaranteeing reader identification with the masculine characters depicted. Loosmore recollected that he was motivated 'to get into action … [by] excitement, *Boys Own Paper*.'[23] These stories, which were a central part of boys' 'fantasy life' fuelling their imaginations, were 'windows into the ideologies of masculinity' that were circulating at this time.[24]

Illustrated histories were another aspect of the masculine pleasure-culture of war and were a key site for inculcating idealised notions of martial masculinity, facilitating boys' negotiation into manhood. Loosmore believed that his peer group was influenced in particular by Arthur Mee's *Children's Encyclopaedia*. Urging me to read it, he recalled that 'it helped to shape a generation. It contains an extraordinary number of poems that extol heroism and self-sacrifice. It gave boys of my generation the notion that it was praiseworthy to serve, and, if necessary, die for one's country.'[25] Mee's encyclopedia, which had been published in fortnightly editions between 1908 and 1910 and reprinted throughout the inter-war period, was a product of a bygone era which celebrated a chauvinist view of British imperialism and 'muscular Christianity'. 'Quit you like a man: be strong' one issue exhorted.[26] While the encyclopedia incorporated values and attitudes that were historically and culturally specific to the Edwardian period, its continued reprinting between the wars meant that it was consumed by a later generation who absorbed attitudes of 'self-sacrifice … you soaked this in … This was the ethos, the climate of the times.'[27] Loosmore's recollections about this publication demonstrate its impact and influence on a generation of eager young men, keen to flex their patriotic muscles.

While it is impossible to be exact about the impact of models of desirable masculine behaviour that were disseminated in popular literature and consumed by youth in this period, given they could be read at a purely superficial level, and while they did not necessarily determine behaviour, it can be asserted that they shaped views and values. Decades after the war had ended, Loosmore still held to their importance. As Orwell noted, many men are 'carrying through life an imaginative background which they acquired in childhood'.[28] The external role models depicted in these war stories and poems fuelled teenage boys' inner or psychic desires, and, as Dawson asserts, provided 'shared forms of fantasy and play through which their own masculinity could be imaginatively secured'.[29]

Many young men raised on this literature were eager to serve when conflict erupted again, seemingly undeterred by the prospect of sustaining horrific injuries and impervious to thoughts of their own mortality. 'None of us were under any illusions what would happen if we did get caught', asserted Jedburgh Ron Brierley.[30] Operating behind German lines dressed in the battledress uniform of their country with the insignia of their previous regiment and a Special Forces badge, most Jedburghs thought it unlikely that the German Army would adhere to the Geneva Convention. Indeed, Hitler's Commando Order of October 1942 stated bluntly that irregulars would be shot without trial. Jedburgh Bernard Knox recalled that upon receipt of their gear and supplies, they did not have to provide a signature:

> That was a sign that we were regarded as lost – together with our equipment – the moment we got on the plane. But none of us had the slightest doubt that what we were doing was absolutely right and, of course, that carried us through. Nobody, not one man, bugged out. They were baying to get into the field.[31]

Post-war accounts often emphasise how dangerous their missions should have been and this serves to bolster their masculine credentials which were threatened by the ultimate failure of most of the Jed teams. While Brierley and Knox were fatalistic about their chances of survival, others emphasised their invincibility. Fred Bailey, for example, asserted: 'We knew there was a likelihood [of dying but] you never thought it would happen to you. Always going to be the other chap.'[32] Bill Colby, an American Jedburgh who went on to serve as Director General of the Central Intelligence Agency (CIA), ascribed the enthusiasm to serve as youthful arrogance:

> None of us dwelt on the dangers of what we were preparing to do ... The usual young man's conceit that he is invulnerable and immortal enveloped us all. Everything was dealt with as a joke; in a sense we were far too much caught up in the adventure that we were undertaking to be afraid.[33]

War allowed men 'soaked' in heroic literature to live the manly virtues they had imbibed through popular juvenile culture. Far from being dissuaded by the brutalities of the First World War, their consumption of military masculinity raised a high bar for their attainment of patriotic manliness.

'KEEN TO BE IN THE THICK OF THE ACTION': UNDERAGE VOLUNTEERING FOR WAR SERVICE

None of the men with whom I was in contact had any recollections of the earlier war, the oldest having been born in 1914, but despite this, they held it in fascination.[34] All had heard stories of the conflict told by their relatives. Of the five million British men who served during the First World War, six in every seven men returned. The war was undoubtedly the seminal experience of their lives and in talking to their sons and nephews, however vaguely, they passed on to the next generation the impression that to serve was noteworthy. There is little hard evidence to substantiate the widely held view that veterans were disinclined to speak about their war experiences. They were probably reluctant to narrate the more traumatic aspects of their own experience, or to speak of the monotonous bits, and were instead much more likely to focus on foregrounding the positive and the heroic. Tommy MacPherson recalled 'We had been brought up at the knees of our elders on the tales of the First World War.'[35] Dick Rubinstein had often overheard his father talking to his friends about volunteering, and as tension escalated in Europe in the mid-1930s, fuelled by the Anschluss, sixteen-year-old Rubinstein thought, 'well come on chum, it's about time perhaps you did something yourself'.[36] Like the men of his father's generation, martial service comprised an important test of masculinity and a way in which men could show what they were made of. Rubinstein constructed a lengthy narrative of volunteering and manoeuvring himself into the action. In his half-term holidays from public school in March 1938, he went to Chelsea Barracks to join the Territorial Army:

> I had to put my age up a year [Laughter]. The adjutant of the unit I went to see said 'how old are you son?' I said '16' and he said '… you're a big chap so why don't you go outside and we'll start this conversation again' [Laughter] and they let me in.[37]

Recruiting officers colluded with enthusiastic underage teenage boys, much as they had in the First World War.[38] Rubinstein was mobilised for the Munich Crisis in September 1938 and delighted in informing his headmaster that he would not be coming to school as he had been called up to an anti-aircraft unit. Following a fortnight's service, and conflict being averted, he returned to school and to his form master's withering put down: 'You may think you're a bloody hero but to me you're just a schoolboy.'

Rubinstein, like many men of his generation, remained impervious to anti-war disillusionment and was part of the flood of volunteers who joined the Territorial Army as war looked increasingly likely. He was later mobilised and was based in London tracking enemy planes in a Searchlights unit. By 1943 he was eager to 'get out' of anti-aircraft as he 'realised that it wasn't going to be very long before somebody tapped me on the shoulder and said you should be doing something a bit more active'. The pressure to play a more dynamic role than that assigned by the forces was often self-imposed, rather than an external one. Working alongside Auxiliary Territorial Service (ATS) women had the potential to undermine young physically fit men, who were 'rankled' by their presence and emasculated by their own implied passivity.[39] This may have prompted Rubinstein to seek a more vigorously combatant wartime role in which women were prevented from participating. He approached the RAF, the Artillery, the Commandos and the Royal Army Service Corps seeking to transfer, all of which would have offered the opportunity to go overseas, but was unsuccessful each time. With a growing sense of frustration that he was not seeing action, he decided to apply for 'the very next thing that comes in' which was a request for volunteers for special operations work in occupied Europe:

> My hand was going like this [shakes frantically] and I thought surely if you're going to live with yourself mate, you'd better go on with it ... And generally we were fed up with what we had been doing in the Army. We wanted to do something ... I wanted to have some control over what I was doing, and anyway it sounded exciting and one thought one would have parachute wings and even a green beret perhaps. And of course vanity plays a part in this. The bravest thing I did was to respond to this bloody letter. It would have been a braver thing to have stepped out of it ... [but I] didn't have the guts to do this, you were going to go on and do it even if you shat your trousers [Laughter].[40]

Rubinstein recognised the seriousness of volunteering for special duties, enlisted so that he might 'live with himself' and overcame his anxiety. While fear preoccupied him, withdrawing from the Jedburghs and returning to his unit would have been more deeply emasculating.

A recurring motif in post-war narratives is that of 'taking control'. Ron Brierley wanted some influence over his posting. Too young to be called up for active service, he volunteered during the Battle of Britain to join a Young Soldiers' Battalion. When he came of conscription age and available for posting overseas, he applied to join the Royal Tank Regiment, 'a far better way to see the war through than stamping around on your feet'.[41] In 1943 he saw a notice on his unit board asking for people with basic knowledge of radio and a willingness to undergo parachute training to volunteer. He had 'still not heard a shot fired in anger' and was 'keen to be in the thick of the action' so put his name forward. Gary Sheffield has noted that soldiers manoeuvred themselves into comparatively 'safe' units of the forces.[42] By contrast, the men who volunteered for hazardous work navigated their way into dangerous roles in a bid to access an experience they had read, heard about and internalised as part of their masculine identity. In doing so, they strove to meet their own perceptions of what constituted acceptable wartime service. Their choice of unit was thus predicated on the unsafe, the less protected. This was despite the fact that they were cognisant of the extreme danger of their role. In fact, proximity to danger and action was a prerequisite to prevent 'missing out'.

The notion of 'doing one's bit' was another common trope in retrospective testimonies of underage volunteering. Sixteen-year-old Harry Verlander was keen to be 'doing something' and recalled 'the frustration of not actually doing anything positive about this war'.[43] Recognising that 'the boys in uniform' were 'getting all the girls', he acquired a khaki uniform in 1941 by joining the Home Guard, an organisation established by Anthony Eden in response to public pressure at the height of the invasion threat in May 1940.[44] The following year he applied to join the King's Royal Rifle Corps, backdating his birth date by two years, and then regularly responded to requests for volunteers to join parachute regiments and commandos because 'angry young men such as me were getting worried. We felt we were not doing enough; we wanted to get back at the Germans before it was too late and dosh out some of our own medicine … Vengeance was on our minds.'[45]

Rubenstein, Brierley and Verlander each volunteered for service prior to reaching the age of conscription and then, 'feeling unappreciated' and 'fed up' with being deployed in Britain and imagining themselves playing a more active role in the war in which they might 'get to grips with the enemy',[46] they made repeated attempts to escape what they perceived to be a dull posting. '[W]hen you're an 18-year-old lad you can't wait to get in there', asserted Fred Bailey.[47] Youthfulness was, then, a key element in narratives of volunteering. Their heroic posturings took different forms but shared much in common; as we saw above, Rubinstein imagined himself in the green beret of Special Forces and proudly sporting the parachute wings badge on his shoulder, visual signifiers attesting to his membership of an elite unit. Fred Bailey, who volunteered for the Royal Armoured Corps on his eighteenth birthday, saw himself as a 'soldier hero' of the North Africa campaign: 'The battle was raging in the desert and I sort of visualised myself out there in a tank.'[48] Glyn Loosmore wanted to 'follow in the steps of Lawrence of Arabia' and, similarly, Bill Colby, who 'fantasized myself' as something akin to Lawrence, recollected buying a copy of *Seven Pillars of Wisdom* and 'pos[ing] as heroes' with his friends.[49] Eighteen-year-old Arthur Brown was also spurred on by the glamour and pluck of volunteering for special duties, and recalled thinking, upon recruitment to the unit that, 'We were heroes already'. His wish fulfilment of joining the Special Forces led to the imagining of his superiority over others; he considered himself a 'brassneck', brimming with 'brazenness, self-confidence'.[50] Young men were especially susceptible to heroic notions regarding special duties and what constituted acceptable military service and used the framework of the 'soldier hero' in their retrospective accounts of volunteering for special duties. Their proximity to a youth culture which valorised sacrifice, nobility and heroic impulsiveness made them fully primed volunteers for roles of danger, pluck and derring-do. Their collective play-acting of manly heroism was to contrast significantly with their experience.

'A MAN FOND OF RISK AND ADVENTURE': RECRUITING FOR SPECIAL DUTIES

Recruitment of personnel for the Jedburghs took place in the latter half of 1943. They needed men who could adapt to the conditions of irregular warfare while also able to organise surprise attacks and military operations.[51] They wanted 'the unconventional, unsubmissive types, the spirited individualist … the troublemakers'.[52] A Student Assessment Board (SAB) gauged to what extent (ranked +, 0, or −) volunteers possessed the thirty-two 'special qualities' that were listed on a form as comprising the ideal recruit: he was to be 'a man of the world' who was 'fond of risk and adventure', 'an aggressive active type' who 'will have enthusiasm for the work' and 'will retain a steady morale', 'a good fighting soldier' with 'good physical stamina' who can 'command others', has 'self-confidence' and 'the will to win and the belief that they will win', a 'man of integrity' who was 'considerate of others', 'a practical sort of man' who 'has plenty of personal initiative' and will 'take decisions decisively'.[53] The language used on the form cataloguing the desirable physical and mental qualities that recruits ought to exhibit mirrors the key stereotypical signifiers of idealised martial masculinity: experience, adventure, aggression, action, drive, physicality, leadership, self-assurance, resolve, honour, pragmatism and resourcefulness. This rigid set of desired characteristics flattens masculinity to a one-dimensional, singular and hegemonic form. Not only does the SAB form make clear what kind of man was required, but it also made evident the exclusion of women.

While SOE and OSS recruited female agents to serve as wireless operators and couriers in France and the Netherlands, the Jedburghs were exclusively male. 'This was sheer bloody fighting, there would have been no role for females here', asserted Dick Rubinstein. 'It wasn't a female environment at all. I don't want to over-dramatise it but it was rough.'[54] The need to withstand punishing circumstances was recognised by headquarters who required the men who passed the SAB to have 'A1 physical fitness and [an] ability to endure possibly extremely hard conditions'.[55] Those that began the Jedburgh training, which commenced on 1 January 1944, were the elite and they were prepared for conditions that they might face behind enemy lines. It was very different to the basic British Army training they had already undertaken; it resembled the physically demanding modern techniques of Commando instruction. The first six weeks included demolitions and weapons training, guerrilla tactics, street fighting and physical training. American Jedburgh Robert Kehoe recalled the 'semireligious dedication to the pushup as being the true mark of manhood'.[56] This competitive ritual, in which recruits measured their manliness against that of their comrades, was an important aspect of male bonding. They were trained in 'ungentlemanly' techniques such as silent killing and unarmed combat. After this initial phase of basic training, they received six weeks of operational training where they were taught how to live off the land and given practical displays of killing animals. On a survival training exercise, they were handed a live sheep and a bag of flour and told 'that's your supper'.[57] The substitution of home, along with all its 'softening' comforts, with the austerity of the great outdoors fashioned a 'hard masculinity' which toughened them up and inculcated manly qualities of grit and determination. The brutal, visceral, sweaty, bloody ungentlemanliness that was cultivated during the training contrasted with the high ideals of noble and sacrificial manliness that they had consumed in their youth.

Parachute training functioned as a vital part of the preparation as this was the method by which the men were infiltrated into occupied France. Those who had parachuted previously often embellished their tales according to Kehoe and 'the listener's ability to absorb tales of gore [was] regarded as a sign of toughness'.[58] The exclusively male unit and the physically demanding nature of the training created a distinct 'soldierly' identity forged in the absence of women and confirmed the

Jedburghs' elite status. As veterans of the service attested: 'we were a bit of an elite', 'something unique, something a bit special', 'it was something to have been a Jed'.[59] This hardened masculinity withstood the bizarre ritual of selecting the multinational teams: a British or American officer teamed up with a French officer and a 'courtship' took place in which the couple were considered 'engaged'. If the men worked well together their 'marriage' was officially announced on the noticeboard. If not, they 'divorced' and selected another mate. A wireless operator of any nationality was then chosen by the couple as their 'child'.[60] The 'family' were then ready for special ops. Family virtues and patriarchal structuring remained at the heart of masculine subjectivities and were cleverly, if amusingly, mobilised here to further cement bonds forged through the hardship of training.

On Active Service: Special Duties Behind Enemy Lines

The first team to be infiltrated was Team Hugh which parachuted into the Châteauroux area in central France on 5/6 June 1944. Team Hilary reported that 'we were received everywhere as heroes' and Team George recalled being greeted as liberators: 'Girls showered the men with kisses and poured them wine and handed them bouquets of flowers.'[61] This was because, as William Crawshay noted, 'We were the boys carrying the goodies', or as Fred Bailey asserted 'the goose that laid the golden egg!'[62] Consequently, they 'lived like fighting cocks'.[63] They basked in the public affirmation of their heroic status. For some, their fantasies were becoming reality. Team Hamish sent a message to London saying, '[we] need mines and booby traps … Been playing games with Boche patrols. It's fun.'[64] Arthur Brown recollected: 'I regarded myself as a boy mucking about in war.'[65] At the liberation of French towns and villages, Jedburghs were frequently feted as heroic emancipators. Harry Verlander recalled being introduced as 'the first English parachutist' to the crowds at Niort on 6 September 1944. 'Over eager females' tried to 'grab hold' of him, 'ladies of all ages' 'smothered' him in 'well meaning kisses' and young women handed him their 'visiting cards' printed with their addresses.[66] Team Gerald participated in the liberation of eight towns and were often met by the mayor, given champagne and flowers and were 'kissed by hundreds of French girls'.[67] Another way in which accounts conformed to the heroic was through the recognition that the physically challenging circumstances in which these men had found themselves encouraged homosocial comradeship. Team Gerald, for example, recorded: 'In our team we had constantly a spirit of cooperation between the three members and I feel sure that the three of us will be life long friends having faced the same dangers.'[68] In these ways the debriefing reports and post-war accounts shore up the heroic image of the irregular soldier. Looking back on his wartime experience with the Jedburghs, Bill Colby noted that this was:

> more than an episode or an adventure. It had a major impact on me personally of course, transforming the young and somewhat shy student I was before into a man with confidence, knowing that I could face risk and danger and hold my own in a company of free spirits exulting in their bravery.[69]

While there is plenty of evidence of action, female adoration and camaraderie in the testimonies, which conform to the classic heroic narrative and assist what oral historians call 'psychic composure', what is particularly striking are the elements that have the potential to unsettle the veteran, to lead to disequilibrium or 'discomposure': the repeated references to the delays, and consequently arriving in France too late to contribute, and to the lack of weaponry to effect action.[70] The promises of both noble manliness, which had been nurtured in their youth, and gritty heroic masculinity, promoted during the specialist training, were left largely unfulfilled by a war careering towards its conclusion while crack troops sat on the sidelines stewing in frustration.

Only one team was infiltrated on the night of 5/6 June 1944, while the other ninety-two were deployed over the course of the next three months. The rapidity with which the Allies advanced meant that many teams were held back. Indeed, some teams were still in Britain on 25 August when Paris was liberated. The men who had volunteered for special duties were greatly frustrated by the delay to the start of their missions. While on standby awaiting deployment, the men whiled away the time playing ball games, attending dances, and visiting the cinema and local pubs. Leo Marks, the head of SOE's coding section, was due to give a lecture but was advised by the commanding officer not to come as the previous two speakers had received 'a very rough reception': the Jedburghs, who 'had been promised a key role on D-Day and were angry at their exclusion' were 'in a state of near mutiny'. He ignored the advice and adopted a belligerent tone, using profane language to explain the thousands of attempts made by his coding staff to crack indecipherable messages: 'listen, you bastards ... we happen to be cunts enough to believe that you're worth it.' He ended by quoting the last line of John Milton's poem 'On His Blindness': 'they also serve who only stand and wait.'[71]

These were men who were 'ready and raring to go', eager to fulfil their masculine fantasies of active military participation.[72] Consequently, many Jedburghs believed they had been infiltrated too late to be of full use. The relative rapidity with which the Allied forces pushed through France meant that some found the area they had parachuted into had already been liberated while others were soon overrun: several teams' missions lasted less than a week. Fifty-two teams, over half the total, commented on this in their debriefing reports. Team Scion, who were infiltrated on 30 August, noted 'we were "workers of the eleventh hour"', 'unable to perform a real Jedburgh task' and considered they had been dropped five months too late.[73] Similarly, Team Douglas were 'regarded as "after the battle troops"'.[74] Team Maurice also wrote of their dissatisfaction and sense of abandonment, making evident their feeling of emasculation: '[b]y the time we arrived in France, our state of mind was somewhat that of a woman whose lover has left without saying goodbye.'[75] This was also a recurring motif in the interviews: Fred Bailey, for example, returned to this issue six times, Dick Rubenstein, who recalled that many of the men were on a training scheme in Britain when news of D-Day circulated, recalled 'we were all a bit disgusted' and Arthur Brown remembered 'we all said "oh God we've missed it!" This was a great source of anger among the Jeds ... Didn't like it one bit.'[76] The rage aimed at the military machine for failing to effectively use them was one way in which they might recoup their lost masculine status: they constructed lengthy narratives of being highly trained elite Special Forces personnel who were prepared to fight and even die but were let down by the decision to delay their entry. The postponement led a number of teams to believe their missions had failed. The despondency felt by the author of Team Andrew's report is palpable: 'I was perhaps of some use as a clothes peg for British uniform ... Mission Andrew was a failure.'[77] Dick Rubenstein, who parachuted on 8 August 1944, returning eighteen days later, noted 'there wasn't really more for us to do ... [M]y work in France was not of great military significance.'[78] He concluded his account of his operations in France: 'that was Rubinstein's role in France and he wasn't very pleased with it. I was just disappointed that's all, but you know it's the luck of the draw.'[79] Looking through his photograph album after the interview, he said of one image of him in his military uniform 'not very manly'. The reality of undertaking special duties, which had failed to live up to their boyish fantasies that had motivated them to volunteer, had the potential to lead to discomposure. This could call into question the coherent masculine identity that the interviewee had carefully constructed up to that point in the oral history interview. This was especially apparent with Oliver Brown. When I asked him what being decorated after the war meant to him, he responded:

> I would have preferred to [hesitation] had [hesitation] something else other than the OBE [Order of the British Empire], although the one I would have preferred to have got is a minor decoration. I'd have rather had an MC [Military Cross] than an OBE. An MC is more a fighting man's medal. The OBE is an organiser's medal. I mean um, they're known in the services, the OBE, for 'other bugger's efforts' [laughter] or 'on bottom earned'! [laughter] I would rather pass that [MC] on to my family than an organising [medal]. I mean I'd rather felt that the family would recognise me as a fighting soldier than an organising soldier.[80]

For others, it was their specific role that prevented them from fulfilling their fantasies of heroic action. Wireless operators were essential for maintaining contact with Allied headquarters and were often prohibited by their leaders from engaging in combat operations. Jack Grinham was envious of his team members who had greater opportunities to ambush the enemy: 'I had to stay at the farm with my radio so I missed all the fun, and to my disgust never fired a shot in anger.'[81]

The failure of headquarters to deliver supplies as promised was another source of frustration. Seventeen team reports noted that requests went unanswered. Team Ivor stated: 'In six weeks, to arm approximately 5000 men we received but 5 aircraft, one of which dropped precisely one package… They might as well have sent us knitting needles.'[82] Their inability to secure supplies for the resistance undermined their authority and served to emasculate them. The disparaging reference to knitting needles undoubtedly refers to the connotations of this implement of productive feminine leisure that was a central plank of the female war effort in the two world wars. The strength of feeling was also evident in Team George's report:

When we received the message giving us the order to attack, as we were about to be over run without having received the armament for the 4,000 men we had at that time organized and for the 5,000 who would very soon be ready, we cried like kids considering our useless set, our useless work and all the dangers that patriots of Loire Inferieure had gone through to get to that point, and remembering how many guys in prison or under the earth had paid for the trouble they had looking for useless grounds and organizing useless reception committees – for planes which never came … We were feeling very depressed, considering what could have been done if we had received the arms and money we were begging for in time.[83]

The Jedburghs' sense of impotence, expressed so vividly in personal accounts ('depressed', 'disgust', 'disappointed', 'not very glorious', 'a failure', 'not very pleased', 'useless'), is evidence that the fantasies of action that had motivated them to enlist played out very differently in reality. Knitting, crying and begging were hardly the manly actions and virtues that they had imbibed in their youth.

CONCLUSION

Gendered expectations of warfare were not insignificant to the men who volunteered to join the Jedburghs. Having internalised the flat-tened and heroic masculinity of their inter-war childhoods, perceptions of their own manliness shaped outlooks and actions. The Special Forces presented an opportunity to assert masculinity as something brave, dar-ing and individualistic. They ultimately held themselves to a standard of masculinity that their actual experience of war could not deliver. While occupied France provided a space in which heroic masculinity could be played out, for many the reality did not live up to the fantasy: long delays in infiltration resulted in a belief that they had not been fully utilised, failure to drop the required supplies rendered them impotent, the cos-seted role of wireless operator prevented some from seeing any action and the presentation of 'organising' rather than 'fighting' medals was a further blow to masculinity. Many men who were denied active overseas service (whether it was because of being in a reserved occupation, con-scripted to work in the mines as a 'Bevin Boy' or because of undertaking a 'safer' military role on the home front) experienced a strong sense of emasculation. This feeling of impotence was heightened for the men who had been trained to see themselves as the elite, elevated above others in the military, and who expected to have the opportunity to act heroically. This caused a great internal conflict. The primacy of active service was so important to some men that to have it removed caused clear ruptures in their masculine sense of self. Their disappointment and disgust decades later demonstrate the potency of these ideals and the impotency of frustrated manliness. It was no coincidence that so many of the ninety British Jedburghs turned to the Empire to reconstitute their masculinities, volunteering to join Force 136 for further action. Operating as three-man British Jed teams, they tested their manhood in an altogether different kind of guerrilla warfare in the Burmese jungle. The colonial arena provided a landscape for the fulfilment of their imperial soldier hero desires.

Notes

1. J. Mackenzie (1987), 'The Imperial Pioneer and Hunter and the British Masculine Stereotype', in J.A. Mangan and J. Walvin (eds), *Manliness and Morality: Middle Class Masculinity in Britain and America, 1800–1940* (Manchester: Manchester University Press), pp. 179–191.
2. C. Peniston-Bird (2012), '"All in it Together and Backs to the Wall": Relating Patriotism and the People's War in the 21st Century', *Oral History*, 40:2, pp. 69–80.
3. M. Connelly and D.R. Willcox (2005), 'Are you Tough Enough? The Image of the Special Forces in British Popular Culture, 1939–2004', *Historical Journal of Film, Radio and Television*, 25:1, pp. 1–25, here pp. 4, 19, 3.
4. G. Dawson (1994), *Soldier Heroes: British Adventure, Empire and the Imagining of Masculinities* (London: Routledge), p. 1.
5. J. Tosh (2005), 'Masculinities in an Industrializing Society: Britain, 1800–1914', *Journal of British Studies*, 44:2, pp. 330–342.
6. M. Roper (2005), 'Between Manliness and Masculinity: The "War Generation" and the Psychology of Fear in Britain, 1914–1950', *Journal of British Studies*, 44:2, pp. 343–362.
7. R.W. Connell (1995), *Masculinities* (Cambridge: Polity Press), p. 77.
8. P. Wilkinson (1997), *Foreign Fields: The Story of an SOE Operative* (London: I.B. Tauris), p. 128; P. Wilkinson, interviewed by Juliette Pattinson, 19 December 1998; TNA, HS7/17 Jedburgh History Vol. I.
9. A. Brown (1995), *The Jedburghs: A Short History* (unpublished); G. Loosmore (n.d.) *A Postscript to Arthur Brown's The Jedburghs: A Short History* (unpublished); R. Ford (2004), *Steel from the Sky: the Jedburgh Raiders, France, 1944* (London: Orion); W. Irwin (2005) *The Jedburghs: The Secret History of the Allied Special Forces. France 1944* (New York:

Public Affairs); C. Beavan (2006), *Operation Jedburgh: D-Day and America's First Shadow War* (New York: Viking).

10. B.F. Jones (2016), *Eisenhower's Guerrillas: The Jedburghs, the Maquis and the Liberation of France* (Oxford: Oxford University Press).

11. G. Mosse (1996), *The Image of Man: the Creation of Modern Masculinity* (Oxford: Oxford University Press); E. Showalter (1985),'Male Hysteria: W.H.R. Rivers and the Lessons of Shell Shock', in *The Female Malady: Women, Madness and English Culture* (New York: Pantheon), pp. 167–194.

12. A. Light (1991), *Forever England: Femininity, Literature and Conservatism between the Wars* (Abingdon: Routledge); S.O. Rose (2004), 'Temperate Heroes: Concepts of Masculinity in Second World War Britain', in S. Dudink, K. Hagemann and J. Tosh (eds), *Masculinities in Politics and War: Gendering Modern History* (Manchester: Manchester University Press), pp. 177–195.

13. J. Meyer (2009), *Men of War: Masculinity and the First World War in Britain* (Basingstoke: Palgrave), p. 7.

14. V. Brittain (1933), *Testament of Youth* (New York: Macmillan), p. 560.

15. Brooke had sold 300,000 copies by 1929, Owen 1400. H. Strachan (1997), 'The Soldier's Experience in Two World Wars: Some Historiographical Comparisons', in P. Addison and A. Calder (eds), *Time to Kill: The Soldier's Experience of War in the West, 1939–1945* (London: Pimlico), pp. 369–378, here p. 370.

16. G. Loosmore, letter written to J. Pattinson, 9 October 2000.

17. Loosmore, interviewed by C. Wood, 16 March 1998, IWM SA 17949.

18. First published on 29 June 1916 in *The New Witness*.

19. Wilfred Owen, 'Anthem for Doomed Youth', October–December 1917.

20. Ibid.

21. K. Boyd (1991), 'Knowing Your Place: The Tensions of Manliness in Boys' Story Papers, 1918–39', in M. Roper and J. Tosh (eds), *Manful Assertions: Masculinities in Britain since 1800* (London: Routledge), pp. 145–167, here p. 146.

22. G. Orwell (1957), 'Boys' Weeklies', in *Selected Essays* (Harmondsworth: Penguin), pp. 175–203, here pp. 196–202.

23. Loosmore, IWM SA 17949.

24. K. Boyd (2003), *Manliness and the Boys' Story Paper in Britain: A Cultural History, 1855–1940* (Basingstoke: Palgrave), p. 3.

25. Loosmore, letter.

26. Mee, *Children's Encyclopaedia*, Vol. 6, p. 546.

27. Loosmore, IWM SA 17949.

28. Orwell, 'Boys' Weeklies', p. 200.

29. Dawson, *Soldier Heroes*, p. 4.

30. R. Brierley, interviewed by J. Pattinson, 5 August 1999.

31. R. Miller (2003), *Behind the Lines: The Oral History of Special Operations in World War II* (London: Pimlico), p. 146.
32. F. Bailey, interviewed by Juliette Pattinson, 12 August 2016.
33. W. Colby (1978), *Honourable Men: My Life in the CIA* (New York: Simon & Schuster), p. 36.
34. For a fuller discussion of enlistment narratives, see J. Morley (2013), 'An Examination of the Influence of the First World War on Attitudes to Service in the Second World War', unpublished PhD thesis, QMUL.
35. Ronald ('Tommy') MacPherson, interviewed by C. Wood, 14 February 1998, IWM SA 17912.
36. D. Rubenstein, interviewed by J. Pattinson, 18 August 1999.
37. Ibid.
38. 250,000 underage boys served in the First World War. R. van Emden (2005), *Boy Soldiers of the Great War* (London: Headline).
39. J. Schwarzkopf (2009), 'Combatant or Non-Combatant? The Ambiguous Status of Women in British Anti-Aircraft Batteries during the Second World War', *War & Society*, 28:2, pp. 105–131, here p. 119.
40. Rubenstein, interview.
41. Ibid.
42. G.D. Sheffield (1997), 'The Shadow of the Somme: The Influence of the First World War on British Soldiers' Perceptions and Behaviour in the Second World War', in Addison and Calder, *Time to Kill*, pp. 29–39, p. 32.
43. H. Verlander, http://evacueetosoe.com/Author.html. Accessed 5 April 2016; H. Verlander (2010) *My War in SOE* (Bromley: Independent Books), p. 75.
44. P. Summerfield and C. Peniston-Bird (2007), *Contesting Home Defense: Men, Women, and the Home Guard in the Second World War* (Manchester: Manchester University Press).
45. Verlander, *My War in SOE*, p. 36.
46. F. Bailey, interviewed by M. Cox, 11 May 2009.
47. F. Bailey, interviewed by J. Pattinson, 12 August 2016.
48. Ibid.
49. Loosmore, IWM SA 17949; Colby, *Honourable Men*, p. 36.
50. A. Brown, interviewed by J. Pattinson, 24 August 1999.
51. TNA, HS7/17 Jedburgh History Vol. I.
52. K. Carew (2016), *Dadland* (London: Vintage), p. 27.
53. TNA, HS7/18 Jedburgh History Vol. II.
54. Rubenstein, interview.
55. TNA, HS7/17 Jedburgh History Vol. I.
56. R.R. Kehoe (1997), '1944: An Allied Team with the French Resistance', uploaded in 2007 to: https://www.cia.gov/library/center-for-the-study-of-intelligence/csi-publications/csi-studies/studies/winter98_99/art03.html. Accessed 5 April 2016.

57. S. Cannicott (n.d.), *Journey of a Jed* (London: Special Forces Club), p. 25.
58. Kehoe, '1944: An Allied Team'.
59. Rubenstein, interview; Brierley, interview; R. Leney, interviewed by Juliette Pattinson, 17 November 1999.
60. Miller, *Behind the Lines*/Stanley Cannicort, IWM Documents.
61. TNA HS6/524 Team Hilary; Cannicott, *Journey of a Jed*, p. 74.
62. IWM SA 12521; F. Bailey, interviewed by M. Cox, 11 May 2009.
63. J. Sharp, interviewed by M. Cox, 11 May 2009.
64. TNA HS6/520 Team Hamish.
65. Brown, interview.
66. Verlander, *My War in SOE*, p. 116.
67. TNA HS6/513 Team Gerald.
68. TNA HS6/513 Team Gerald.
69. Colby, *Honourable Men*, p. 54.
70. P. Summerfield (2000), 'Discomposing the Subject: Intersubjectivities in Oral History', in T. Cosslett, C. Lury and P. Summerfield (eds), *Feminism and Autobiography: Texts, Theories, Methods* (New York: Routledge), pp. 91–106.
71. L. Marks (1998), *Between Silk and Cyanide: the Story of S.O.E.'s Code War* (London: HarperCollins), pp. 528, 534, 535.
72. J. Grinham, letter written to J. Pattinson, 16 February 2000.
73. TNA HS6/558 Team Scion; TNA HS7/19 Jedburgh History Vol. III. Report on Team Scion.
74. TNA HS6/502 Team Douglas.
75. TNA HS6/542 Team Maurice.
76. Rubenstein, interview; A. Brown, interview.
77. TNA HS6/477 Team Andrew.
78. D. Rubinstein, *Churchill's Secret Army*.
79. Rubenstein, interview.
80. O. Brown, interview.
81. Grinham, letter.
82. TNA HS6/528 Team Ivor.
83. TNA HS6/511 Team George.

Acknowledgements I would like to thank Nigel Perrin and Emily Manktelow for their insightful comments on this chapter.

CHAPTER 3

'Man, Lunatic or Corpse': Fear, Wounding and Death in the British Army, 1939–45

Emma Newlands

In November 1942 Lieutenant Neil McCallum was deployed with the Eighth Army at the Second Battle of El Alamein. He wrote in his diary:

> It is the end of two years transformation from raw rookie in Britain to battle-reinforcement in Africa. This is the last metamorphosis and whatever emerges will be man, lunatic or corpse. One can sink no further into anonymity, be stripped no more of the idiosyncrasies of personality and taste. I am now what my civilisation has been striving to create for so long, a technically valuable, humanly worthless piece of flesh and blood, animate, responsive, and supposedly faithful until death.[1]

McCallum was part of a reinforcement draft of young officers assembled by the War Office for overseas service in July 1942. He was one of over two-and-a-half million million soldiers who served overseas during the Second World War. The majority of these men were, like McCallum, conscripts, recruited under the British Government's National Service Acts.[2] McCallum's experience of military service up to this point had been fairly typical. He had undergone sixteen weeks of general service

E. Newlands (✉)
University of Strathclyde, Glasgow, UK
e-mail: e.newlands@strath.ac.uk

© The Author(s) 2018
L. Robb and J. Pattinson (eds.), *Men, Masculinities and Male Culture in the Second World War*, Genders and Sexualities in History,
https://doi.org/ 10.1057/978-1-349-95290-8_3

47

training at Richmond Barracks in London, where he had been given an army number and uniform, had his hair shaved, and ate, slept and worked alongside a squad of other men. He had been schooled in weapons instruction, physical training, route marching and drill. Selected for officer training, McCallum spent a further six months at a depot in Winchester for technical and leadership instruction, more physical training and drill. After three months in the Home Defence Forces, and a period of further training in Norwich, McCallum travelled to Glasgow, where he boarded a ship to Egypt. Seven weeks later he arrived in the Suez area, where he spent two months being trained in desert warfare and became physically acclimatised to the hot environment. He was then sent forward to Alamein.[3] Thus, for almost two years, McCallum had been subject to a range of physical interventions by the authorities that were designed to transform him into an effective military machine, a 'technically valuable piece of flesh and blood'. Having been honed and primed for warfare, his body was expected to remain disciplined and obedient, even in the difficult circumstances of engagement with the enemy where its damage and destruction were imminent.

This chapter examines official and individual responses to fear, wounding and death in order to explore what happened to soldiers' bodies in combat: the moment for which men had long been prepared. Between 1939 and 1945 almost a quarter of a million British soldiers, one out of every ten, were wounded while on active service overseas. A further 150,000 personnel died as a result of military action. These figures respectively represented 86 and 42 per cent of all British service casualties.[4] For men who were not physically injured, fear of action could be just as debilitating. As Joanna Bourke notes, 'whatever a soldier's rank, fear was his persistent adversary and its effects upon the body were particularly evident in wartime'.[5] Physical manifestations included trembling hands, sweating palms, chronic gastrointestinal problems and the malfunctioning of the nervous system. Nevertheless, we know very little about these moments of problematic bodily performance in the context of the Second World War.[6] The medical treatment and rehabilitation of wounded servicemen have been the focus of scholarly attention. In his study of the British Army overseas, Mark Harrison argues that well-practised medicine in the field was crucial to military successes. Improvements in disease prevention and combat casualty care stemmed not only from new developments in hygiene, surgery and technology, but from a unique 'medical consciousness' among British officers who recognised the importance of manpower conservation.[7] Julie Anderson has considered what happened to wounded and disabled bodies once they left the battlefield and the hospital, arguing that wartime experience led to a 'modern, organised system of rehabilitation' that drew on combined medical, industrial and social expertise.[8] Nevertheless, the question of what happened to soldiers in the moments leading up to action and at the time of injury remains unexplored. Similarly, the question of what happened to soldiers' bodies once they had expired is largely unknown.[9] All of these issues will be examined in this chapter. The methods used by the military authorities to counter the physiological effects of fear, the army's medical arrangements and official burial regulations will all be explored. These procedures, I suggest, were designed to control, order and organise men's bodies in the pursuit of manpower efficiency, even when they were injured or killed.

More importantly, this chapter examines the experiences of front-lines troops; the foot soldiers, tank crews and artillerymen exposed to the full rigours of warfare.[10] Between a third and one-quarter of British troops served in combat roles between 1939 and 1945.[11] As such, their accounts have largely been forgotten within the popular memory of the Second World War, which as John Ellis notes 'owes more to fond allusions to foreign climes, sunshine, good health and periodic binges than to any real conception of conditions at the front'.[12] This chapter looks beyond this nostalgic version of war service to examine the complexities of ordinary military experience.[13] Through an analysis of soldiers' personal testimonies, it explores the ways in which men felt and expressed fear, suffering and loss through their responses to the danger and damage that war could inflict on their bodies and on others around them. Scrutinising the bodily experiences of soldiers in this way opens up a number of key themes such as control, agency and resistance, gender identities, emotional responses to war, and memories of armed conflict.[14] Personal accounts of military service have been found in soldiers' memoirs, diaries and, predominantly, through a selection of oral history interviews held in the Imperial War Museum's sound archive. While these sources are subject to all the caveats that surround the use of personal testimonies, they are highly revealing: not only do they provide insight into intricacies of military experience, they help us to understand how soldiers have constructed their narratives of wartime service by inextricably linking 'memory, subjectivity and the materiality of the body'.[15]

FEAR

For British front-line troops, military service between 1939 and 1945 meant long marches and patrols, night-time ambushes and large-scale attacks. Deployed to Africa, Asia, the Mediterranean and North West Europe, British soldiers fought in a range of terrains and climates. They experienced a world characterised by noise, danger, discomfort and almost constant uncertainty. Although training had been designed to indoctrinate men into the military command structure and develop a combative mindset, the reality of active service could still come as a profound shock. Describing his first experience of action during the Normandy campaign in June 1944, Private Eric Woods explained that:

> All hell broke loose. It [training] isn't the same. You don't have the dust and the smell of bodies that have been lying about in the sun for several days. The horror was not there. The smells and sights contributed to the horror ... It was a sight one will never forget.[16]

Wood's memories of combat were therefore inextricably linked to bodily sensations. He described the shock of battle with reference to certain sights and smells, which he vividly remembered over fifty years later.

In such an unforgiving environment, men could also succumb to a sense of fear that was intrinsically physical. Some men were worried about what could happen to their bodies, or specific bodily parts. Lionel Leach served as an officer with the Royal Artillery in Abyssinia. He explained that: 'I always had a fear that I would have my elbow blown off.'[17] For infantryman John Jarvis the prospect of losing his legs was worse than death:

> The only one thing that worried me all the time in my service was this bleedin' thought I had about getting shot in the legs, getting me legs off. And I think if I'd had the courage, if I'd getting shot in the legs and I knew me legs was to come off, I'd have shot myself, you know. I dreaded it that much. Apart from that, nothing perturbed me at all. I wasn't perturbed about nothing, you know.[18]

John even contemplated suicide as a preferable alternative to permanent disability and concentrated his fear on the possibility of being shot in the legs. Indeed, he suggested that nothing else about combat worried him at all. The face and genitalia also merited special protection among troops. According to military psychiatrists, these were the parts of the body that men tried to cover first during air raids.[19] In his memoir McCallum described a young subaltern named Lofty who remarked before arriving in Egypt: 'I don't mind being killed. What gets me is being wounded, blind or something.' McCallum replied: 'The old story, eyes and genitals. You're too young, my little friend, to have the latter.'[20] Youth, masculinity, anatomy and emotions were therefore closely intertwined as soldiers subscribed to a phallic sense of maleness.[21] Perhaps vanity played a part and men did not want to be disfigured. Yet fear of blindness was also equated with fear of castration, an injury that represented impotence and emasculation.[22]

Other soldiers' fears were manifested through their bodies, resulting in shaking, sweating, dizziness and insomnia.[23] Bodily responses to fear were most commonly located in the stomach. Soldiers reported 'gut-wrenching' and 'gut-strangling' sensations.[24] Of particular concern to the medical authorities from early on in the war were high rates of abdominal complaints in both the military and civilian populations. By 1942 gastric disorders, or 'military dyspepsia', were responsible for 17 per cent of discharges for disease in the army and RAF. Medical professionals increasingly explained these conditions in emotional rather than purely physiological terms.[25] American psychiatrists P.M. Lichtenstein and S.M. Small explained in their *Handbook of Military Psychiatry*:

> Gastric hypertension, nausea, vomiting, cramps and diarrhea [*sic*] are commonly observed in both the British and American armies. The British consider 'dyspepsia' as the largest single type of disease among the military ill, and it has been recently reported as the second major medical problem, the first being the psychiatric one – among our own military sick. There is general agreement that psychologic factors, especially prolonged emotional strains such as chronic anxiety, tension and resentment, play a part.[26]

According to some military personnel, however, dyspeptic soldiers were simply malingerers who took advantage of difficulties in diagnosing abdominal disorders.[27] In his memoir, Scots Guards Officer George MacDonald Fraser described the suspicion directed towards one man before an attack against the Japanese in Burma:

> When I pressed his lower right abdomen he yelped. I told him to report to the M.O. and went over to tell Peel, who was falling the section in. "He'll

have to go sick", I said. "Aye", said Forster. "Sick wid nerves". I said it might be appendicitis – being from a medical family you feel obliged to give idiotic diagnoses every so often – and Forster spat and said: "I doot it". Peel said nothing, and we moved off to the assembly point. It wasn't appendicitis, but I'm not saying Forster was right; the man was in pain, and it would have taken an expert to determine what caused it. What was interesting was the section's indifference; whether he was sick or scared made no odds, since either would make him an unreliable quantity in action, and it was never referred to again.[28]

Despite the distrust levelled towards this soldier by some of the men, he was ultimately considered of no military value. Regardless of whether he really was sick, was incapacitated through fear or was feigning his symptoms, he was a hazard to the military mission and was removed from the group.

Concerned about the potential of fear to undermine the military mission, army leaders and medical staff employed a range of bodily strategies to counter its harmful effects. As had been common practice during the First World War, some troops were issued with a rum ration before going into battle. A quarter-pint measure, sometimes added to tea or cocoa, was thought to be enough to loosen men's inhibitions without making them sick.[29] According to British Army psychiatrist Lieutenant-Colonel S.A. MacKeith, it 'was likely to be good for a period of waiting and might be good for going over the top'.[30] Officer Henry Wilmot issued rum to his men in Italy because it gave them 'Dutch courage'.[31] Lieutenant John Cordwell-Horstall claimed that it was a 'battle winner' at Monte Cassino.[32] Certainly, soldiers who received rum felt that it was beneficial. Infantryman Ernest Harvey, who was given some before going into action in France in 1944, recalled that 'it put some heat into the body', while Herbert Beddows, who had rum on board a landing craft headed for the Normandy beaches in 1944, remembered that 'it fortified me a little and that was very nice'.[33] As such, the army was able to bolster and reinforce men's bodies against the effects of fear.

Yet fear could also be cumulative, something that took hold when a man's courage had run out.[34] Reflecting on the European campaign, D-Day veteran Geoffrey Picot explained in his memoir:

If casualties in battle tend to be around twenty per cent, if you have fought five battles and are still safe, if the army has advanced only thirty miles from the coast and it's still 600 miles to Berlin, what are your chances of surviving till the end? That is the fear that eats away at you. Every man has only a finite supply of courage. It can get used up. Then you must have a long rest for bravery to grow again.[35]

From a medical perspective, repeated exposure to hazards left men unable to overcome theirfears and susceptible to more serious psychological conditions, including hysteria, neurasthenia and battle exhaustion. Symptoms included violent shaking, deafness, blindness, mutism and paralysis.[36] Soldiers who suffered from these conditions were a serious drain on manpower, accounting for between 10 and 30 per cent of all casualties overseas.[37] Efforts to prevent men from succumbing to more serious psychiatric conditions again often centred on the physical. The Army Medical Service set up forward psychiatric centres where men received hot food, sweet tea, a bath, a change of clothes and, if needed, a sedative.[38] The rationale behind these centres was to prevent men who were showing slightly neurotic tendencies from developing acute anxiety states. The centres were generally successful as sixty-five per cent of men returned to full combatant duties within a week.[39] According to a medical report from India, 'the men improved out of all recognition with nothing more than sleep, food, a wash and a change of clothing'.[40]

Despite all of the measures adopted by the military and medical authorities to regulate men's emotions, soldiers' testimonies reveal that being in the combat zone invoked a range of responses. Confronted with threats to their bodies, some men were able to convert their fears into action. Officer William Scroggie first went into battle during the Allied advance on the Gothic Line in Italy in 1944. Later describing how he felt he stated: 'I discovered that there is nothing more exhilarating in the world than combat. You behave as if your body belonged to someone else. You have no fear, no worries. You're on some kind of alternative high and it's just tremendously exciting and exhilarating.'[41] In his memoir, Scots Guards officer W.A. Elliot described his first encounter with the enemy during an ambush in Italy:

An awful savagery now seemed to take hold of us as we rushed along the embankment shouting oaths and shooting at Germans who were lying there. I felt as if some wild animal had got me by the throat and I had to keep shooting or else my normal self would return bringing fear along with it. There was even a savage pleasure in it. One German was truculent, refusing to double back down the line, and while we were arguing and threatening him, other Germans fired at us out of a trench. I shot him point blank; the effect was electric.[42]

Elliot's story suggests an out-of-body experience. He felt as if an animal had got hold of him, which kept his fear at bay. As the attack continued, he experienced a sense of energy and exhilaration culminating in an 'electric effect' as he confronted the prospect of death and his fear was transformed into pleasure.

For others, being in the combat zone was simply too frightening. Some soldiers resorted to harming their own bodies in order to get out of the front line. Self-inflicted wounds were a court-martial offence punishable by detention. Between 1939 and 1945, 265 British soldiers serving overseas were found guilty of this crime.[43] Charles Bennett remembered a fellow soldier in Italy who 'shot himself in the foot cos he couldn't stand the shelling'.[44] On active service in India in 1944, William Cornell also encountered a man who shot himself in the foot before going into combat. He recalled:

> I heard a rifle shot go off right next door to where I was in my slit trench. I went over and said 'what have you done?' He said 'my gun went off accidentally.' I said 'you're in trouble, you know that?' He said 'I know.' He'd blown all his toes off with his own rifle. He said 'I can't face it. I can't go on any further.' I said 'but there's none of us been hurt yet.' He said 'I know but I can't face it. I can't face what's coming.' The medics came and he was escorted away. No doubt he ended up in a detention centre somewhere in India, minus two toes.[45]

Such was the extent that men would go to in order to escape the possibility of death and serious bodily injury. By inflicting wounds on themselves, soldiers could control the damage to their bodies, rather than taking their chances with the enemy.

Men who ventured into battle also found that when fear took over they were unable to put their training into practice. Ronald Petts served with the Royal Army Medical Corps in North West Europe. He explained: 'I learned the lesson that it's no good accepting the fact that an apparent corpse lying there is in fact dead. I came across a number of men who were not really wounded but absolutely transfixed with fear, just lying there, frozen.'[46] Sent in as part of the Allied beach landings on D-Day, William Spearman noticed how some men were unable to advance. He explained:

> You stay and die or you get off and live. People doing it for the first time, no matter how many times you tell them, they don't realise it, and nobody gets off the beach. Any one of us could tell you, they wouldn't get off. They were transfixed with fright. They couldn't get off. We were transfixed with fright but we had the knowledge that you either stopped and died or got off and got away.

While Spearman was able to convert his own fear into action in order to ensure his survival, he was unable to persuade the other men to do so. His repetition of the word 'transfixed' suggests a hypnotic state, a loss of control over mind and body, something that some of the men could not overcome, as they remained motionless with horror. A similar story was told by McCallum when he described the plight of one man in his unit during the Battle of the Mareth Line in Tunisia in 1943:

> One of the men in the company lay down and began to sob. He was one of the older men, almost forty, old enough to be the father of some of the youngsters with us. How to explain to him in the middle of battle that he should be up on his feet with his rifle in his hand – aggressively tough – and not spend his glorious patriotic hour lying on the ground moaning for his wife and family in the suburban home? There was no time to explain, to argue, to plead. He was beyond the direct order of oblique persuasion. He was left lying, the tears on his face mixed with sand and earth.[47]

Perhaps considered as a father figure, this soldier was expected to demonstrate his manliness in front of the younger recruits. Yet he was unable to so in the heat of battle. In such instances the body was rendered useless, leaving men incapable of performing their military duties, even in the face of death. As McCallum noted, the older man was supposed to be ready for action and 'aggressively tough', yet his emotion overrode his ability to continue with the task at hand. Recognising that he was beyond help, the other men in the unit had no choice but to leave him lying on the ground and continue without him.

Even men who tried to repress the manifestations of their fears could be powerless to do so. Try as he might to stop, John Buchanan would 'involuntarily twitch with fear' before going into battle in France. Patrol activity was a particularly nerve-wracking experience involving forays into enemy-occupied territory. Describing a night patrol in Belgium, infantry-man Rex Wingfield wrote in his memoir that 'we shivered. We shook. We shuddered. Our teeth chattered. We were bathed in sweat. Our mus-cles twitched and strained as we fought to stop ourselves from vomiting. It was no good. We leaned over the wall.'[48] It seems that these men's rational calculations were overwhelmed by their emotional bodies. At the moment for which their bodies had long been trained and prepared for, they became become most individualistic, betraying the instructions of military superiors and the soldiers themselves.

WOUNDING

In addition to dealing with the emotional effects of war on the body, the army also had to retrieve, transport and treat the almost quarter-of-a-million men who were physically wounded as a result of military service. In order to preserve manpower it was imperative that soldiers who could resume active duties were returned as quickly as possible to combat thea-tres, while those with injuries too severe were discharged and returned to civilian life. To this end, the army put in place a series of medical posts that moved men gradually away from fighting zones to supply bases. The chain of evacuation began with regimental aid posts near the front, fol-lowed by advanced dressing stations, field dressing stations, field surgical units, casualty clearing stations and general hospitals at the rear. Within this chain of evacuation worked teams of stretcher squads, ambulance crews, nurses, medical officers and surgeons. These medical personnel sorted and prioritised bodies according to a system of triage that ranked patients according to severity of wounds and chances of survival. Based on the French word 'trier', meaning to sort, triage had been applied in the armed forces since the eighteenth century.[49] It was designed to streamline the delivery of treatment and maximise the use of resources.[50] As such, men with the poorest odds were made as comfortable as pos-sible and were often given morphine to ease their pain. Medical orderly Joseph Day served in Egypt and recalled that 'they sometimes gave lethal doses in order to stop the suffering'.[51] Ronald Petts, an officer in the Royal Army Medical Corps in Germany, likewise explained, 'you knew how many grains would be an overdose and send him quickly on his way. The great thing was to knock out his pain and his consciousness.'[52] Implementing triage could, however, be ethically challenging for medical staff. Army surgeon John Watts was assigned to a busy casualty clearing station in Normandy on D-Day, where he was confronted with one particular case of abdominal wounding. He noted in his memoir:

> I had ten cases awaiting operation, all of them with a reasonable chance if they were operated on in time. This man's plight seemed so desperate that even if operated on he would have little chance of survival. Despondently I arranged for him to have a large dose of morphia to ease his pain, and instructed the stretcher bearers to put him in a corner to die. Then back to my cellar and the ten cases.[53]

Soldiers who were treated at medical facilities entered into a target-driven system in which clear optimums and limits were set for staff working in different operational settings. In field dressing stations, where surgeries were not performed, the Army Medical Services stipulated that 250 soldiers should be treated every 24 hours. In field surgical units a lower rate was set at one man every hour. The army's emphasis on speed and efficiency was recognised by soldiers like John Buchanan, who was hit with shrapnel in his back and chose to go absent without leave from a field hospital in France. He explained, 'when you go back to these places you're impersonal. You're just a number. So I said "I'm going back." They didn't stop me. They wanted rid of us anyway, one way or another.'[54] It is clear that John felt dehumanised by a system that was designed to do exactly that: treat his body as a cog in the wider military machine.

Similar to veterans' accounts of fear, there is a clear sense of detachment between body and self in soldiers' stories of wounding. In their testimonies, men commonly describe a feeling of alienation from their bodies. Arthur Thompson was hit by enemy shelling in Normandy in 1944 and lost his right leg. He explained that 'When it's chopped off like that you don't feel any pain. I was amazed. As soon as I moved, that was when I knew I'd lost my leg because it dropped off. You felt the bones grating but there was no pain with it. You felt the bone grating as it dropped off and it was just fastened on with skin at the back.'[55] Upon being hit by Japanese shellfire in northern India in 1944, Arthur McCrystal likewise experienced 'no pain as such … I mean, nothing would work but there was no knowledge of anything. I didn't know what had happened, in fact.'[56] In his memoir, W.A. Elliot described being hit by Japanese shelling in Rangoon. He also noted that 'I found myself in the curious position of thinking that I was looking down on myself. My reactions were "my God, I must be absolutely riddled", as I noticed in a detached way, blood beginning to flow down my left side.'[57] Within these narratives, the men focus on describing the bodily damage caused by injury rather than any felt experience of pain.[58] All three claimed that they were unaware that they had been wounded, or did not realise the extent of their wounds until they noticed clinical signs. Elliot realised that he had been hit when he saw 'blood beginning to flow'. Arthur Thompson became aware of his severed leg when it 'dropped off', while Arthur McCrystal was only aware that 'nothing would work'. Although it is clear that injury brought their bodies into a heightened state of consciousness, the men experienced their wounds as something 'other' to the self.[59] This is also evident in rifleman William Dilworth's testimony. He was hit by an enemy mine while on night patrol in Italy. Like other soldiers, Dilworth claimed that he felt no immediate pain. Initially rendered unconscious by the blast, he started to search for his wounds when he came round:

> I started putting my hands between my body; funny thing how you put your hands into feel for your heart first. If you'd been hit in the heart you'd have been dead anyway so you wouldn't have been able to feel. It's a silly thing but it's automatic. So you feel, nothing there, pushing me hands in between the earth and me body, nothing wrong. I put my hands round the back and my hand sunk into my stomach, from the back. Well that's how it feels, because the nerve endings are so tender then that even a tiny hole feels as though it's a great big hole, you know. And I thought my hand had gone straight in and there was nothing, so I thought to myself, I'm gonna die. I've got no stomach or anything. I'm gonna die. I could imagine this great big hole in my back.[60]

While Dilworth became acutely aware of his body at this point, he experienced it in a disconnected and unfamiliar way. He searched for his injuries with his hands, suggesting that he could not sense any pain directly. Once found, he had a distorted view of his wounds, that there 'was a great big hole' in his back. His locating of his wounds brought his body into a heightened state of consciousness as he came to anticipate the extent of the damage caused. As his testimony continued, Dilworth accounted for each one of his injuries by reference to specific bodily parts:

I was wounded in this leg, in the foot here. One ball bearing went in here. One ball bearing went in there because the one that hit me in the back spun me round and of course the rest of them were coming at me sideways, you see. Well that's the only reason they, we can think of. In actual fact I was hit twice in the back. One by the spine and one just slightly off from the spine. And all in total I've had nine operations on my spine, on my back.[61]

Dilworth focused on the number, location and nature of his injuries when constructing his wounding narrative. Although he could not describe the sensation of being wounded or recollect the exact circumstances that led to his injuries, he was able to use physical markers to explain these past events. In this respect, his body literally connected him to his wartime experience.[62]

A soldier's ability to cope with his injuries could also cause a sense of disconnect between body and self. The experience of being wounded confronted men with a direct challenge to military expectations of resilience and forbearance.[63] This is clear in the testimony of Leslie Perry, who found an unusual way of controlling his emotions after losing his left leg and his right arm in a mine blast in Normandy. When he was collected by the stretcher bearers Perry began to sing because 'I was frightened to make myself look stupid by crying. I didn't want to cry. I felt like I wanted to but I didn't want to. I didn't want to let myself down.'[64] Officer Ernest Lanning, on the other hand, did cry after being shot in the leg while serving in North Africa in 1942. He recalled, 'my mind was perfectly clear except, "what an undisciplined, ridiculous thing to do, stop." But I couldn't stop it.'[65] Lanning's conflict between his body and his mind is clear. Although he willed himself to stop crying—something that he considered unprofessional and unsoldierly—he was unable to take control of his emotions. These testimonies suggest that, although some were more successful than others, soldiers tried hard to live up to military masculine ideals. Men clearly wanted to be stoic and tough. These were standards against which they measured themselves.

DEATH

The war-damaged bodies of the living were not the only concern for the British military authorities overseas between 1939 and 1945. An effective system for processing and disposing of dead bodies was also crucial for fighting efficiency. Although regulations for the handling and treatment of dead bodies in combat had been in place since the end of the nineteenth century, these had been based predominantly on the principle of protecting the integrity of the deceased.[66] During the Second World War military leaders and medical staff considered mutilated and decomposing bodies as dangerous, as a potential source of disease and a threat to discipline and morale. Field-Marshal Montgomery explained that: 'A corpse in a ditch or a grave by the side of the road will remind him [the soldier] of the peril of his position. He will suddenly realise that he himself is liable to be killed.'[67] Among 'special causes of stress' the army pamphlet *Psychiatric Casualties* also listed 'the sight of the dead or of specifically unpleasant wounds'.[68] This was especially important given the nature of the damage caused to the body by more destructive weapons. During the First World War 80 per cent of all injuries had been from gunshot. Between 1939 and 1945, however, over 85 per cent of wounds were from mortars, grenades, aerial bombs, shells and mines. Rather than causing a clean bullet wound, these weapons often inflicted multiple injuries and removed whole areas of tissue and muscle.[69] The management of dead bodies was the responsibility of the Graves Service, which set burial regulations, arranged cemeteries and kept records for identification purposes.[70] The handling and burial of the dead was, however, down to the men themselves. Soldiers who cleared battlefields, dug graves and performed funerals had to adhere to a strict code of procedure. Field Service Regulations stipulated that all bodies were to be searched and, if possible, identified. Each corpse was to be buried in a single, standardised grave of no more than six feet long, two feet wide and two feet deep, with no more than one foot between each plot. Soldiers were instructed to mark graves with pegs, labels, bottles or tins, with a piece of paper with the deceased's information placed inside. Graves Registration Units followed behind the troops and used the information to register deaths, move bodies or place on a permanent cross.[71] In death, as in life, the soldier's body was subject to specific codes and regulations in order to ensure an efficient and sanitary disposal and prevent the corpse from contaminating the bodies and the minds of other men.

Despite the army's efforts to sanitise death, however, encounters with corpses could be incredibly difficult for individual soldiers. As a medical officer, Ronald Petts was used to seeing the destruction to bodies caused by war. Yet Ronald, who had served in the non-combatant corps as a religious conscientious objector before transferring to the medical services, was still deeply affected by the death of a young soldier hit by close grenade in Germany:

> I was completely shocked. I opened up his tunic and his gut was completely smashed. As I opened up his tunic and belt and trousers his whole gut just fell away. A visual thing that stays in my mind, most incredibly, one looked into the middle of the thigh and various tendons. The tendons were holding a coin with the King's head on it, as if it was held in a collection, you know from his pocket. This coin was right deep in his thigh, held in place by tendons. This effigy of the sovereign and the lad of eighteen dying for his country. All that I could do, I mean he was on his way, all I could do was to hold him like a mother for a moment and give him a big shot of morphia.[72]

Confrontations with mutilated and dismembered bodies could have a deeper impact still, altering soldiers' sense of what was meaningful about their lives and the world around them. Before being injured himself, William Dilworth, who had been in the Salvation Army, was sent to clear the dead from the battlefield at Anzio in 1944:

> There was one leg with the boot and the gaiters and everything sticking out from under this bush. So I bent down, got hold of the ankle and tugged to pull the whole body out from under the bush where it had been blown. I fell over backwards holding it from the knee down in my hand. I looked at the stump where it was all raw and bloody and everything. I looked up and I said, 'There's no bloody God', and from that moment, I've never been religious. I packed up religion altogether then because I thought to myself, to allow this to happen to anybody, even if its enemy or not, there can't be a God, so from now on I'm not a religious man.[73]

The incompleteness of this body and the severe damage that it had endured were so shocking to Dilworth that he came to question the cause for which he was fighting and ultimately lost his, previously steadfast, religious beliefs. The impact of this experience lasted far beyond his wartime service as his convictions were permanently changed by his encounter with the corpse.

As the authorities had anticipated, the sight of corpses also reminded the soldier of his own potential death. Assigned to collect the dead after battle in North Africa, Harold Atkins recalled that 'this was possibly one of the most unpleasant tasks that anybody had to perform, particularly if you are an infantryman and you're still going to do some more fighting. You're aware that there by the grace of God go I.'[74] For D-Day veteran Leonard Harkins the sight of the dead on the beaches came as a real shock, 'especially when you look in a tank and see bodies like that and thinking, well, tomorrow you could be the same'.[75]

Yet the sight of dead bodies did not always provoke an emotional response. Tank driver Alfred Court explained how his initial apprehension over seeing dead bodies quickly disappeared.

> I always wondered what I would feel like when I saw a dead person. Yet, I found that I could go over and look at a dead person, turn him over, flies all around him, and think 'Oh he's dead, hard luck chum.' I didn't think he's somebody's son or somebody's husband. Just okay, that's just it. I always remember seeing a twenty-five pounder quad [Morris C8 tractor for pulling twenty-five pound guns] that had been hit by a shell. The driver was still in it and all his trousers had been burned off. I remember turning round to one chap and saying 'he looks like a bit of roast pork.'[76]

By describing the corpse that he found in the quad bike as a piece of meat, Court objectified and dehumanised this soldier's body. Perhaps this was simply an observation based on how the corpse looked. Yet it appears that Court was immediately indifferent when confronted with the sight of death, despite his pervious concerns over how he would react. Other soldiers found the process of desensitisation more gradual, occurring as death became an everyday reality. Private Rubin Wharmby served in North West Europe and explained that 'you get used to it. At first you see them and, you know, it's sick, and then you don't bother.'[77] William Tichard, a gunner in Normandy, also stated that 'you were getting used to seeing that, dead people. You know, it grew on you ... It was heartbreaking but you had a job to do.'[78] Focusing on the task became a valuable coping mechanism for men confronted regularly with death. George MacDonald Fraser described the reaction of his unit to the deaths of two fellow servicemen in Burma:

> There was no outward show of sorrow, no reminiscences or eulogies, no Hollywood heart-searchings or phoney philosophy ... It was not callousness or indifference or lack of feeling for two comrades who had been

alive that morning and were now names for the war memorial: it was just that there was nothing to be said. It was part of war; men died, more would die, that was the past and what mattered now was the business in hand; those who lived would get on with it. Whatever sorrow was felt, there was no point in brooding about it, much less in making, for form's sake, a parade of it. Better and healthier to forget about it, and look to tomorrow.[79]

While they were upset by the deaths of their friends, Fraser and his men concentrated primarily on the military mission. Rather than dwelling on the loss of their comrades, they had learned to focus on the task to which they had been assigned.

Soldiers also found practical uses for dead bodies. Some suggest that corpses became makeshift signposts. Rubin Wharmby claimed that 'we used to use them for landmarks'.[80] William Corbould likewise explained that on the way to Monte Cassino, 'We were told, "Turn right at the dead New Zealander. Keep going until you come across an Italian. Turn right at the next German," et cetera, et cetera, et cetera. It sounds as if I'm being very crude. It sounds as if I'm not telling the truth, but that is in fact how we found our way.'[81] In the African desert, the men in Neil McCallum's unit used dead bodies as chairs and even worked out the most comfortable way of sitting on them. McCallum noted that 'to use a corpse as a seat it should be turned on its face. It is difficult to sit on a dead chest, and besides, the face is obtrusive. But the small of the back is rather like a saddle.'[82] It seems to have been the faces of the bodies that made them human. Once turned around, they were converted into furniture of the combat theatre, part of the scenery of war.

Conclusion

The damage and distress caused to the body by war were of key concern to the British military authorities of the Second World War, who continued to implement strategies to protect the efficiency of fighting men. Through training, soldiers had been physically and psychologically toughened, taught to overcome pain and deprivation and to conduct themselves proficiently as part of a fighting unit. Nevertheless, in the combat area, the army did not leave men's bodies alone. Aware that fear could seriously undermine the fighting capabilities of individual men, officers and medical staff issued rum, provided hot meals, clean clothes and opportunities to rest. They did not simply hope that men would resist their fears, but tried to bolster and reinforce their bodies against its harmful effects. Since maintaining manpower was of paramount importance, wounded bodies were also subject to strict codes of military management. Injured soldiers entered into an official sorting process in which their bodies were categorised and treated in a system designed, first and foremost, to salvage and restore them to active duty. Efforts to organise soldiers' bodies extended even into death. In the field, corpses were searched and identified according to a set code of instructions. Bodies were treated in ways that robbed them of their individuality. Even the sizes of graves made no effort to memorialise the individual. This was not simply to prevent the spread of disease, but to remove the corpse's symbolic presence as the reminder of men's own mortality.

What impact did these processes of control and rationalisation have on the experiences of soldiers? Veterans' accounts tell us that confrontations with fear, wounding and death provoked a multitude of responses because combat was ultimately the moment when efforts to discipline the body were tested against the impulses of individual men. While some soldiers experienced battle as exhilarating and exciting, others found the prospect of action overwhelming. Terrified soldiers shook, shuddered and were transfixed with fright. Men who were desperate resorted to harming their own bodies rather than risk going into action. Men who wanted to repress the physical manifestations of their anxieties found that they were powerless to do so. When faced with the enemy, some were literally paralysed with fear, even when inaction almost certainly meant death. Other soldiers tried desperately, but without success, not to vomit and to control their shaking and shivering. Perhaps these accounts can be read as evidence of the success of military authority by the fact that the men experienced their bodies as a source of frustration or constraint. The tension that men experienced between body and will and the disappointment they expressed suggest that they were guided by a set of dispositions that were imposed from 'outside'.[83] The importance of military culture can also be seen in soldiers' accounts of wounding. While some men reported feeling no physical pain, others struggled to maintain the appearance of stoic masculinity by repressing what they did physically feel. Finally, the sight of dead and incapacitated bodies confronted men with their own fragile existence. Seeing bits of bodies and flesh challenged their perceptions of the war and indeed the wider world around them.

Official and individual responses to fear, wounding and death highlight the centrality of the body to the conduct and experience of warfare between 1939 and 1945. Significantly, they reveal a complex and often difficult relationship that existed between the military, medicine and wartime recruits. When exposed to hazards and hardships, bodies shuddered, shook and vomited, absconded, bled and died. Bodies were unpredictable, dangerous and difficult to control, for both the military authorities and the soldiers themselves.

NOTES

1. J. McCallum (1959), *Journey with a Pistol* (London: Victor Gollanz), p. 45.
2. The National Archives, Kew (hereafter TNA) WO277/12, Army and A.T.S. 1939–1946, appendix C, p. 80.
3. McCallum, *Journey with a Pistol*, pp. 9–35.
4. Parliamentary Debates, *Strength and Casualties of the Auxiliary Services of the United Kingdom* (Cmd. 6832), p. 8. Navy casualties equated to 50,758 killed and 14,663 wounded and RAF losses amounted to 69,606 killed and 23,839 wounded.
5. J. Bourke (2005), *Fear: A Cultural History* (London: Virago), pp. 199–200.
6. See D. Leder (1990), *The Absent Body* (London: University of Chicago Press).
7. M. Harrison (2004), *Medicine and Victory: British Military Medicine in the Second World War* (Oxford: Oxford University Press), p. 2.
8. J. Anderson (2011), *War, Disability and Rehabilitation in Britain: 'Soul of a Nation'* (Manchester: Manchester University Press), pp. 4, 44.
9. An exception is G. Moshenka (2017), 'Token Scraps of Men: White Lies, Coffins and Second World War Air Crash Casualties', in P. Cornish and A. Saunders (eds), *Bodies in Conflict* (London: Routledge), pp. 133–143.
10. In all theatres, riflemen made up the majority of war wounded and dead. J. Ellis (2009), *The Sharp End: The Fighting Man in World War II* (London: Aurum Press), p. 164; D. French (2000), *Raising Churchill's Army: The British Army and the War against Germany, 1919–1945* (Oxford: Oxford University Press), p. 147.
11. Ellis, *The Sharp End*, pp. 156–157.
12. Ibid., p. 53.
13. Recent publications include: R. Doherty (2008), *Ubique: The Royal Artillery in the Second World War* (Stroud: History Press); J. Devine (2010), *Forgotten Voices of Dunkirk* (London: Ebury Press); A Beevor

(2010), *D-Day: The Battle for Normandy* (London: Penguin); F. McLynn (2010), *The Burma Campaign: Disaster into Triumph, 1942–1945* (London: Bodley Head). For a more in-depth discussion of the popular memory of the British Armed Forces in the Second World War, see M. Francis (2014), 'Remembering War, Forgetting Empire? Representations of the North African Campaign', in L. Noakes and J. Pattinson (eds), *British Cultural Memory and the Second World War* (London: Bloomsbury), pp. 111–132; P. Summerfield (2010), 'Dunkirk and the Popular Memory of Britain at War', *Journal of Contemporary History*, 45:4, pp. 788–811.

14. J. Bourke (2017), *The Story of Pain: From Prayer to Painkillers* (Oxford: Oxford University Press); L. Bending (2000), *The Representation of Bodily Pain in Late Nineteenth-Century English Culture* (London: Clarendon Press); E. Hallam, J. Hockey and G. Howarth (2001), 'The Body in Death', in N. Watson and S. Cunningham-Burley (eds), *Reframing the Body* (Basingstoke: Palgrave); C. Shilling (2003), *The Body and Social Theory* (London: Sage), pp. 153–171.

15. S. Smith and J. Watson (2001), *Reading Autobiography* (Minneapolis: University of Minnesota Press), p. 37.

16. Imperial War Museum, London, Sound Archive (hereafter IWM SA) 16754, Eric Woods reel 5.

17. IWM SA, 8286, Lionel Leach, reel 2.

18. IWM SA, 16715, John Thomas Jarvis, reel 6.

19. TNA CAB21/914, 'Summary of Lectures on Psychological Aspects of War', p. 14.

20. McCallum, *Journey with a Pistol*, p. 28.

21. See, for example, R.W. Connell (2005), *Masculinities* (Cambridge: Polity Press), p. 54; C. Jarvis (2004), *The Male Body at War: American Masculinity during World War II* (DeKalb: Northern Illinois University Press), p. 87.

22. D. Bolt (2014), *The Metanarrative of Blindness: A Re-Reading of Twentieth Century Anglophone Writing* (Ann Arbor: University of Michigan Press), pp. 58–59.

23. Bourke, *Fear*, p. 200.

24. IWM SA, 13299, Dominic Neill, reel 8; IWM SA, 12710, John Avery, reel 22.

25. E. Jones (2012), '"The Gut War": Functional Somatic Disorders in the UK during the Second World War', *History of Human Sciences* 25:5, pp. 30–48; I. Miller (2010), 'The Mind and Stomach at War: Stress and Abdominal Illness in Britain c.1939–1945', *Medical History* 54, pp. 95–110.

26. P.M. Lichtenstein and S.M. Small (1943), *A Handbook of Military Psychiatry* (New York: W.W. Norton and Company), p. 141.

27. 'Dyspepsia in the Army', *British Medical Journal*, 14 December 1940, p. 836.
28. G. MacDonald Fraser (1992), *Quartered Safe Out Here: A Recollection of the War in Burma* (London: Harvill), pp. 106–107.
29. S. Longden (2007), *To the Victor the Spoils: Soldiers Lives from D-Day to VE-Day* (London: Robinson), pp. 68–70.
30. S.A. MacKeith, 'Presentation to Northern Command, York, 3 March 1945', unpublished report cited in E. Jones and N.T. Fear (2011), 'Alcohol Use and Misuse Within the Military: A Review', *International Review of Psychiatry*, 23, 168.
31. IWM SA, 22666, Henry Wilmott, reel 3.
32. IWM SA, 24921, John Coldwell-Horstall, reel 5.
33. IWM SA, 14977, Ernest Harvey, reel 7; IWM SA, 20372, Herbert Beddows, reel 2.
34. A. Allport (2015), *Browned Off and Bloody Minded: The British Soldier Goes to War, 1939–1945* (New Haven, CT, and London: Yale University Press), p. 244.
35. G. Picot (1993), *Accidental Warrior: In the Front Line from Normandy till Victory* (London: Penguin), p. 301.
36. B. Shephard (2002), *A War of Nerves: Soldiers and Psychiatrists, 1914–1994* (London: Pimlico), p. 188.
37. F.A.E. Crew (1953), *The Army Medical Services: Administration, Volume I* (London: HMSO), p. 489.
38. TNA WO32/11550, Report on a conference on psychiatry in forward areas, p. 4.
39. Crew, *The Army Medical Services*, p. 489.
40. TNA WO32/11550, Report on a conference on psychiatry in forward areas, August 1944, p. 5.
41. IWM SA, 13281, William Scroggie, reel 3.
42. W.A. Elliot (1996), *Esprit de Corps: A Scots Guards Officer on Active Service, 1943–1945* (Wimborne: Michael Russell), p. 35.
43. It is likely that court-martial records significantly underestimate the true extent of self-inflicted wounds. Cases were difficult to prove and often went unreported by officers who sympathised with their men or were worried about effects on morale TNA WO277/7, Brigadier A.B. MacPherson, Discipline 1939–1945 (1950), Appendix 1(a) Comprehensive summary of court-martial convictions (British other ranks), 1 December 1939–31 August 1945.
44. IWM SA, 13230, Charles Bennett, reel 3.
45. IWM SA 14981, William Cornell, reel 8.
46. IWM SA 9732, Ronald Petts, reel 10.
47. McCallum, *Journey with a Pistol*, p. 89.

48. R.M. Wingfield (1955), *The Only Way Out: An Infantryman's Autobiography of the North–West Europe Campaign, August 1944–February 1945* (London: Hutchinson), pp. 114–116.
49. A. Carden Coyne (2014), *The Politics of Wounds: Military Patients and Medical Power in the First World War* (Oxford: Oxford University Press), p. 23.
50. Lt.-Col. Debenham and Lt.-Col. A.B. Kerr (1945), 'Triage of Battle Casualties', *Journal of the Royal Army Medical Corps*, 84:5, pp. 125–129, here p. 125.
51. IWM SA, 12412, Joseph Day, reel 5.
52. IWM SA, 9732, Ronald Petts, reel 10.
53. J.C. Watts (1955), *Surgeon at War* (London: Allen and Unwin), p. 93.
54. IWM SA, 19867, John Buchanan, reel 6.
55. IWM SA, 13370, Arthur Thompson, reel 1.
56. IWM SA, 19066, Arthur McCrystal, reel 3.
57. Elliot, *Esprit de Corps*, p. 117.
58. E. Scarry (1985), *The Body in Pain: The Making and Unmaking of the World* (Oxford: Oxford University Press), p. 15.
59. Shilling, *The Body and Social Theory*, p. 184.
60. IWM SA, 18435, William Dilworth, reel 5.
61. Ibid.
62. K.A. Burnett and M. Holmes (2001), 'Bodies, Battlefields and Biographies: Scars and the Construction of the Body as Heritage', in S. Cunningham-Burley and K. Backett-Milburn (eds), *Exploring the Body* (Basingstoke: Palgrave), pp. 21–36.
63. A. Carden-Coyne (2013), 'Men in Pain: Silence, Stories and Soldiers' Bodies', in Cornish and Saunders (eds), *Bodies in Conflict*, pp. 53–64, here p. 54.
64. IWM SA, 20009, Leslie Perry, reel 4.
65. IWM SA, 19056, Ernest Lanning, reel 6.
66. Institute of International Law (1880), *The Laws of War on Land* (Oxford: Institute of International Law), articles 19–20.
67. Field-Marshal Viscount Montgomery, 'Morale in battle', *British Medical Journal*, 9 November 1946, p. 703.
68. General Headquarters, Middle East Forces (1942), *Psychiatric Casualties: Hints to Medical Officers* (Cairo: Middle East Forces), pp. 6–7.
69. Ellis, *The Sharp End*, p. 178.
70. War Office (1930), *Field Service Regulations, Volume I: Organization and Administration* (London: HMSO), pp. 114–115.
71. War Office, *Field Service Regulations, Volume I*, p. 376.
72. IWM SA, 9732, Ronald Petts, reel 10.
73. IWM SA, 18435, William Dilworth, reel 5.

74. IWM SA, 12440, Harold Atkins, reel 7.
75. IWM SA, Leonard Harkins, reel 4.
76. IWM SA, 16059, Alfred Court, reel 3.
77. IWM SA, 18741, Rubin Wharmby, reel 3.
78. IWM SA, 20620, William Tichard, reel 3.
79. MacDonald Fraser, *Quartered Safe Out Here*, pp. 88–89.
80. IWM SA, 18741, Rubin Wharmby, reel 3.
81. IWM SA, 23216, William Corbould, reel 4.
82. McCallum, *Journey with a Pistol*, p. 107.
83. E. Goffman (1963), *Behaviour in Public Place: Notes on the Social Organization of Gatherings* (New York: Free Press), p. 35.

CHAPTER 4

'Pinky Smith Looks Gorgeous!' Female Impersonators and Male Bonding in Prisoner of War Camps for British Servicemen in Europe

Clare Makepeace

I have studied all our best actresses; B—McI----- for style and personality, S-m C----h for sauciness and sex appeal, L-------e W----n for conversation, and J---n D----n for modesty and charm. T-m B----y I decided was not the sort of woman my mother would like me to be, so I left him out of it.[1]

In July 1944, the ninth issue of *Touchstone* magazine, a monthly edition published in Oflag VIIB, carried a satirical article entitled 'How To Be A Woman'. The article provided guidelines on how a prisoner of war (hereafter POW) might break into 'the realm of womanhood'. Oflag VIIB was one of 248 POW camps established in Germany in the Second World War.[2] Short for Offizierlagern, meaning a camp for officers, Oflag VIIB was located in the town of Eichstätt in Bavaria, and housed around 1800 POWs, the vast majority of whom were British.[3] They were among

C. Makepeace (✉)
Birkbeck College, University of London, London, UK
e-mail: claremakepeace@hotmail.com

© The Author(s) 2018
L. Robb and J. Pattinson (eds.), *Men, Masculinities and Male Culture in the Second World War*, Genders and Sexualities in History,
https://doi.org/ 10.1057/978-1-349-95290-8_4

71

the 142,319 men taken prisoner while serving in the UK armed forces in the war against Germany.[4] 'Pickaxe', the anonymous author of the article, was critical in that only 'manhood' has been stressed 'as the ultimate goal of every right thinking schoolboy', brought up, as they were, on the 'Kipling theory "and what is more you'll be a man my son"'. This, he declared, was 'deliberate one sided propaganda', for 'a little intelligent logical thinking should soon make it clear that there are equal, if not superior, opportunities in being a woman'. Pickaxe conceded that, at home, where there 'are so many who have been at the game since they were born', there might be little worth in making the effort but, in the POW camp, where women were scarce, 'the obvious advantages which would accrue to a charming, well dressed, sweet-voiced bundle of femininity are so vast, no one can doubt for a moment that it is a business proposition'. The 'actresses' in Oflag VIIB (Eichstätt), which Pickaxe referred to in the epigraph above, had 'succeeded in breaking into the realm of womanhood' but they, he declared, 'surround the whole thing with a screen of mystery (as do women everywhere), and make it out to be a divine gift'. This, he asserted, was nonsense as '[p]ractically anyone can make a reasonable shot at it'. The rest of the article advised the readers of *Touchstone* how 'womanhood' might be achieved: by, for example, wearing the appropriate undergarments, modulating one's speaking voice to be as high as possible and learning how to behave femininely. With this, plus 'hard work and close attention to detail', readers were assured they would 'look like a woman and will perhaps too begin to feel like one'.[5]

'How to be a Woman' is probably one of the most explicit pieces of evidence that brings to historians' attention the need to examine the experiences of POWs and civilian internees *as men* or *as women*. The reader of Pickaxe's satirical thoughts is made acutely aware of the all-male environment of POW camps, and how they responded to the absence of the opposite sex in camps. Numerous other aspects of wartime incarceration demand that the experience of it be studied as a gendered one. With conceptions of masculinity being so strongly linked to performance in battle in so many societies, past and present, the act of being captured could arouse suspicions that a combatant had, in literary scholar Robin Gerster's words, 'effectively forfeited his manhood'.[6] For male inmates, the 'enforced passivity' of wartime incarceration, according to historian Stephen Garton, 'conjures up a feminised condition'.[7] Female civilian internees, meanwhile, were held in, what historian

Christina Twomey describes as, 'the ambiguous zone' of an internment camp, being away from the 'supposedly natural feminine realm of the domestic "home"'.[8]

It is surprising, therefore, that only a limited number of histories on wartime incarceration have systemically applied gender as a category of analysis to the lives of military prisoners and civilian internees. Foremost among these are studies by Christina Twomey and Bernice Archer on Australian and British POWs and civilian internees held in the Far East between 1941 and 1945; works by Frank Biess and Matthias Reiss on German POWs in the Second World War; Iris Rachamimov's study of German-speaking POWs in Russia in the 1914–1918 war; and Brian Feltman's work on German POWs held in Britain during the Great War.[9] These scholars have looked at the extent to which wartime incarceration was an emasculating or de-feminising experience, how gender roles were maintained in captivity and in what ways men and women transgressed from them.

Despite a prolific number of accounts having been written on the lives of British POWs held in Europe during the Second World War, none of these have critically considered their experiences of captivity *as men*.[10] This chapter is taken from a broader cultural history of the lives of British POWs held in Germany and Italy during the Second World War, which seeks to understand how these men made sense of, and found meaning in, their experience of war from behind barbed wire.[11] One of the most challenging aspects of captivity that POWs had to make sense of was their all-male environment; a way in which they did so was through the existence of female impersonators in the camps.

This chapter explores how POWs reacted to female impersonators in captivity, accessed through the personal narratives written by fourteen men during imprisonment: their diaries, correspondence and logbooks. The latter resemble small, hard-backed notebooks and were issued by the Young Men's Christian Association (YMCA) in Geneva in the final year of the war with the purpose of being a place where POWs could, for example, draw sketches, store recipes, record sporting achievements, gather poetry, collect autographs, collate photographs or write a diary. Contemporary, rather than retrospective, written accounts have been focused upon in this chapter to ensure that these men's attitudes towards female impersonators reflect understandings of sexuality during the Second World War, rather than attitudes formed in more recent times. Most of these fourteen men were officers or senior non-commissioned officers (NCOs). Due to the provisions of the 1929 Geneva Convention, of which Britain, Germany and Italy were all signatories, these ranks were not permitted to be put to work and so were held in central camps, either oflags or stalags (Stammlagern), which housed prisoners with the rank of NCO and below. In these central camps, prisoners had both time on their hands and little or no contact with the outside population. This contrasted with other ranks, who were forced to labour long days for the Third Reich, so having far less time to create such entertainments. They also had less of a need: POWs who were put to work often came across, and even had affairs with, female civilian women.[12]

This chapter first describes how and where female impersonators featured in these central POW camps. The chapter proposes that men in drag provided prisoners with a release from their single-sex society and that POWs' admiration for these 'women' enabled them to assert their collective male superiority. However, it goes on to demonstrate the limits of this 'safety valve' interpretation of drag, and argues that prisoners' attitudes towards these female impersonators blurred the boundaries of male heterosexual desire. The chapter ends by suggesting that this reflects a fluidity in attitudes towards male sexuality, more generally, during this era.

'THE UNFORTUNATE SYNTHETIC FEMALE HAD TO BE TAUGHT TO WALK "TOE TO HEEL"'

Female impersonators were not an uncommon sight for servicemen in the two world wars. In the Great War, division and battalion concert parties became a 'practically universal' feature of life on the western and eastern front which, according to historian J.G. Fuller, in his study on troop morale, acted to promote *esprit de corps*.[13] Scholar David Boxwell has also described plays that featured military men in drag as occurring with 'startling frequency'. These performances took cross-dressing from being a marginal activity and placed it at the heart of this most public and mainstream of institutions.[14] This tradition of cross-dressing extended to the sphere of captivity. Historian Iris Rachamimov describes drag performances as being 'lively and ubiquitous' in officer camps for German-speaking prisoners held in Russia during the Great War. Theatre life was important in recreating, among these prisoners, a 'prewar sense of comfort, power, and self-worth' and female impersonators were at the centre of this 'theatrical sociability', performing women's roles both onstage and often maintaining their feminine persona in everyday life in the camps, by being addressed only by their feminine names or having a circle of admirers wash and iron their women's clothing.[15] In the Second World War, this tradition continued. Female impersonators, for example, were very popular components of American military shows.[16] Professor of Theatre Sears Eldredge has documented the central role played by female impersonators in hospital and relocation camps in Thailand in the Second World War. Although all the musical and theatrical producers and performers gained 'special recognition', he writes 'none were more precious to the POWs than the female impersonators'.[17]

The female impersonators in POW camps in Europe during the Second World War were, therefore, neither an unprecedented nor unusual phenomenon. The realm in which they most consistently appeared was on the stage. As the war progressed, and POW camps became more established, theatre productions became increasingly sophisticated affairs. By 1944, Oflag 79 (Brunswick), which housed just over 2000 POWs, had two separate stages, each with their own theatre companies. Similarly, Stalag 383 (Hohenfels) had two stages with several hundred seats. Each of the 6000 prisoners held there could look forward to watching a show once every fortnight.[18]

These theatrical performances were, according to the diaries and logbooks kept by POWs, the most popular activity in the camps. This is unsurprising given the time and manpower required to produce a performance, and the distraction an actual performance offered to audience and cast alike. Those watching the productions could imagine themselves elsewhere; those who participated in them could experience different material comforts from those available in captivity and, temporarily, become someone other than a POW. Preparing for performances probably involved a greater number of POWs than other activities that were widespread in the camps, such as sports or study. For example, in addition to those involved in the cast, prisoners were needed for the building of the theatre, set design and construction; costume creation and make-up; production of programmes, tickets and advertising posters; dressing the actors before the performances and serving as ushers and programme sellers during it.[19]

The popularity of these performances is revealed through descriptions contained in POWs' diaries, and compilations of lists of these shows in numerous logbooks. Sometimes these titles are accompanied by illustrations of sets, stages and audiences.[20] These personal narratives often also contain photographs of these performances. As the sophistication of these productions increased, the guards took photographs of the casts and the sets, or gave the POWs film to do likewise.[21] The camp authorities regarded the theatre as a good way to keep prisoners busy, and guards seemed genuinely to appreciate the performances, often occupying the front row.[22] Programmes of these performances were also pasted into POWs' diaries and logbooks. Some men even took the time and care to copy programmes out and then adorned them with signatures from the cast.[23]

Female impersonators were prominent in these performances. In some camps, it was the same POW who featured repeatedly in the female roles. One name that appears often, and mentioned by Pickaxe, was Brian McIrvine. He had been a professional actor before the war and had often been cast in female roles in his school plays. In captivity, he first played a female character in early May 1941, at Oflag VIIC (Laufen), in a piece called *The Forget-Me-Love Knot*.[24] At the end of the month, he featured as 'Linda Swansdown' in *Behind the Scenes*, a play written by POWs. This was Swansdown's debut and 'she' was to appear subsequently in plays that had been specially written in POW camps. When at Oflag VIB (Warburg), McIrvine starred as the leading lady in the pantomime *Citronella*, performed at Christmas 1941.[25] After being transferred to Oflag VIIB (Eichstätt), he appeared as the mother and the girlfriend of the protagonist in Noel Coward's *Post-Mortem*, a gloomy and bitter anti-war play; as Mrs Manningham in Patrick Hamilton's 1938 play *Gaslight*; and as one of ten female roles in the pantomime *Dossing Dulcie* (Fig. 4.1).[26]

Creating a female presence onstage was a lengthy and involved process, an insight into which is provided through the programme of a 'Special POW Matinee' production of Noel Coward's *Blithe Spirit*, staged at the Duchess Theatre in London's West End in July 1945. *Blithe Spirit* was performed in various POW camps. This matinee performance was a repeat of an original production held in September 1943 at Campo PG 78 (Sulmona), short for *Campo concentramento di prigioneri di Guerra*.[27] Out of a cast of seven, five were female parts. The play sees a successful novelist, Charles Condomine, inviting a medium, Madame Arcati, into his home, hoping to gather material for his next book. Madame Arcati summons up the ghost of Charles' first wife, which only Charles can see. His second wife thinks he has gone insane but then, after watching a vase float across the room, accepts the ghost

Fig. 4.1 Brian McIrvine (on the *left*) playing the protagonist's girlfriend in *Post-Mortem* at Oflag VIIB (Eichstätt). (Image used with permission of Jonathan Goodliffe.)

is present. The two wives then compete for possession of their husband and with much haunting and bawling, Charles wonders if he wants to be with either woman at all.

The programme produced to accompany the post-war performance tells us about the efforts involved to teach the five male cast members to be female 'without any suggestion of burlesque'. Rehearsal time averaged about six hours per day for about three months. Elocution and expression were given priority, followed closely by deportment, stage movements and gestures. 'The unfortunate synthetic female', this programme explained, 'had to be taught to walk "toe to heel," to take small steps, not to turn his broad back to the audience and to slide gracefully into his chair'. Cast members also had to endure having their 'unsightly masculine limb [*sic*]' shaved, eyebrows plucked, hair grown long and being made up with grease-paint, cosmetics and nail varnish.[28]

The programme also describes how prisoners created the requisite costumes for the production. The ingenuity of POWs and civilian internees to create utilitarian objects out of their scarce material resources has been well-documented by historians.[29] Their inventiveness is also evident in this context. Dresses were designed from those in magazines; material for them was taken from white shirts as well as clothing from private parcels sent to British POWs from home. Mosquito netting and pilfered sheets were also used. One man spent about a month hand stitching a dress. Another devoted hours to manufacturing a pair of ladies' shoes. Madame Arcati's wig was ingeniously created strand by strand from Red Cross parcel string.[30] These parcels were, in theory, meant to be received by POWs each week, providing them with perishables such as condensed milk, biscuits, sugar, jam, tea, oats, butter, dried eggs, salmon and liver pâté. The tightly twisted string that bound these packages became a valued resource for prisoners, used to make items such as brushes, hammocks and cricket balls, as well as to simulate female hair.[31]

POWs also created costumes through other means. At Oflag VA (Weinsburg), where British POWs reportedly had good relations with their captors, the costumes for the pantomime *Puss in Boots* were loaned from an opera company in Stuttgart. They gave the camp a complete set of wigs, hats, dresses and stockings for every part, and POWs supplemented these with various garments of their own, such as pyjamas, trousers, pullovers and socks.[32] Similarly, at Campo PG 35 (Padula), the guards went to Naples and purchased wallpaper, curtain material, dresses, make-up and wigs for the plays.[33] In other camps, this cooperation occurred at a more illicit level. One guard brought curling tongs into Stalag 383 (Hohenfels) for which, according to Sergeant Major Andrew Hawarden, he was 'suitably rewarded in kind'. This probably meant he was given soap, good quality cigarettes or coffee, items that POWs were sent from home but that could not be obtained in Germany, even on the black market.[34] Theatrical productions aside, these examples provide an insight into just how informal relationships between prisoners and guards could be.

While female impersonators most commonly appeared onstage, their presence is also recorded in several other settings. At Oflag VIB (Warburg), Major Edmund Booth wrote of having a 'conjurer' to dinner, who was an RAF officer known locally as 'Margaret'.[35] Sergeant David Nell recorded in his diary a New Year's Eve party, at Stalag IVB (Mühlberg), where entertainers performed in his billet and 'some fellows dressed up as girls'.[36] From the same camp, Warrant Officer Alexander East wrote of the hut next door to his holding sewing parties, in which 'all members dress and make up in feminine garb'. He thought that others had 'tea parties with "waitresses"'.[37] Hawarden noted a 'few' 'ladies' were at a fancy dress ball at Stalag XXA (Thorn). He was later transferred to Stalag 383 (Hohenfels) where dances were held twice a week at which several lads dressed as ladies. Stalag 383 also had 'fancy dress dances', where special prizes included one for the 'best dressed girl'.[38]

There was, therefore, a desire among British POWs held in camps in Germany and Italy to create a female presence in their homosocial environment. Individuals were ready to turn themselves into women and numerous men welcomed their presence. In itself, this shows the all-male society had limited reach for these men, and that the male bond was not sovereign.[39] As the next section shows, the type of females that POWs created and admired reinforces the idea that they needed women, who were as realistic as possible, to be with them in the camps.

'When We Come Home We Shall Be Very Critical of How Women Play Feminine Parts'

POWs went to great lengths in their cross-dressing to ensure the difference between the female impersonator and a genetic woman was as minimal as possible. These were mimetic performances. They stand in contrast to female impersonation as a form of mimicry, which is exemplified by the pantomime dame. Mimetic cross-dressing elicited the most comment from POWs in the personal narratives studied for this chapter and these men almost unanimously declared how impressed they were by the results.[40] Some based their praise on the fact that they had not seen a woman for months. According to Commander Geoffrey Lambert, some of those onstage at Marlag 'O' (Westertimke), a camp established for Royal Navy officers, 'make pretty good girls … at least they look good to us who haven't seen a decent one for a long time'.[41] At the second theatre show Wing Commander Noel Hyde saw at Stalag Luft III (Sagan), one of seven permanent camps set up for air force POWs, he commented on how 'The Popsie [girl] looked + spoke just like the real thing—or at least, as far as I can remember!'[42] He had been shot down two and a half years previously. Similarly, when Nell saw the play *Boy Meets Girl* at Stalag IVB (Mühlberg), he found 'the acting was very convincing. When a man is dressed as a woman he looks astoundingly like the authentic article. But none of us have been on speaking terms with a woman for some time: perhaps that is something to do with it'.[43] Others declared the authenticity of these female impersonators in more unequivocal terms. For East, also at Stalag IVB (Mühlberg), the 'feminine parts' of *Blithe Spirit* were taken 'with great accomplishment … at times we forgot that theirs was just impersonation'.[44] Captain John Mansel, after seeing *Pasquinade* at Oflag VIIB (Eichstätt), wrote of McIrvine's performance, 'I'm bloody sure if he was billed as a girl at a London Theatre no—one would question her sex. It's unbelievable.'[45] Gunner Cyril King revealed his disbelief, and pre-empted the incredulity of others, when he wrote above a photograph, pasted into his logbook, of a female impersonator at Stalag VIIIC (Sagan): 'A French Officer—not female' (Fig. 4.2).

Perhaps the greatest compliment given to these performances is through Hawarden's confused use of punctuation in recording the success of *H.M.S. Pinafore*, a Gilbert and Sullivan collaboration, at Stalag 383 (Hohenfels):

> Went to see 'H. M. S. Pinafore' tonight – another marvellous show. I didn't know we had so many good singers in Camp. The 'Male Part' of the chorus singing is very good – as good as I've heard at home. Five hundred handkerchiefs were used in making dresses for the six girls.

Hawarden's use of quotation marks to qualify the 'male part' of the chorus, rather than the girls, indicates the extent to which female impersonators successfully challenged gender categories.[46]

These comments fit in with the so-called 'safety valve' interpretation of drag, put forward by anthropologists. In this interpretation, drag provides men with a release from the abnormal state of a single-sex society.[47] This would also explain why POWs favoured mimetic performances: pantomime dames would not have offered prisoners the same release from their homosocial environment because they draw attention to the fact that their impersonation is a performance.[48] Numerous POWs explicitly wrote in their personal narratives of how the function of female impersonators was to make their captive society a more normal one. Hawarden recorded that at dances held at Stalag 383 (Hohenfels) every Wednesday and Saturday, 'As usual several lads dress as ladies to give it a proper atmosphere'. At one performance of *Cinderella,* at Oflag

Fig. 4.2 Gunner Cyril King's annotated photograph of a female impersonator. IWM 85/50/1, C.G. King, logbook, unpaginated

XIIB (Hadamar), which Captain Richard Angove attended, an 'usher-ette & programme girl' as well as 'a dear old flower seller' worked at the theatre, 'all contributing to the creation of the right theatre spirit before the show started'. Meanwhile, Mansel qualified his initial reaction to McIrvine and another female impersonator entering the canteen dress-ing room at Oflag VIIB (Eichstätt) when he wrote in his diary that they made him 'feel most uncomfortable—or comfortable?'[49]

In the 'safety valve' interpretation of drag, anthropologists gener-ally agree that the basic societal order is not questioned. Cross-dressers affirm the two-gender/two-sex system by reintroducing a female ele-ment into an all-male environment.[50] Sexual inversion can also be, as his-torian Natalie Zemon Davis explains,

> ultimately sources of order and stability in a hierarchical society. They can clarify the structure by the process of reversing it. They can provide an expression of, and a safety valve for, conflicts within the system … But, so it is argued, they do not question the basic order of society itself.[51]

Echoing this idea are the ways in which POWs used these performances by female impersonators to assert the hierarchical gender order, by declaring men were better at being female than some women were them-selves. Mansel, for example, commented on how McIrvine in *Citronella*, 'is staggering and in a dance with the Prince, himself quite excellent, per-forms a dance at which the average girl would make but a poor attempt'. Major George Matthews similarly wrote to his wife, from Stalag XXIA (Schildberg), that the 'beauty chorus' in the musical comedy, *Windbag the Sailor*, did such a good job that 'When our "girls" come home the Tiller girls will have to take up Domestic Scenes!! As for our leading lady—well, that resection [removal] of Adam's rib was quite unneces-sary.'[52] On another occasion, when in Stalag Luft III (Sagan), Matthews told his wife how, at one concert, 'the "ladies" were clad in the latest Paris models' and that 'when we come home we shall be very critical of how women play feminine parts'.[53]

There is, of course, a certain jocularity to these comments but, at the same time, embedded within them is the claim that men were better at being female than some women were themselves. These observations support the conclusions of other scholars and historians who have sim-ilarly noted how men in the past used cross-dressing to achieve domi-nance over women, by claiming they were better at being female than biological women.[54] In this way, although cross-dressers were praised for their femininity, they paradoxically enabled prisoners to uphold the traditional gender hierarchy and to assert their collective male superiority.

Also significant in these comments is the type of femininity these prisoners constructed and admired. The 'females' to which these men refer were not of a quotidian womanliness, but were like 'Paris models' and dressed in evening gowns. These reactions to female impersonators are revealing for men's understandings of an ideal woman at this time, and the function women were intended to provide: a typically middle class construct of a woman both glamorous and of whom mother would approve.

A 'Pleasurable and Haunting Experience for Hundreds of Men'

Historians and other scholars have also readily pointed out that there are limits to this 'safety valve' interpretation of drag, arguing that cross-dressing can serve to destabilise gender identities.[55] In his analysis of cross-dressing in the theatre on the British front lines during the First World War, David Boxwell notes:

> the form and content of the drag performer's 'act,' strongly dependent as it was on multiple entendre, close physical contact with other men (both in and out of drag), and the illusion of eroticized, idealized and objectified femininity, disrupted the boundaries that contained the act as a necessary release in an all-male environment. A spectator's desiring and approving gaze on a soldier in drag was not simply a matter of pleasure in a 'surrogate' woman; rather, his gaze was directed at a fellow man in drag, a fellow soldier in his own military organization.[56]

In other words, when POWs showed admiration for female impersonators, it entailed the possibility that they were transgressing the boundaries of male heterosexual desire.[57] This is, perhaps, what Mansel referred to when he wondered whether the two female impersonators he saw in the canteen dressing room made him feel 'uncomfortable—or comfortable?'[58] Others were similarly unsettled by their admiration. East, who attended an 'excellent party' put on by the army at Stalag IVB (Mühlberg) where one of the 'fellows dressed as a girl and fooled the audience beautifully', noted that 'Many could be seen squirming in their seats'. Sergeant Navigator G. Hall described 'Junior Booth', a female impersonator at Stalag Luft VI (Heydekrug), as having 'flaxen hair, wide, baby-blue eyes, cheeks like rosy apples ... and a charming smile'. Gazing at him, when dressed as a woman, was, noted Hall, 'both [a] pleasurable and haunting experience for hundreds of men'.[59] The uncomfortableness, squirming and haunting that these men experienced suggest these female impersonators provoked a desire among their audience and, perhaps also, an uneasiness knowing they were ultimately desiring another man.

These potential transgressions are also brought to the fore when these men discuss the personal attractiveness of the female impersonators in the camps. Hyde, in a letter home, described Dick Whittington's girlfriend in Oflag XXIB's (Schubin) 1942 pantomime as 'extremely popsie like and very attractive at that', while Angove said the 'usherette' and 'programme girl' at *Cinderella* were 'made up to kill'. When 'Linda Swansdown' opened the Fun Fair at Oflag VIB (Warburg), dressed in a two-piece costume, McIrvine was reported to Mansel as looking 'simply ravishing!' The same adjective was used by East to describe Stalag IVB's (Mühlberg) leading female impersonator, 'Sugar' Townley, who appeared in the musical show *Spring Time for Jennifer*, while Corporal Jack White described Don 'Pinky' Smith, the star of *Up the Pole*, a variety show performed at Stalag 383 (Hohenfels) in May 1944, as 'gorgeous'.[60]

Don 'Pinky' Smith, featured in Fig. 4.3, was photographed and turned into a camp pin-up at Stalag 383 (Hohenfels) and, according to White, 14,000 orders were placed for a copy of the image. This extraordinarily 'big order' was also recorded in Hawarden's diary, in June 1944; 'even one for myself', he noted. The photograph forms part of his papers held at the Imperial War Museum.[61]

In the 'safety valve' interpretation of drag, the cross-dressing contained in a performance is limited to it and, when the play ends, the female impersonators return to being, and are again seen as, men.[62] In this way, such performances did not threaten masculinity because they are temporal and confined to the stage.[63] However, both the naming of 'Pinky' and 'her' being turned into a pin-up indicate this impersonator continued to have a female presence offstage. Further evidence also shows that the behaviour of, and effect created by, female impersonators went beyond the boundaries of the theatre. Before performances at Oflag VIIB (Eichstätt), those POWs playing the female roles had their own separate 'ladies' dressing room in the canteen. During a

Fig. 4.3 'Pinky' Smith, who starred in the play *Up the Pole* at Stalag 383 (Hohenfels). (Image used with permission of Mrs Sandra Hawarden-Lord, from the private papers of Sergeant Major A. Hawarden, IWM 66/12/1.)

revue entitled *Albany Club*, at Stalag Luft III (Sagan), Squadron Leader C.N.S. Campbell recorded, shortly after the war, that at each performance, a senior officer was the guest of honour and he was granted the privilege of having the leading lady at his table when she was not performing. Similarly, at one debate, at Campo PG 35 (Padula), on 'This house believes in Father Xmas', Angove recorded in his diary how 'one of the "ladies" of the forthcoming pantomime', who spoke on behalf of the 'women's point of view ... brought the house down & was very nearly mobbed at the end at the end of the show'. Mansel also recorded how some POWs found McIrvine to be a 'great embarrassment' when he visited their room. The embarrassment, it seems, took the form of bashfulness, given that one POW could not 'refuse giving him anything he-she- [*sic*] has come to ask for'.[64]

These different examples illustrate that cross-dressing did not just provide POWs with temporary release from their all-male society, but could also cause prisoners to contravene acceptable heterosexual behaviour. On the occasions when POWs noted this was happening, they appear to have held contradictory attitudes as to what was tolerable behaviour and what was improper. East, who complimented the female impersonator 'Sugar' Townley, wrote just a few days later of how Townley was accused by other prisoners of 'being very effeminate as he puts polish on his nails and affects a long-bob hair style. In civvy life he was a beauty expert at a big Toronto department store.' His description stops there. There is no accompanying interpretation of Townley's sexual identity. However, when East observed that the hut next door to him, in Stalag IVB (Mühlberg), was 'now holding sewing parties in which all members dress and make up in feminine garb' as well as 'tea parties with "waitresses"', he had reacted with incredulity: 'It is an extraordinary thing that some men have the inclination to impersonate women in these surroundings.'[65] Similarly, while Hawarden requested a photograph of 'Pinky' Smith, he responded negatively to one concert, held at Stalag XXA (Thorn), where one of the lads was dressed as a waitress called Angela and would 'offer herself to be kissed by the highest bidder'. He considered this 'a little unsavoury', although clearly others did not, as the Welfare Fund benefited from it by 400 marks, approximately £26, the equivalent of £1000 today.[66] Hawarden's critique of 'Angela' could be related to the homosexual undertones of men kissing other men, or may have also been influenced by the hypersexual femininity displayed by this female impersonator, compared to the more acceptable demure glamour of 'Pinky'. Meanwhile, while Hawarden also considered it acceptable for men to dress up as women at dances, this form of male intimacy was frowned upon by the British authorities in other camps. In 1943, an imprisoned medical officer, Lieutenant Trevor Gibbens, recorded that the custom of men 'holding dances, under shaded lights, in which half of them were dressed as women ... died out under official pressure'.[67]

These attitudes indicate that ideas held by POWs regarding acceptable heterosexual behaviour were not clear-cut. This is further supported by the type of personal narrative in which these men commented on female impersonators: almost all the quotations referring to these mimetic performances are taken from letters written to wives, or diaries written with a public audience in mind. The only exception was Mansel. It is hard to discern which of his entries were written for a family member to read and which were written purely for himself. In other words, these POWs do not show any compunction about discussing their equivocal reactions to female impersonators. This could indicate the extent to which attitudes around male sexuality were transgressive in the homosocial POW camp, but it could also illustrate something broader about British society at this time.

While in today's terms, sexuality forms a crucial element of all men's identities and experiences, the vast majority subscribing to a coherent sexual identity of homosexuality or heterosexuality, scholars have shown that this was not always the case. Helen Smith, in her study of men who desired other men in industrial England during the first half of the twentieth century, has argued that 'sexual fluidity' was common among working men, and their communities, in the north. Sex between men was something ordinary—another form of human contact. There was a 'tolerance' of, or 'ambivalence towards', male same-sex desire.[68] Historian Emma Vickers, meanwhile, has shown how the Second World War fostered a '"for the duration" toleration' of same-sex desire and, 'in some cases, acceptance'. The unavailability of women, as well as the fear of contracting venereal disease, led to, and legitimated, the practice of homosex, that is sexual activity between men that makes no assumption about sexual identity. Each ship, unit and squadron possessed its 'own, often implicit, guidelines' as to whether or not it was permissible, and whether an 'openly queer recruit was ostracised or accepted was subjective and often unit-specific'. After the war, sexual identity and sexual activity became much more firmly linked together, and the 'boundaries between queer and normal began to solidify'.[69]

Smith's and Vickers' work suggest why POWs showed contradictory attitudes towards what was acceptable and unacceptable in terms of same-sex desire: ideas surrounding 'normal' male sexual behaviour at this time were much more fluid than they are today. Their findings might also help explain the notable silence on homosexuality in the letters, diaries and logbooks written by POWs. Seldom do these men comment on the presence of homosexuality, or homosex, in the camps.[70] This does not necessarily mean that homosexuality was comparatively rare in the central camps, as other historians writing on captivity have concluded.[71] POWs may simply have chosen not to comment on it. Observations made by psychiatrists and doctors at the time suggest two reasons for this, both of which echo Smith's and Vickers' findings. First, that POWs might have been indifferent towards homosex in the camps. This is suggested in one report, based on the work of psychiatrists who interviewed almost twenty percent of ex-POWs over the summer of 1945. It concluded that 'homosexualism [sic] although it did occur, does not seem to have been practised more frequently than in non-prison groups' and that 'on the whole a very realistic attitude would seem to have been adopted towards this side of life'.[72] The report does not explain what is meant by this 'realistic attitude'; one interpretation might be that, in lieu of a female presence, such practice was considered acceptable. Imprisoned medical officer Archie Cochrane seems to suggest this. He concluded the general incidence of 'actual sodomy' was 'probably very low' but, where it did occur, there were two groups of cases. One group consisted of men who had been 'active homosexual[s]' before the war, one of whom told Cochrane that 'POWs were much more easily seduced than civilians'. The other group consisted of regular soldiers among whom 'there seems to be a vague homosexual tradition' and they 'turned to it when bored'.[73] The idea that POWs turned to homosexuality when bored, or were seduced into it, suggests that such behaviour was regarded with a certain degree of pragmatism.

The other reason for POWs' silence may lie in there being no clear language attached to same-sex experiences at this time. Helen Smith has observed that 'Language is key to developing, categorising and solidifying sexual identities' and suggests 'homosexuality was not spoken of because there was no clear, widespread understanding in the community of what it meant as an identity'. Homosexual Londoners, where a queer subculture existed, came into contact with new public discourses about homosexuality, as did middle- and upper-class homosexuals who lived outside the capital but who were able to access London's nightlife and read books written by sexologists.[74] The idea that the word 'homosexuality' did not automatically signify a widely recognised sexual identity is reflected in the writing of Gibbens, through his attachment of various adjectives to describe the noun. He wrote of 'visible homosexuality', which varied from camp to camp; 'emotional homosexuality', which was not common but regarded with 'unusual tolerance'; and, 'unconscious homosexuality', or 'intimate friendships', which was very widespread.[75] It is hard to know what Gibbens meant by these different types of homosexuality, but such adjectives indicate no fixed meaning was attached to the word, and it could refer to both the act of sex and friendship.[76]

Conclusion

Female impersonators were one of the ways in which POWs made sense of their all-male environment. They went to great lengths to create mimetic cross-dressers and were unreserved in the admiration they showed for them. The existence of female impersonators provided prisoners with a release from their homosocial world, enabling them to recreate a 'normal' society. They even enabled POWs to assert the hierarchical gender order, by declaring these men were better at being female than some women were themselves. The type of femininity portrayed, and admired, through female impersonators is also indicative of men's understandings of an ideal woman at this time. She was both glamorous and someone of whom mother would approve.

Yet, at the same time, POWs' admiration for these men in drag entailed transgressions of the gender order. Prisoners continued to show affection for these actors even when their performance had ended. POWs wrote of the attractiveness of these 'women', and the unsettling effects they could have on them. Prisoners also displayed contradictory attitudes as to what was acceptable male heterosexual behaviour and what was improper, and they showed no compunction in discussing their equivocal reactions to female impersonators in their letters home or their diaries written for a public audience. This could indicate the extent to which attitudes around male sexuality were transgressive in the homosocial POW camp but, when analysed alongside how POWs responded to homosexuality in the camps, it may also illustrate a fluidity in attitudes towards male sexuality in British society during this era more generally.

NOTES

1. These names were redacted in the original article.
2. These camps were usually defined by a Roman numeral and a letter: The Roman numeral indicated the military district to which the camp was attached; the letter distinguished between camps in the same district. Some had an Arabic number; in the middle of the war, these were used because the Roman numeral and letter system had become overloaded. A. Gilbert (2007), *POW: Allied Prisoners in Europe, 1939–1945* (London: John Murray), p. 66.
3. Archives of the International Committee of the Red Cross (hereafter AICRC), C SC, Germany, Oflag VIIB, 22 August 1944.
4. (1946) *Strength and Casualties of the Armed Forces and Auxiliary Services of the United Kingdom 1939 to 1945* (London: HMSO), p. 9, Table 9: 'Total number of prisoners of war of the armed forces of the United Kingdom captured by the enemy as reported to 28th February 1946'.
5. Pickaxe, (1944), 'How to be a Woman', *Touchstone*, 9 (July/August), p. 9.
6. J.S. Goldstein (2001), *Gender and War: How Gender Shapes the War System and Vice Versa* (Cambridge: Cambridge University Press), pp. 252, 331; R. Gerster (1987), *Big-Noting: The Heroic Theme in Australian War Writing* (Melbourne: Melbourne University Press), p. 228.
7. S. Garton (1996), *The Cost of War: Australians Return* (Melbourne: Oxford University Press), p. 210.
8. C. Twomey (2009), 'Double Displacement: Western Women's Return Home from Japanese Internment in the Second World War', *Gender and History*, 21:3, pp. 670–684, here p. 677.
9. C. Twomey (2007), 'Emaciation or Emasculation: Photographic Images, White Masculinity and Captivity by the Japanese in World War Two', *Journal of Men's Studies*, 15:3, pp. 295–310; B. Archer (2004), *A Patchwork of Internment: The Internment of Western Civilians under the Japanese, 1941–1945* (London: RoutledgeCurzon); F. Biess (2006), *Homecomings: Returning POWs and the Legacies of Defeat in Postwar Germany* (Princeton: Princeton University Press); M. Reiss (2012), 'The Importance of Being Men: The Afrika-Korps in American Captivity', *Journal of Social History*, 46:1, pp. 23–47; I. Rachamimov (2012), 'Camp Domesticity: Shifting Gender Boundaries in WWI Internment Camps', in G. Carr and H. Mytum (eds), *Cultural Heritage and Prisoners of War: Creativity Behind Barbed Wire* (New York: Routledge), pp. 291–305; B.K. Feltman (2015), *The Stigma of Surrender: German Prisoners, British Captors, and Manhood in the Great War and Beyond* (Chapel Hill: University of South Carolina). For the experience,

impact and legacy of captivity among men from Australia, Britain and France during the Second World War, see J. Pattinson, L. Noakes and W. Ugolini (2014), 'Incarcerated Masculinities: Male POWs and the Second World War', *Journal of War and Culture Studies*, 7: 3 pp. 179–190.

10. See, for example, Gilbert, *POW*; S. Longden (2008), *Dunkirk: The Men They Left Behind* (London: Constable); S.P. MacKenzie (2004), *The Colditz Myth: British and Commonwealth Prisoners of War in Nazi Germany* (Oxford: Oxford University Press); D. Rolf (1988), *Prisoners of the Reich: Germany's Captives 1939–1945* (Sevenoaks: Coronet).

11. C. Makepeace (forthcoming), *Captives of War: British Prisoners of War in Europe in the Second World War* (Cambridge: Cambridge University Press).

12. MacKenzie, *The Colditz Myth*, p. 214.

13. J.G. Fuller (1990), *Troop Morale and Popular Culture in the British and Dominion Armies, 1914–1918* (Oxford: Clarendon Press), pp. 96, 102–103.

14. D.A. Boxwell (2002), 'The Follies of War: Cross-Dressing and Popular Theatre on the British Front Lines, 1914–1918', *Modernism/modernity*, 9:1, pp. 1–20, here p. 4.

15. I. Rachamimov (2006), 'The Disruptive Comforts of Drag: (Trans) Gender Performances among Prisoners of War in Russia, 1914–1920', *American Historical Review*, 111:2, pp. 362–382, here pp. 363–364.

16. L. Halladay (2009), 'A Lovely War: Male to Female Cross-Dressing and Canadian Military Entertainment in World War II', in S.P. Schacht and L. Underwood (eds), *The Drag Queen Anthology: The Absolutely Fabulous but Flawlessly Customary World of Female Impersonators* (New York: Routledge), pp.19–34, here p. 27.

17. S.A. Eldredge (2014), *Captive Audiences/Captive Performers: Music and Theatre as Strategies for Survival on the Thailand-Burma Railway 1942–1945* (Macalester College), p. 516. http://digitalcommons.macalester.edu/thdabooks/1. Accessed 7 January 2016.

18. MacKenzie, *The Colditz Myth*, p. 210; (hereafter ACICR), C SC, Germany, Oflag 79, 19 September 1944.

19. For these benefits, see also Feltman, *Stigma of Surrender*, p. 128.

20. See, for example, IWM, 86/89/1, W.M.G. Bompas, diary, pp. 20–21; p. 29; p. 32; IWM 88/5/1, A.C. Howard, logbook, p. 77; IWM Documents.234, L. McDermott-Brown, diary, p. 54; pp. 168–171; IWM 95/3/1, H.C. Macey, logbook, pp. 37–40; IWM Documents.8127, A.G. Edwards, logbook, pp. 64–65.

21. See, for example, IWM 05/3/1, L.G.F. Upshall, logbook, cardboard pages. On taking photographs, see IWM 66/132/1, A. Hawarden,

diary entry, 25 March 1944; Ted Barris (2013), *The Great Escape: The Canadian Story* (Toronto: Dundurn Press), p. 130.

22. M. Gillies (2011), *The Barbed-Wire University: The Real Lives of Prisoners of War in the Second World War* (London: Aurum Press), p. 299; MacKenzie, *The Colditz Myth*, p. 210.

23. Upshall, logbook, cardboard pages; IWM 05/57/1 (+ con shelf), E.G. Ball, logbook, pp. 12–13; IWM 81/5/1, P.N. Buckley, logbook, pp. 51–52; Bompas, logbook, cardboard pages; IWM P308, H.F. Shipp, logbook, p. 107; Macey, logbook, pp. 94–95.

24. Private collection of Andrew McIrvine, autobiography of Brian McIrvine, unpaginated.

25. IWM Documents.11736, Lieutenant H. Dros MC, logbook, p. 2; Jonathan Goodliffe, 'Michael Goodliffe: Wartime Shakespearean Actor and Producer', http://www.mgoodliffe.co.uk/. Accessed 18 November 2015.

26. Dros, Logbook, pp. 28, 38; Goodliffe, 'Michael Goodliffe'.

27. Originally, each camp in Italy was distinguished by their place name but, from early 1942, they were also given an Arabic number. W.W. Mason (1954), *Prisoners of War: Official History of New Zealand in the Second World War 1939–1945* (London: Oxford University Press), p. 112.

28. IWM 86/17/1, A.G. Hickmott, The Falcon Company Special P.O.W. Matinee of Blithe Spirit, Duchess Theatre, 16 July 1945.

29. Carr and Mytum, *Cultural Heritage and Prisoners of War*.

30. The Falcon Company Special P.O.W. Matinee of Blithe Spirit, Duchess Theatre, 16 July 1945.

31. Gilbert, *POW*, pp. 100–101; Gillies, *The Barbed-Wire University*, p. 31.

32. IWM P382 (+Conf Shelf), J.S. Naylor, diary entry, 28 December 1943; ACICR, C SC, Germany, Oflag VA, 27 November 1943.

33. IWM 66/174/1, R.L. Angove, diary entry, 3 January 1943.

34. Hawarden, diary entry, 24 January 1944.

35. IWM P370, E. Booth, diary entry, 25 April 1942.

36. IWM PP/MCR/215, D. Nell, diary entry, 1 January 1944.

37. IWM 87/34/1, A.J. East, diary entry, 4 March 1944.

38. Hawarden, diary entries, 9 November 1941, 6 December 1942.

39. This compares, for example, to the type of bonding identified by Thomas Kühne in Nazi Germany where, in the all-male camp or barrack, the male bond was independent of the rest of the world, in particular from women. See T. Kühne (2010), *Belonging and Genocide: Hitler's Community, 1918–1945* (New Haven, CT: Yale University Press), p. 47.

40. Other scholars have emphasised this mimetic function of female impersonators in the First World War. See Boxwell, 'The Follies of War', p. 13; Fuller, *Troop Morale and Popular Culture*, pp. 105–106; Rachamimov,

'The Disruptive Comforts of Drag', p. 377. For one POW who is exceptional in deriding attempts at female impersonation, see Second World War Experience Centre, 2007.531, D.H. Webster, letter to his family, 1 December 1943.

41. IWM 90/19/1, G.T. Lambert, letter to his wife, 7 February 1944.

42. IWM 88/14/1, N.C. Hyde, letter to his wife, 27 September 1943.

43. Nell, diary entry, 5 February 1944.

44. East, diary entry, 18 December 1943.

45. IWM 99/68/1, J.W.M. Mansel, diary entry, 26 February 1943.

46. Hawarden, diary entry, 27 July 1943. For insight into the usage of quotation marks in such contexts, see Rachamimov, 'Camp Domesticity'; Rachamimov, 'The Disruptive Comforts of Drag', p. 381.

47. Rachamimov, 'The Disruptive Comforts of Drag', p. 375; N. Zemon Davis (1987), *Society and Culture in Early Modern France: Eight Essays by Natalie Zemon Davis* (Cambridge: Polity Press), p. 130.

48. P. Baker and J. Stanley (2003), *Hello Sailor! The Hidden History of Gay Life at Sea* (London: Longman), pp. 134–135.

49. Hawarden, diary entry, 6 November 1942; Angove, diary entry, 28 February 1945; Mansel, diary entry, 6 January 1944.

50. P. Boag (2011), *Re-dressing America's Frontier Past* (Berkeley: University of California Press), p. 17; E. Vickers (2015), *Queen and Country: Same-Sex Desire in the British Armed Forces, 1939–1945* (Manchester: Manchester University Press), p. 98.

51. Davis, *Society and Culture in Early Modern France*, p. 130.

52. The Tiller Girls were a dance troupe founded by John Tiller in 1890.

53. Mansel, diary entry, 1 January 1942; IWM 03/12/1, G.B. Matthews, letters to his wife, 23 November 1941, 13 December 1942.

54. S.M. and S. Gubar (1989), *No Man's Land: The Place of the Woman Writer in the Twentieth Century, Volume 2: Sexchanges* (New Haven, CT: Yale University Press), pp. 334–335; S.R. Ullman (1987), *Sex Seen: The Emergence of Modern Sexuality in America* (Berkeley: University of California Press), pp. 53–54.

55. Rachamimov, 'The Disruptive Comforts of Drag', pp. 364, 376; Eldredge, *Captive Audiences/Captive Performers*, p. 530; Boxwell, 'The Follies of War', p. 17.

56. Boxwell, 'The Follies of War', p. 17. For a similar assessment of the role of cross-dressing in the armed forces, see M. Garber (1992), *Vested Interests: Cross-Dressing and Cultural Anxiety* (New York: Routledge), pp. 55–56.

57. For a discussion of this in relation to the performances of female impersonators in early twentieth-century America, see Ullman, *Sex Seen*, p. 54.

58. Mansel, diary entry, 6 January 1944.

59. East, diary entry, 27 November 1943; IWM Documents. 172, G. Hall, diary entry, 25 July 1943.

60. Hyde, letter to his wife, 30 December 1942; Angove, diary entry, 28 February 1945; Mansel, diary entry, 3 January 1942; East, diary entry, 12 December 1944; IWM 01/25/1, J.G. White, diary entry, 2 May 1944.

61. White, diary entry, 11 May 1944; Hawarden, diary entry, 15 June 1944.

62. Rachamimov, 'The Disruptive Comforts of Drag', p. 375.

63. Vickers, *Queen and Country*, p. 92.

64. Mansel, diary entry, 6 January 1944; IWM Docs 2728, Squadron Leader C.N.S. Campbell, diary entry 2 December 1942, written in 1949; Angove, diary entry, 23 December 1942; Mansel, diary entry, 21 January 1944.

65. East, diary entries, 12 December 1944, 9 February 1945, 4 March 1944.

66. Hawarden, diary entry, 8 October 1941. It is difficult to establish a precise approximation for this value. Mansel indicates that 15 marks was the equivalent of £1 in 1941; Mansel, diary entry, 9 August 1941.

67. Gibbens is referring either to Oflag IX A/Z or Stalag 344, T.C.N. Gibbens (1948), 'The Psychology of the Prisoner-of-War', MD thesis, University of Cambridge, p. 20.

68. H. Smith (2015), *Masculinity, Class and Same-Sex Desire in Industrial England, 1895–1957* (Basingstoke: Palgrave Macmillan,), pp. 3, 14, 21, 80, 117.

69. Vickers, *Queen and Country*, pp. 7, 58, 61, 62, 69.

70. Out of seventy-eight contemporary personal narratives I have consulted for my forthcoming book, only three discuss homosexuality; see IWM 05/57/1, F.G. Blyth, letter to his wife, 4 June 1944; Mansel, diary entry, 10 February 1944; Hall, diary entry, 25 July 1943. The latter two comment on how they did not come across it.

71. MacKenzie writes that the extent of active homosexuality among British POWs is open to debate but most of the evidence he cites suggests it was uncommon. Gilbert concludes that in officer and other non-working camps homosexual activity was minimal while in the larger other ranks' camps there were instances of quite overt homosexual behaviour; Gilbert, *POW*, p. 118; MacKenzie, *The Colditz Myth*, p. 212.

72. TNA (The National Archives) WO 32/10757, R.F. Barbour, 'Interim Report on Returned Prisoners of War', 29 August 1945.

73. A.L. Cochrane (1946) 'Notes on the Psychology of Prisoners of War', *British Medical Journal*, 1:4442, p. 283.

74. Smith, *Masculinity, Class and Same-Sex Desire*, pp. 34, 80, 116, 158, 161, 184, 186.

75. Gibbens, 'The Psychology of the Prisoner-of-War', p. 21.

76. See also Smith, *Masculinity, Class and Same-Sex Desire*, p. 123.

Acknowledgements With thanks to the Trustees of the Imperial War Museum for allowing access to the collections and to each of the copyright holders. While every effort has been made to trace all copyright holders, the author and the Imperial War Museum would be grateful for any information which might help to trace the family of Captain Richard Angove, Major Edmund Booth, Warrant Officer Alexander East, Sergeant Navigator G. Hall, Wing Commander Noel Hyde, Commander Geoffrey Lambert, Sergeant David Nell, Corporal Jack White. Thanks also to Andrew McIrvine for supplying a copy of his father's autobiography and to Jonathan Goodliffe, for his correspondence on his father's performances. This chapter draws upon material from within Clare Makepeace (2017), *Captives of War: British Prisoners of War in Europe in the Second World War* (Cambridge: Cambridge University Press), reproduced with permission.

CHAPTER 5

Becoming 'a Man' During the Battle of Britain: Combat, Masculinity and Rites of Passage in the Memoirs of 'the Few'

Frances Houghton

In mid-1940, a freshly minted airman joined 92 Squadron at Kenley airfield. Some months shy of his nineteenth birthday, Geoffrey Wellum was delighted to find himself surrounded by fighter pilots, the 'idols' of his boyhood, and watched as the rest of his new squadron took off on their first operation.[1] When these pilots later returned to the mess, he was startled to see that a dramatic change had been wrought upon both their countenance and their attitude. In his bestselling war memoir, *First Light* (2002), he recollected that this event 'gave me my first intimation of what war is all about. These pilots were no longer young men with little care in the world, they were older mature men.'[2] Wellum surmised that his new comrades had undergone an important transition, acquiring a kind of knowledge that disconnected them from as yet untested members of the squadron. Ascribing their acquisition of a new 'adult' masculinity to the experience of battle, he devoted much attention in his

F. Houghton (✉)
University of Manchester, Manchester, UK
e-mail: frances.eileen.houghton@gmail.com

L. Robb and J. Pattinson (eds.), *Men, Masculinities and Male Culture in the Second World War*, Genders and Sexualities in History,
https://doi.org/ 10.1057/978-1-349-95290-8_5

memoir to charting his own perceptions of a similar sense of self-transformation when he too became a fully operational fighter pilot, a process encapsulated in the strapline to his memoir: *The True Story of the Boy who Became a Man in the War-torn Skies above Britain.*

This chapter examines a number of similar autobiographical accounts published by veterans who believed that they had transitioned from 'boys' to 'men' in the cockpits of their Spitfires and Hurricanes in mid-1940, exploring interpretations of combat as a rite of initiation into 'manhood'. Although the notion that military action offers an important test of manly character is as old as war itself, post-war memoirs of ex-fighter pilots were particularly insistent that aerial combat functioned as a meaningful ceremony in which the pilot traversed the boundary between boyhood and manhood.[3] The stage upon which this particular rite of passage was performed was the long summer of intensive air fighting in 1940, in which Fighter Command desperately strove to avert the threat of German invasion of the British Isles.[4] Through the valiant defensive action of a woefully outnumbered band of pilots, the Battle of Britain and 'the Few' who won it rapidly became legendary.[5] Although the Battle of Britain is traditionally dated from 10 July to 31 October 1940, several memoirists took a rather more flexible view of these dates, perceiving the RAF's protection of the evacuation of the British Expeditionary Force from Dunkirk in late May/early June as the preliminary stages of the battle. Correspondingly, this chapter follows the memoirists' expanded timeline of the Battle of Britain *period*, from the evacuation of Dunkirk to the close of battle in late October. Many of the former aircrew who chose to write and publish post-war memoirs had only just begun to filter through into operational flying as these opening stages of the battle commenced. In retrospect, these veterans ascribed considerable personal significance to the Battle of Britain period as a catalyst for transformation in both their martial identities as aircrew and their own concepts of masculine self. Fighting in the Battle of Britain, they collectively asserted, made 'men' out of 'boys', and they deployed the unique privileges of reflective auto/biographical writing to map these shifts in their masculine identity.

Surprisingly little scholarly attention has been paid to the ways in which post-war autobiographical writing allowed military veterans to self-assess how they had been altered by the experience of war. This chapter seeks to remedy this omission by indicating how these valuable documents may be drawn upon as repositories of reconstructed experience and identity. Autobiographical acts have been described as the history of an author observing himself,[6] granting opportunities to add consciousness to lived experience of an event.[7] As Samuel Hynes comments in his literary overview of twentieth-century soldiers' tales, personal testimonies of war relate two stories. They tell of servicemen's actions, the 'things men do in war', but they also tell the counter-story of the 'things war does' to men.[8] The interiority of these narratives proffers deeper comprehension of how former combatants interpreted conflict as shaping their sense of self. Indeed, if war, as Elaine Scarry insists, served to 'unmake' identity, then the act of writing a war memoir allowed the veteran to reassemble the pieces of that identity and to chart a sense of self-progression from inexperienced youth to war-hardened adult, cementing that process of masculine development into the historical record of warfare.[9] While Richard Hillary's famous memoir, *The Last Enemy* (1942), displayed a revealing sense of *Selbstbesinnung* (self-contemplation), and other wartime-published narratives also exhibited brief flashes of interiority, it was in the post-war memoirs of ex-fighter aircrew that a subjective sense of self-awareness became markedly pronounced, since the authors benefited from valuable time for reflection on the process of becoming 'a man' during wartime. In these later accounts, the former flyers actively reviewed their expectations that battle would function as a ceremonial ritual to incorporate them into a fascinating world of 'men'.

The reconstructive nature of post-war memoirs carries important implications for studies of war and masculinity. As Michael Roper's excellent analysis of ex-soldiers' narratives from the First World War observes, veteran accounts provide 'a useful point of entry into the history of twentieth-century masculinity' because they involve a dialogue between the codes of manliness which surrounded a generation of youth as it grew up, and more internally focused concepts of the adult self.[10] Indeed, in any study of masculinity, as Graham Dawson explains, it is necessary to distinguish between representations of masculinities in cultural images and narratives, and the complexities of an identity as it is actually lived out.[11] The veterans of 'the Few' were poignantly aware of a chasm between the fighter pilot's desirable and 'real' masculine identities, and firmly established the dissimilarity in their narratives. Correspondingly, by illustrating a number of key differences between the masculinities imagined and lived out by the men of Fighter Command, this study is intended to contribute to the burgeoning field of literature interrogating war and masculinities.[12]

Published between 1956 and 2010, most of the eleven memoirs upon which this study focuses will undoubtedly be familiar to historians of the wartime RAF, and they continue to be popular with the interested general reader.[13] Nevertheless, the full scope of these particular books as historical sources has yet to be explored. Veteran reconstructions of masculinity remain a significantly understudied topic, but the personal testimonies of these men prove vital for historians who wish to probe subjective understandings of a sense of masculine self among veterans of the Second World War. They also allow us to chart these authors' perceptions of the ways in which their own understandings of war and manliness shifted. In evaluating tensions in the airman's self-constructions of martial masculinity, these memoirs bear witness to John Tosh's argument that masculinity is composed of both a 'psychic' identity, in which male subjectivities are shaped during childhood, and a 'social' identity, in which masculinity is bound up with peer recognition and performance in the public sphere.[14] Accordingly, this chapter enquires first into the ex-fighter pilots' understandings of the representations which moulded their boyhood visions of the airman's manliness and secondly into the 'social', or 'martial', identity that they composed through their performance in combat in 1940.[15]

'BOY'S-EYE VIEW': THE SCHOOLBOY'S APPROACH TO WAR

The post-war memoirs of 'the Few' testify to Dawson's memorable assertion that masculinities 'are lived out in the flesh, but fashioned in the imagination'.[16] As children and adolescents, 'the Few' shared an idealised image of the airman as the epitome of heroic manly identity which was founded on tropes of the adventure of flight, a fantasy that former fighter pilot Hugh Dundas dubbed the 'schoolboy approach' to war.[17] War in general furnishes opportunities to 'imagine and test desirable masculinities', but in inter-war Britain, air combat appeared an especially enticing proving ground for combatants to play out their boyish ideals of heroic manliness.[18] Strikingly, the ways in which the flyer veterans framed their juvenile fantasies and assumptions about battle indicate conditioning from an early age to anticipate an accelerated development of the masculine self through war in the air. For many of the men who would become 'the Few', during their formative years as schoolboys and adolescents, early foundations had been laid which equated an idealised adult masculinity with a martial identity as a pilot. For example, popular illustrated youth papers such as the *Gem*, or the *Magnet*, which sold weekly in excess of 200,000 copies between 1925 and 1935, increasingly identified the 'principal schoolboy heroes' of their stories 'with a future destiny as air pilots'.[19] Wellum articulated this synonymy of identities, explaining that aircrew training would 'make not only a pilot of me but, also, a man capable of doing a man's job in a man's life'.[20] Similarly, although at twenty-four years of age in 1940, the future ace, 'Johnnie' Johnson, was a little further from his schooldays, his recollection that 'I was anxious to prove myself in combat and mix on equal terms with men' suggests that he too still held a boyish preconception that 'real' men, the nadir of manliness, were airmen.[21]

Boyhood constructions of the airman's supreme manliness in these narratives derived, in the first instance, from the celebration of the flyer in inter-war popular British culture. The 'schoolboy approach' to war as it is documented in these memoirs was formed against a wider cultural backdrop of public fascination with aviators. The 'allure of the flying ace' cast a bewitching spell over male British youth during the inter-war period. With the RAF's shrewd capitalisation upon popular images of the flyer as an airborne superman, airmen became lionised as a superior breed of heroes who were daring and resourceful masters of a new, powerful technology, a perception which is key to understanding the desirable masculinity associated with the fighter pilot to which these memoirists aspired. As Tosh and Roper observe, 'masculinity is always bound up with negotiations about power'.[22] With his expert control over his flying machine, and his ability to dictate his own movements in the air, the fighter pilot could be regarded as a special kind of man, a tremendously powerful being who correspondingly possessed a heightened sense of masculinity.

Yet despite the evident synthesis of idealised identities of 'man' and 'pilot' in these memoirs, it was the sense of heroic martial masculinity popularly attached to military flyers, with its emphasis on intense bravery and great skill, which these authors most wanted to emulate. Stereotypical images of the First World War fighter pilots offered a paradigm of manly virtue to the boys who would become 'the Few'; as memoirist Roger Hall attested, 'They were all heroes to me'.[23] In 1918, a biography of Albert Ball VC, perhaps the most famous British ace, was published. Ball had particularly captured the British public's imagination, becoming celebrated for his youthfulness, courage and determination before he was killed at the age of twenty in 1917. His exploits entranced the next generation of boys who would succeed him as fighter pilots. Memoirist Geoffrey Page, for instance, remembered that when he undertook officer cadet training at RAF Cranwell in late 1939, he was convinced he was ready to be a pilot simply on the basis that he 'knew practically all there was to know about Albert Ball: how he flew, how he fought, how he won his Victoria Cross, how he died.'[24] Reflecting upon his former hero worship, Page explained that: 'As an officer cadet of nineteen, my thoughts were boyishly clear and simple. All I wanted was to be a fighter pilot like my hero, Captain Albert Ball.'[25]

The First World War's creation of a myth that the air war offered a return to romantic illusions of knightly chivalry in combat was central to the 'schoolboy approach' to war as it is retrospectively documented in these memoirs. The air war above the Western Front had lifted battle literally and metaphorically away from the squalor of the trenches, seemingly granting an arena in which small-scale gentlemanly duels were fought by a brotherhood of heroic pilot-knights errant. The image of the airman thus emerged from this war as chivalrous/heroic, endorsed by Prime Minister David Lloyd George, who venerated the flyers as 'the Chivalry of the air' in the House of Commons in 1917, and the poet Sir Henry Newbolt, who mused that 'our airmen are singularly like the knights of the old romances'.[26] The biographers of Albert Ball also ensured that he was commemorated as 'a young knight of gentle manner who learnt to fly and to kill at a time when all the world was killing'.[27] The memoirs of 'the Few' suggest that because of the seductive appeal of this established 'knights of the air' myth, the aspirant fighter pilot could subscribe to a belief that he 'knew' what he would face in his own forthcoming battles. Based on his knowledge of Ball's life and death, Page recalled that: 'I also thought I knew about war in the air. I imagined it to be Arthurian—about chivalry.'[28] A fantasy was created among the next generation of pilots that future battle would also involve medieval traditions of fair play. For the apprentice fighter pilot, chivalry seemed to offer a guideline for the theory and practice of heroic masculine behaviour in battle. As Allen Frantzen remarks in his study of chivalry and sacrifice in the First World War, medieval warriors 'created a code for examining and evaluating masculine conduct in competitive contexts'.[29] For youths who were entranced by the deeds of aircrew like Ball, therefore, the associations of chivalry and air warfare effectively proposed a code of conduct which additionally affirmed the heroic masculinity of the fighter pilot.

The cinema also visually confirmed that war in the air manufactured heroes out of men. Edmund Goulding's remake of *Dawn Patrol* in 1938 held a particular appeal for adolescent males and was seen by memoirist W.G.G. Duncan Smith four times in May 1939.[30] Centring upon the exploits of a Royal Flying Corps (RFC) squadron on the Western Front, and starring Basil Rathbone, David Niven and Errol Flynn, champions of many cinematic swashbuckling escapades throughout the 1930s, this film helped to condition expectations that battle would prove noble and exciting. Boys' literature also supplied the inter-war generation of adolescents with a plethora of fictional paradigms upon which to model their future behaviour as combatants. In her study of boys' story papers, Kelly Boyd notes that these texts offer valuable 'windows into the ideologies of masculinity which informed readers' lives'.[31] Aimed at a broader market than the public school elite, this literature was widely read by the distinctly middle-class youth who became the memoirists of 'the Few'. While considerable investigation into the social backgrounds of 'the Few' has demonstrated that it was more egalitarian than traditionally assumed, the vast majority of men who later published memoirs of their experiences as members of Fighter Command in 1940 were drawn from the middle classes.[32] Crucially, Boyd posits that the heroes with which juvenile readers were presented in these stories were seldom 'supermen' who emerged fully formed with no need for initiation into manliness, and many tales 'centred around the protagonist's development from rough approximation into fully-fledged man'.[33] It is evident from the postwar memoirs of 'the Few' that their ultimate youthful manly hero—or, as popular historian Patrick Bishop dryly remarks, 'Fighter Command's single most effective recruiting sergeant'—was James 'Biggles' Bigglesworth, the creation of Captain W.E. Johns, whom we encountered earlier in Doyle's chapter.[34] As a fictional flyer in the wartime RFC, Biggles enjoyed astonishing aerial adventures which served as an early introduction to air combat for many Second World War airmen who seem to have half-believed that the character was real. Indeed, memoirist Bobby Oxspring synthesised this fictional fighter pilot with the image of his own father, who had been an RFC pilot: 'To me', he remembered, 'my father was Biggles'.[35] Biggles' influence seems to have had a formative impact upon his young readers, especially those who would themselves go on to publish books about their own war experiences. Like his real-life counterparts in the later conflict, Biggles began his story as a 'boy' and became a 'man' through the aegis of combat. While it is difficult to prove conclusively that the memoirists of 'the Few' modelled the trajectory of their narratives upon the sojourn of Biggles, it is apparent that the concept of aerial combat as a rite of passage into manhood was already a familiar and common theme for these youngsters.

The crux of the 'schoolboy approach' to combat was the ability of youth to fashion fantasies of battle based entirely upon stirring accounts of moments of especial martial glory, to the detriment of any element of undesirable realism. The model of war as adventure upon which 'the Few' had been brought up dominated their expectations of combat, and, at this stage, death was not a concept that they easily grasped. Some overlooked it altogether in the manner of Tony Bartley, who reported that on the eve of his first operation, he was 'too excited' to gain much sleep, and spent the night dreaming of what might await him: 'It never entered my head that I could be killed. All I could imagine was shooting the Luftwaffe out of the sky, with the boys beside me, and winning honour and glory for myself and the squadron.'[36] Others comprehended potential death in absurdly romanticised and melodramatic terms. Dundas, 'fascinated by the idea of war' from an early age, spent many hours at prep school lost in a reverie in which he led 'a thousand forlorn hopes, died a hundred deaths in a manner which aroused the astonished admiration of the entire nation'.[37] If the harsh facts of death in wartime intruded at all upon these youthful dreams therefore, they left only the lightest of traces. Yet it is worth noting that these harsh facts were fully available to the youngsters, should they have opted to recognise them. The extant body of scholarship which has investigated the 'cult of the airman' in inter-war Britain has tended to gloss over the fact that all of the cultural models which shaped the myth of the flyer fully communicated the more unpleasant possibilities of war. For example, while *Dawn Patrol* undeniably glamorised chivalrous aspects of the air war of 1914–1918, it was also a pacifist script that depicted grief, depression, dangerous levels of alcohol consumption and emotional scarring among the men of the RFC. The 'Biggles' books were, as Bishop comments, 'practically documentary in their starkness'.[38] They spared their young readers from neither scenes of violent death nor images of flyers whose nerves were worn to shreds on the Western Front. Given that W.E. Johns was ruthless in killing off or crippling a number of friendly characters in his tales of the air war, memoirist Tim Vigors' comment that he had imagined war as being 'like a Biggles book, where the heroes always survived and it was generally only the baddies who got the chop', indicates that the adolescent fighter pilot-to-be indulged in a pleasurable degree of selective reading.[39] Perhaps the most telling indication of the judicious nature of this 'boy's-eye view' of war is provided by Page, the devotee of Albert Ball.[40] Despite proudly claiming to know 'practically all there was to know' about Ball, including the grisly manner of his demise, the veteran still reflected that 'death and injury had no part' in his adolescent 'Arthurian' vision of war.[41] In reviewing their early expectations of battle, the memoirists of 'the Few' thus indicate that they stubbornly subscribed to a shared fantasy that participation in the exhilarating adventure of air warfare would bestow upon them idealised standards of heroic adult masculinity. Founding these illusions upon a boy's 'popular masculine pleasure-culture' of aerial battle in inter-war Britain, they confidently predicted that acquiring the status of a flyer would propel them into the coveted manliness of the men of the air.[42]

Growing 'a Little Older': Reviewing Battle as a Rite of Passage

Ethnographer Arnold van Gennep claims that certain conditions must be fulfilled in order to traverse socially constructed boundaries, or 'rites of passage', and that 'special acts' invariably accompany progression from one group or life stage to the next.[43] In reviewing their experiences of the Battle of Britain, the memoirists of Fighter Command suggested that their boyish aspirations of becoming 'a man' were bound up with associations of flight as a glorious adventure. With hindsight, however, they perceived that the 'special act' which propelled them into an identity as a 'man' was explicitly connected to the performance of violence. In this airborne rite of passage, the critical liminal moment was slightly different for each flyer. Vigors, for instance, identified his first contact with death during pilot training in the lead-up to the Battle of Britain as the point at which he was inducted into manhood. Training was an extremely hazardous time for novice pilots, and fatal accidents were tragically common. The loss of two senior cadets when they misjudged their distances and crashed 'came as a real shock' to Vigors. Up until then, he mused, 'I had regarded flying as a marvellous game'. Only at the funerals of these men did it occur that 'it could easily be me in one of those coffins. Looking back now over all these years, I believe that it was at that moment that I left schooldays behind and became a man.'[44] Page, too, connected his transition from 'boy' to 'man' with finding himself in mortal peril on his first operation, a fighter sweep over northern France during the Dunkirk evacuation. In retrospect, he perceived that this was the critical point at which he cast off boyhood: 'All that remained of youth in those swiftly moving Hurricanes were the physical attributes of our bodies, the minds were no longer carefree and careless. The sordid reality of all that our task implied banished lighter thoughts.'[45] Having distinguished himself only by becoming lost in a huge smoke pall from burning oil storage tanks, Page reported that: 'My first sortie over enemy-held territory was over. I had grown a little older.'[46] Unlike Page, however, Dundas and Tom Neil did not feel that they had progressed into manhood simply by dint of cheating death in the air. Both memoirists indicated that it was only the act of destroying the enemy that allowed the crossing of the threshold into the elite circle of the pilot-warrior. Neil recorded that he did not have time to discharge his guns during his first few operations, and this left him feeling 'almost ashamed', 'like something of an outsider', in the crew room.[47] Dundas, too, singularly failed to loose off his weapons during his inaugural sortie. Nevertheless, the memoirist reported that after this 'inglorious' first brush with the enemy, he returned to the airfield at Rochford, supposing himself to be 'transformed, Walter Mitty-like: now a debonair young fighter pilot, rising twenty, proud and delighted that he had fired his gun in a real dog-fight, even though he had not hit anything, sat in the cockpit which had so recently been occupied by a frightened child.'[48] The gentle self-mockery with which this anecdote is related suggests that the 'schoolboy approach' remained in the ascendant for the young Dundas, who proudly imagined that he had undergone the much anticipated rite of passage into manhood. Nevertheless, deploying a suggestive retrospective awareness that the real transition—that is to say, acquiring a full knowledge that war involved death—had yet to occur, the memoirist identified the liminal point in his rite of passage as the first time he actually succeeded in scoring hits on two Dornier bomber aircraft: 'I felt twelve feet tall after that combat.'[49] Neil, too, recorded that when he did manage to make his first kill, he returned home 'feeling like a king'.[50] In these narratives of the 'things war does to men', therefore, the memoirists of 'the Few' clearly interpreted the 'sordid reality' of close affiliation with death and killing as the catalyst for the transition which made 'men' out of boys in the air.

The dawning of cognisance that the status of military airman meant a close relationship with extreme violence is associated in these narratives with experiencing visceral fear. Through the creation of a war memoir, the ex-fighter pilot undertook a self-appraisal of how he learned to control this emotion. Accepting Tosh's argument that masculinity is a social identity which 'depends upon performance in the social sphere', the masculine identity of the fighter pilot as it is reconstructed in these narratives was also dependent upon performance in the martial sphere, and there is a revealing disjuncture between the fighter pilot's expectations of heroic battle and the lived experience of terror.[51] Vigors recalled that as he prepared to scramble on his first operation, his mouth dried up:

> For the first time in my life I understood the meaning of the "taste of fear". I suddenly realised that at long last the moment had arrived ... Within an hour I could be battling for my life being shot at with real bullets by a man whose sole intent was to kill me. Up till now it had been something of a game; like a Biggles book, where the heroes always survived and it was generally only the baddies who got the chop. Now it was real war. I was dead scared and knew I had somehow to control this fear and not show it to my fellow pilots.[52]

There is a suggestion here that new pilots judged their own sense of martial masculinity against the behaviour of their experienced comrades. Like Vigors, Wellum was anxious that he should successfully maintain appropriate masculine standards in front of his squadron: 'I'm afraid of being a coward.'[53] Equating good performance in battle with a lack of fear which would develop his sense of military manliness, Wellum anticipated that his first battle would demonstrate whether 'I shall be either a man or a coward.'[54] His illusion that to be a fighter pilot meant to show no fear, and preferably to feel no fear, harks back to Victorian codes of 'manly stoicism', and is clearly intended to illustrate the author's juvenile understanding of the true nature of the airman as combatant in the midtwentieth century.[55]

Overall, the flyer's relationship to fear reveals, as Martin Francis's study demonstrates, an important dimension of the ways in which the airman's sense of masculinity was forged.[56] Francis shows that manly courage among wartime flyers in the Second World War was normatively understood not as nineteenth-century 'unreflective fearlessness', but instead as 'the conquest of fears that were openly acknowledged'.[57] The memoirs of 'the Few' depicted learning to overcome reflexive instincts to run away as an integral part of their rite of passage in 1940, representing the flyer's ability to manage his own terror as a litmus test of manliness. Dundas's narrative provides a particularly instructive illustration of how the former fighter pilot assessed his own masculine development in correlation with his behaviour under fire. His first operation was to protect the remnants of the British Expeditionary Force on the beaches of Dunkirk. Before take-off, Dundas found himself alone with a few moments for quiet contemplation, and depicted a poignant scene in the wash room of the officers' mess at Rochford airfield in which he spoke aloud to his reflection in the mirror: '"Well, Hughie," I said to myself, "you couldn't insure your life now, for love nor money." I said it several times over, because I thought it sounded rather dramatic.'[58] From the vantage point of some forty years later, Dundas ruefully acknowledged this statement as 'trite' and 'trivial', yet he perceived this snapshot of memory to be 'enlightening' because it displayed that his younger self was:

[M]entally aware of the fact that two months before my twentieth birthday, sudden death was an imminent possibility. But it shows me facing this knowledge with a cliché, *Boy's Own Paper* style. Even in that grave moment I still saw Errol Flynn looking over my shoulder in the mirror.[59]

This manifestation of the 'schoolboy approach' to combat suffered a severe blow when he engaged the enemy for the first time: 'I was close to panic in the bewilderment and hot fear of that first dog fight … [T]he consideration which was uppermost in my mind was the desire to stay alive.'[60] Yet with experience and several kills to his credit, Dundas discovered that the initial 'hot fear' of battle gave way to something altogether more calculating:

I heard the tempting tone of an inner voice which said: 'There, now. You have been in action several times and you have done some damage to the enemy. You are still alive and kicking. Even if you pulled out now, no one would be able to say you had not done your bit.'

It was the voice which expressed a sincere desire to stay alive, opposing a sincere desire to engage the enemy. It was muted and easy enough to muffle at that stage. But I was to learn how insistent it could become.[61]

Bartley also confessed to experiencing a desire to turn away from battle once experience had taught him that was legitimately possible. The speeds at which a dogfight took place meant that the skirmish moved in a constant whirl from which it was easy to become displaced, and many fighter pilots were bewildered to suddenly find themselves alone in a patch of sky which had, moments previously, been heaving with aircraft. Under these circumstances, the temptation to return to base could prove compelling: 'it was easy to run away. The sky is a big place to get lost in.'[62] Like Dundas, Bartley overcame the impulse to absent himself from battle. Nevertheless, the fact that these veterans documented an ongoing struggle with the 'inner voice' of fear, and the persistent temptation to escape from the battle arena, demonstrates that they were aware of combat's enforced revision of boyish expectations that battle should prove one either 'a man' or 'a coward'. These retrospective evaluations of their sensibilities and behaviour thus acknowledged that battle forced them to revise idealised adolescent fantasies of military performance. The memoirists indicate that their juvenile notion of heroic martial masculinity, predicated upon the polarisation of courage and cowardice, was reworked into something far more nuanced, and self-compassionate. Moreover, they also portray the authors' growing realisation that the process of becoming a 'man' in aerial combat often meant standing up to the self as much as to the enemy.

The flyer's performance in battle also underpinned his self-construction of manliness in a different way. Despite the fantasies which many of the memoirists in this study initially projected onto aerial battle, their narratives indicate that there was little space to adhere to codes of chivalric behaviour in the frenzied dogfights of 1940. Neil recorded that 'Aircraft, friend and foe, flashed around my head like flies',[63] whilst Bartley was perturbed to find himself flying amid a 'veritable maelstrom of whizzing bullets.'[64] In these conditions, the pilot discovered little inclination to joust with his enemy, and boyish illusions of engaging opponents in chivalric manner rapidly foundered. Under these circumstances, the flyer's choices were condensed into three discrete courses of action: to kill; to be killed; or to run away.[65] The latter option offered aircrew a puzzle to resolve. On the one hand, as Dundas illustrated, the pilot fought ceaselessly to master an 'inner voice' which instructed him to flee from battle. Yet on the other hand, aerial combat demanded a necessary degree of prudence in selecting one's opponent and one of the most important lessons the pilot learned was when to withhold combat. With only sufficient ammunition for between twelve and fifteen seconds of firing, most fighter pilots could not keep their gun-buttons depressed and so were required to employ some calculation in their choice of targets.[66] Here there is an intriguing point of difference in the wartime and post-war narratives of 'the Few'. Wartime-published memoirs of fighter pilots quite cheerfully acknowledged that they cultivated the art of 'not throwing one's life away carelessly', and deliberately sought out weak targets, such as crippled or inexperienced opponents.[67] The post-war memoirists, however, exhibited a revealing degree of reticence on this subject, and an unease with killing frequently lurks beneath the surface of these texts, as it does not in the narratives of men who were still embroiled in the nation's fight for survival when their testimonies were published. The post-war decades that offered the former fighter pilot the space and leisure in which to reflect upon his wartime experiences could also allow long-suppressed anxieties about his wartime identity as a killer to surface. Several veterans questioned whether their violent actions had really been morally acceptable, since certain kills etched themselves into their memories as particularly fraught with horror. Wellum, for instance, experienced an especially emotional reaction to dispatching a Me.109 into the sea, describing his deed as 'just plain cold-blooded murder.'[68] Upon incinerating a Stuka bomber, Page was appalled to realise that he registered 'fascination' alongside 'horror' at his act, perceiving that he returned 'a different person.' In an effort to exorcise his conflicting emotions about this kill, he penned a tortured letter: 'Maybe I am a bit sorry for myself … I enjoy killing. It fascinates me beyond belief to see my bullets striking home and then to see the Hun blow up before me. It also makes me feel sick.'[69]

Boyish constructions of the airman's masculine code of chivalry clearly proved difficult to reconcile for some ex-fighter pilots. As we have seen, gallantry offered a means of evaluating combatant character, but the great aerial battles of 1940 had not provided a forum for the manly qualities of valiant honour that these men had associated with the earlier air war. The distinct absence of openly honourable combat during the Battle of Britain contributed to a sense of unease among some former airmen, who were moved to wonder what this implied about their own manly character. Joanna Bourke argues that chivalry in the air was, where possible, 'evoked to stifle fears of senseless violence', and there is an interesting difference of opinion in some of these memoirs which corroborates this.[70] Although opportunities to display open gallantry in the frenzy of a dogfight were rare, several memoirists insisted that they maintained noble intentions by adhering to a universal 'live and let live' approach to enemy airmen who were forced to bail out of their aircraft. Johnson, for example, insisted that evacuated aircrew:

> should be allowed to drift down to earth without being riddled with cannon fire. It was an act of chivalry which we had inherited from our forebears of the previous war; and despite accounts to the contrary, I never knew of a pilot who was shot at as he drifted helplessly to the ground.[71]

Neil, too, claimed that 'no self-respecting airman, friend or foe' would target a pilot parachuting to safety.[72] Bartley, however, disagreed. Having sustained direct hits to his oil and glycol tanks, he made preparations to launch himself out of his stricken Spitfire. Upon recalling that a friend of his had been shot down while dangling from his parachute, he explained that he changed his mind: 'Escaping airmen over their own territory were fair game in some combatants' log book.'[73] Although officially recorded instances of airmen being gunned down on the strings of their parachutes might well have been accidents caused amid the welter of flying bullets, the existence of a debate about performance of chivalric mercy in these memoirs lends weight to Stefan Goebel's suggestion that such ideals 'fulfilled a compensatory function'.[74]

Arguably, then, the retrospective efforts of authors such as Johnson and Neil to identify at least the vestiges of a code of chivalry in battle offered some reassurance against past and present anxieties that the fighter pilot memoirist might have been brutalised by his violent actions. Yet herein lay a terrible disjuncture between boyish preconceptions of aerial combat and the seasoned masculinity which actually emerged from the 'maelstrom of bullets'.[75] C.S. Lewis was wise enough to recognise in 1940 that, while the image of the fighter pilot certainly lent itself to superficial comparisons with 'Launcelot', the chivalric ideal of the knight in fact seduced flyers with a 'pernicious lie', having been originally imposed upon medieval knights to contain their bloodlust.[76] As veterans, 'the Few' communicated a similar sense that they were deceived in their youthful subscription to a gentlemanly martial identity as 'knights of the air'. For example, Page recorded that: 'I had taken off from the same airfield an innocent, and returned a bloodied fighter pilot, or was it a murderer hiding behind the shield of official approval?'[77] Furthermore, looking back on his boyish 'Arthurian' fantasy of combat, Page reflected:

> In the innocence of youth, I had not yet seen the other side of the coin, with its images of hideous violence, fear, pain and death. I did not know then about vengeance. Neither did I know about the ecstasy of victory. Nor did I remotely suspect the presence within my being of a dormant lust for killing.[78]

Bartley voiced a very similar sense of brutal disconnect between youthful fantasy and a reality born of experience. 'In retrospect', he wrote, 'I realise how pathetically naïve we were in the supreme confidence of youth'.[79] Like Page, he expressed the sense that his progression through battle into manhood had not quite lived up to his hopes, explaining that 'the Few' had been 'fit and fearless, in the beginning. By the end, we were old and tired, and knew what fear was. I had taken a life before I had taken a woman.'[80] There is an uncomfortable suggestion in both memoirs that the longed-for rite of passage into an identity as a man of the air instead produced a masculinity in which youth became warped into manhood by the act of killing. Even Wellum, who had looked forward with such enthusiasm to becoming 'a man capable of doing a man's job in a man's life',[81] insisted that at the age of twenty, he had become instead a 'worn-out bloody fighter pilot at twenty years of age, merely left to live, or rather to exist, on memories, reduced to watching from the wings'.[82] Ultimately, therefore, it is difficult to discern any sense from these memoirs that the Battle of Britain veterans regarded their emergent masculine selves as akin in any way to the heroic projections of their youthful fantasies, despite their heroic image in the eyes of the British public throughout the next seventy years.[83]

Conclusion

To summarise, the Battle of Britain period was presented in the memoirs of 'the Few' as *the* formative experience of their lives, an anvil upon which new adult identities as warrior 'men' were forged. Yet combat failed to provide the desired transition to the heroic paradigm of devil-may-care martial masculinity on which the inter-war teenager's fictional and non-fictional masculine heroes were modelled. Instead, the emergent adult male self bore far more resemblance to Sonya Rose's identification of a wartime 'temperate masculinity', in which bravado was replaced by characteristics such as good humour, emotional reserve and the courage of the 'ordinary' man called upon repeatedly to do his best.[84] The memoirs of 'the Few' indicate that their authors had been forced to recognise that, in the final analysis, pilots were not in fact supermen. In these narratives, ideals of hyper-heroic manliness thus evolved into an awareness that the manly identity of the fighter pilot could be measured instead by his approach to all the unpleasant elements of battle that the young 'Few' had excised from their fantasies of combat. In placing these recollections of 1940 on public record, the memoirists of 'the Few' pointedly emphasised a painful disconnect between their juvenile precepts of manliness and more complex, often conflicted, adult male identity which emerged from their rite of passage. The deliberation with which 'the Few' depicted this gulf between the airman's 'real' and 'imagined' masculine selves indicates an attempt to impart to their reader the sense of shock they received when battle did not turn out to be the gentlemanly affair they anticipated. Page, in particular, shaped his narrative to intensify the impact of combat in all its brutality for his reader, introducing his memoir with a description of the appalling burns he sustained from being shot down. Having set the scene for impending trauma, he returned to the beginning of his life story to relate all his boyish dreams of war. In granting the reader this dreadful foreknowledge of the injuries that awaited him, Page cleverly heightened the sense of innocence betrayed and boyhood corroded. There was also a certain black irony in the fact that the Battle of Britain became a popular romantic myth through much the same cultural mechanisms that had prompted the inter-war generation of boys to volunteer as fighter aircrew. Fighter Command's memoirists did take care to ensure that their own loss of youthfulness was never quite presented as tragic, leaving their audiences in no doubt that their sacrifices in 1940 were worthwhile, and that they had, so far as possible, enjoyed their war. Nevertheless, these personal narratives were deliberately crafted as eulogies for those earlier boyish selves who had so eagerly and vividly anticipated becoming 'men' via aerial combat. There is a clear need for historians of gender and identity to unravel similar veteran ego-documents more fully.

Notes

1. G. Wellum (2002), *First Light: the True Story of the Boy who Became a Man in the War-torn Skies above Britain* (London: Viking), p. 97.
2. Wellum, *First Light*, p. 100.
3. For further discussion of war as a test of manhood, see G. Mosse (1996), *The Image of Man: The Creation of Modern Masculinity* (Oxford: Oxford University Press); G. Dawson (1994), *Soldier Heroes: British Adventure, Empire and the Imagining of Masculinities* (London: Routledge).
4. See J. Terraine (1985), *The Right of the Line: The Royal Air Force in the European War 1939–1945* (London: Hodder and Stoughton); S. Bungay (2000), *The Most Dangerous Enemy: A History of the Battle of Britain* (London: Aurum Press); P. Addison and J. Crang (eds.) *The Burning Blue: A New History of the Battle of Britain* (London: Pimlico).
5. At the beginning of July 1940, 754 RAF Spitfires and Hurricanes found themselves pitted against 1464 German fighters and 1808 bombers. This represented a ratio of 4.5:1. Bungay, *The Most Dangerous Enemy*, p. 107. The attrition rate among RAF aircrew also became legendary, with 544 Fighter Command pilots killed. Bungay, *The Most Dangerous Enemy*, p. 373.
6. S. Spender (1980), 'Confessions and Autobiography', in J. Olney (ed.), *Autobiography: Essays Theoretical and Critical* (Princeton: Princeton University Press), p. 116.
7. G. Grusdorf (1980), 'Conditions and Limits of Autobiography', in Olney (ed.), *Autobiography*, p. 38.
8. S. Hynes (1998), *The Soldiers' Tale* (London: Pimlico), p. 3.
9. E. Scarry (1985), *The Body in Pain* (Oxford: Oxford University Press), p. 122. For a more detailed explanation of how war memoirs allowed the veteran-author to assess the impact of war upon his mind, body and identity, see F. Houghton (2015), '"Remembering with Advantages": British Military Memoirs of the Second World War, 1950–2010', unpublished PhD thesis, University of Edinburgh.
10. M. Roper (2005), 'Between Manliness and Masculinity: The "War Generation" and the Psychology of Fear in Britain, 1914–1950', *Journal of British Studies*, 44:2, pp. 343–362, here pp. 346–347.
11. G. Dawson (1991), 'The Blond Bedouin: Lawrence of Arabia, Imperial Adventure and the Imagining of English-British Masculinity', in J. Tosh and M. Roper (eds), *Manful Assertions: Masculinities in Britain since 1800* (London: Routledge), pp.113–144, here pp. 118–119.
12. Recent examples of this literature include L. Robb (2015), *Men at Work: The Working Man in British Culture, 1939–1945* (Basingstoke: Palgrave Macmillan); J. Meyer (2009), *Men of War: Masculinity and the First*

World War in Britain (Basingstoke: Palgrave Macmillan); M. Francis (2008), *The Flyer: British Culture and the Royal Air Force, 1939–1945* (Oxford: Oxford University Press); S. Dudink, K. Hagemann and J. Tosh (eds) (2004), *Masculinities in Politics and War: Gendering Modern History* (Manchester: Manchester University Press).

13. For instance, Geoffrey Wellum's *First Light* seems to be an almost permanent fixture on the shelves of most high-street bookstores, while the presence of Wellum and his fellow veteran-memoirist, Tom Neil, at the recent seventy-fifth commemorations of the Battle of Britain ensures that the profile of these authors remains high.

14. J. Tosh (1994), 'What Should Historians Do with Masculinity? Reflections on Nineteenth-Century Britain', *History Workshop*, 38, pp. 179–202, here p. 198.

15. John Tosh and Martin Francis have called for gendered histories of men which recognise male domestic roles, quite rightly pointing out that masculinity operates in a complex relationship with female identities. Sex and relationships with women clearly played an important role in many fighter pilots' experiences, but in their own reconstructions of wartime manly identity, these memoirists notably privileged combat as the ultimate induction into manhood, even above more traditional male rites of passage, such as loss of virginity.

16. Dawson, *Soldier Heroes*, p. 1.

17. H. Dundas (1988), *Flying Start: A Fighter Pilot's War Years* (London: Stanley Paul and Co.), p. 23.

18. Dawson, 'The Blond Bedouin', p. 123.

19. O.D. Edwards (2000), 'The Battle of Britain and Children's Literature', in P. Addison and J. Crang (eds), *The Burning Blue: A New History of the Battle of Britain* (London: Pimlico), pp.164–190, here pp. 164–168.

20. Wellum, *First Light*, p. 32.

21. J. Johnson (1956), *Wing Leader* (London: Chatto & Windus), p. 46.

22. Tosh and Roper, *Manful Assertions*, p. 18.

23. R. Hall (1975), *Clouds of Fear* (Folkestone: Bailey Brothers and Swinfen), p. 29.

24. G. Page (1999), *Shot Down in Flames: A World War II Fighter Pilot's Remarkable Tale of Survival* (London: Grub Street), p. 8.

25. Ibid., p. 8.

26. Paris, 'The Rise of the Airmen', here pp. 137, 134.

27. W.A. Briscoe and H.R. Stannard (1918), *Captain Ball, V.C.* (London: Herbert Jenkins), p. 23.

28. Page, *Shot Down in Flames*, p. 8.

29. A. Frantzen (2004), *Bloody Good: Chivalry, Sacrifice and the Great War* (Chicago: University of Chicago Press), p. 3.

30. W.G.G. Duncan Smith (1981), *Spitfire into Battle* (London: John Murray), p. 3.
31. K. Boyd (2003), *Manliness and the Boys' Story Paper in Britain: A Cultural History, 1855–1940* (Basingstoke: Palgrave Macmillan), p. 3.
32. See, for example, T. Mansell (1997), 'Flying Start: Educational and social factors in the recruitment of pilots of the Royal Air Force in the interwar years', *History of Education*, 26:1, pp. 71–90.
33. Boyd, *Manliness and the Boys' Story Paper in Britain*, pp. 175–176.
34. P. Bishop (2003), *Fighter Boys: Saving Britain 1940* (London: HarperCollins), p. 52.
35. B. Oxspring (1984), *Spitfire Command* (London: William Kimber), p. 17.
36. T. Bartley (1997), *Smoke Trails in the Sky*, rev. edn (Wilmslow: Crecy Publishing), p. 25.
37. Dundas, *Flying Start*, p. 3. A 'forlorn hope' traditionally refers to a band of soldiers chosen to participate in an assault on a highly defended position in advance of the main body of troops. The near certainty of death on these missions meant that the junior officer commanding could expect to receive personal advancement, financial reward, and martial glory if he survived.
38. Bishop, *Fighter Boys*, p. 53.
39. T. Vigors (2006), *Life's Too Short to Cry: The Compelling Memoir of a Battle of Britain Ace* (London: Grub Street), p. 152.
40. Dundas, *Flying Start*, p. 1.
41. Page, *Shot Down in Flames*, p. 8.
42. Dawson, *Soldier Heroes*, p. 4.
43. A. Van Gennep (1960), *The Rites of Passage* (London: Routledge & Kegan Paul), p. 3.
44. Vigors, *Life's Too Short to Cry*, p. 96.
45. Page, *Shot Down in Flames*, p. 38.
46. Ibid., p. 40.
47. T. Neil (2010), *Gun Button to Fire: A Hurricane Pilot's Dramatic Story of the Battle of Britain*, rev. edn (Stroud: Amberley Publishing), p. 75.
48. Dundas, *Flying Start*, p. 3.
49. Ibid., p. 31.
50. Neil, *Gun Button to Fire*, p. 89.
51. Tosh, 'What Should Historians Do with Masculinity?', p. 198.
52. Vigors, *Life's Too Short to Cry*, p. 152.
53. Wellum, *First Light*, p. 131.
54. Ibid.
55. For a detailed discussion of fear, masculinity and the flyer, see Francis, *The Flyer*, pp. 106–130.
56. Francis, *The Flyer*, p. 106.

57. Ibid., p. 127.
58. Dundas, *Flying Start*, p. 23.
59. Ibid.
60. Ibid., p. 2.
61. Ibid., p. 31.
62. Bartley, *Smoke Trails in the Sky*, p. 59.
63. Neil, *Gun Button to Fire*, p. 74.
64. Bartley, *Smoke Trails in the Sky*, p. 12.
65. A. Calder (2000), 'The Battle of Britain and Pilots' Memoirs', in Addison and Crang (eds.) *The Burning Blue*, pp.191–206, here p. 194.
66. S. Bungay (2000), *The Most Dangerous Enemy: A History of the Battle of Britain* (London: Aurum Press), p. 240.
67. For example, P. Richey (1941), *Fighter Pilot: A Personal Record of the Campaign in France, September 8th, 1939, to June 13th, 1940* (London: B.T. Batsford), p. 79.
68. Wellum, *First Light*, p. 207.
69. Page, *Shot Down in Flames*, p. 63.
70. J. Bourke (1999), *An Intimate History of Killing: Face-to-Face Killing in Twentieth-Century Warfare* (London: Granta Books), p. 68.
71. Johnson, *Wing Leader*, p. 302.
72. Neil, *Gun Button to Fire*, p. 57.
73. Bartley, *Smoke Trails in the Sky*, p. 37.
74. S. Goebel (2007), *The Great War and Medieval Memory: War, Remembrance and Medievalism in Britain and Germany, 1914–1940* (Cambridge: Cambridge University Press), p. 227.
75. Bartley, *Smoke Trails in the Sky*, p. 12.
76. C.S. Lewis (1986), 'The Necessity of Chivalry' in W. Hooper (ed.), *Present Concerns*, pp. 309–310.
77. Page, *Shot Down in Flames*, p. 63.
78. Ibid., p. 8.
79. Bartley, *Smoke Trails in the Sky*, p. 25.
80. Ibid., p. 58.
81. Wellum, *First Light*, p. 32.
82. Ibid., p. 293.
83. This heroic image has endured due to a plethora of films, war memorials, fiction and non-fiction, plays, and art. See M. Connelly (2004), *We Can Take It! Britain and the Memory of the Second World War* (Harlow: Pearson Longman), pp. 95–105.
84. S.O. Rose (2004), 'Temperate Heroes: Concepts of Masculinity in Second World War Britain', in Dudink, Hagemann and Tosh (eds.) *Masculinities in Politics and War*, pp. 177–195, p. 184.

PART II

The Home Front Man

CHAPTER 6

Rebuilding 'Real Men': Work and Working-Class Male Civilian Bodies in Wartime

Arthur McIvor

The literature on civilian male identities in wartime has largely focused on the ways that masculine hierarchies were reconfigured with the emergence of the 'soldier hero' and hence how adult men on the home front denied access to uniformed service felt diminished.[1] As Linsey Robb has argued, industrial male workers were largely ignored in wartime, and have been since, in cultural representations.[2] Such status and identity corrosion was demoralising and capable of having a deleterious impact on workers' mental health and well-being. Many working men in industrial reserved occupations were denied the opportunity to join the forces in wartime and articulated in oral testimonies a sense of feeling worthless and stripped of purpose.[3] This chapter utilises newly conducted oral interviews from an Arts and Humanities Research Council (AHRC)-funded Reserved Occupations project undertaken by Juliette Pattinson, Linsey Robb and me, as well as a range of other evidence, including archived interviews and published autobiographies, to explore the work experience of adult civilian industrial working-class men in wartime. In particular, it focuses on how war impacted upon male workers' gender identities.

A. McIvor (✉)
University of Strathclyde, Glasgow, UK
e-mail: a.mcivor@strath.ac.uk

© The Author(s) 2018
L. Robb and J. Pattinson (eds.), *Men, Masculinities and Male Culture in the Second World War*, Genders and Sexualities in History,
https://doi.org/ 10.1057/978-1-349-95290-8_6
121

Working men experienced subordination to the economic imperatives of war and degrees of emasculation, but also found ways to express, validate and rebuild masculinity in wartime after the ravages of the 1930s Depression. An array of evidence tells a more complex and contingent story of the agency of male workers on the home front. Masculinities were expressed through bodies and war impacted upon reserved workers' corporeality in myriad ways. Indeed, a wide range of masculinities coexisted in wartime and the job that a worker did was a key factor in positioning men within a fluid status hierarchy. Civilian working-class male bodies in the reserved occupations were regulated, controlled and placed under surveillance in not dissimilar ways to the armed forces and this could be experienced as an emasculating loss of autonomy. Concurrently, in marked contrast to the inter-war Depression, working-class men were now in demand and valued again in wartime with secure work, full employment and higher wages. Men in the reserved heavy industries and munitions work expressed this sense of reconstructed traditional 'breadwinner' masculinity in their oral testimonies through narratives that expressed pride in the job and their skills and physical capacities, in their earning power and in the performance of their patriotic duty as tough wartime 'grafters' exposing their bodies to greater levels of risk and stress, and stoically enduring the long working hours, higher injury and industrial disease rates that characterised the intensified wartime production regime. These dangers also included the risks of aerial bombardment while on the job. The risk threshold was reconfigured and the level of death and disability deemed socially acceptable shifted in wartime. To a degree this reflected *continuities* in workplace culture in which a 'hard man' mode of masculinity was exalted within working-class communities, with a deepened sense of wartime patriotic sacrifice grafted on to this.[4] It is argued here that in tolerating and enduring the assault upon the body in the wartime workplace, facing long gruelling working hours in dangerous conditions doing 'war work', working-class civilian men performed their patriotic duty and validated their masculinity.

SUBORDINATING THE BODY: THE IMPERATIVES OF WARTIME PRODUCTION

Bodies are gendered: the male body, as Connell has argued, is a marker of masculinity. It is read as symbolising strength through physicality and furnishing the capacity to both protect and provide.[5] Work was felt and experienced through men's bodies and working-class masculinity was embodied in a normative figure expressing muscular strength.[6] Miners, for example, attracted interest from writers such as George Orwell and Walter Greenwood because of their honed, powerful, well-built bodies.[7] Muscular masculinity was also deemed, however, to represent inner qualities; a fit body was associated with a fit mind.[8] The capacity to tolerate and endure the toll that heavy industrial work imposed upon the body in hazardous, unhealthy, dirty, repetitive and exhausting work regimes pointed to revered working-class 'hard man' qualities. Workers gained standing and esteem within their peer group for the ability of their bodies to withstand stress, face up to dangers, show no fear and get the job done. Bodies were also currency during wartime, much in demand and subject to contestation between competing interests, while the wartime state found itself drawn into efforts to harness bodies more effectively to the war effort.

In wartime, a powerful popular discourse positioned those risking their lives as combatants at the top of the hierarchy of male identities, while in the workplace, male authority was also undermined and subordinated by the flooding of wartime factories with female 'dilutee' labour. A pervasive sense of civilian masculinity diminished in wartime is referenced frequently in oral testimonies and in the literature, for example in the work of Sonya O. Rose, Penny Summerfield and Corinna Peniston-Bird.[9] There were also other challenges to male autonomy and power in the wartime workplace associated with state intervention—such as the curtailing of collective action with the outlawing of strikes under Order 1305—and with technological and work organisation changes associated with the shift to mass production and 'Fordism' which threatened workers' rights, cherished skills and traditional ways of doing work. Male workers' bodies were also monitored and protected to unprecedented degrees in wartime, with the state-sponsored extension of company medical, nursing and rehabilitation facilities. This reflected the importance of the labouring body on the home front to the successful prosecution of modern mechanised warfare. Previously, such paternalistic state and private company medical surveillance and protection were widely regarded as being appropriate for women and children (for example, the legal banning of employment underground for such categories of labour), but hardly necessary for 'real men'. In discussing such developments in the US context Stephen Meyer has noted: 'their work became unmanly.'[10]

A series of developments in the wartime industrial workplace certainly challenged traditional hegemonic working class masculinity in the UK. The presence of women on the shop floor increased massively as numbers of female employees surged from 26% of the total employed (1938) to a peak of 39% (1943).[11] In some sectors, such as munitions and light and electrical engineering, the remaining working men were surrounded by and had to interact with very different bodies. Many men adapted to this without serious difficulty but for some men this 'feminisation' of work was felt as a threat, raising fears of loss of control over jobs, loss of purpose as the 'breadwinner' and the usurping of masculine roles. Moreover, Fordist, 'scientific' management methods (including time and motion study), were given a sharp stimulus by the needs of the war economy. This was especially well developed in the munitions, vehicles and aircraft sectors, where labour management guru Anne Shaw headed up a wartime government think tank on labour efficiency.[12] As such methods told workers how to do their own jobs better, divorced conceptualisation (thinking) from execution (the 'doing' of the work) and facilitated labour-shedding, the dissemination of such 'modern' ways of organising industrial work represented opportunities for some while being felt by other workers (and especially skilled craftsmen) as deeply threatening, degrading and emasculating. This was all destabilising, leaving working men to ponder whether there would be a return to the precarity of the 1930s or whether there would be jobs for them after the war and, if so, what kind of jobs would be on offer. This raised the spectre of what Charlie Chaplin's prophetic visionary pre-war film *Modern Times* (1936) so beautifully portrayed. Men would be just robotic, servile cogs in the industrial machine; powerless and subject to the whim of ruthless, profit-maximising employers. The surveillance and monitoring of workers, using the stop-watch, rate-fixers and 'efficiency engineers', caricatured so brilliantly in *Modern Times*, was certainly cranked up in wartime Britain. Workers' bodies, their labour process movements and energy intake and expenditure became subject to unprecedented levels of scrutiny, control, direction and protection.

Before the war working-class men typically avoided visits to the doctor unless as a last resort and regularly practised crude self-medication, basic protection (such as muslin rags used as a dust shield) and rudimentary 'first-aid' administered by fellow workmen in the workplace. Being able and willing to take risks at work, endure discomfort, dirt and pain and not show emotions marked a 'real man'.[13] Stimulants such as alcohol, cigarettes and laudanum-based patent medicines were widely resorted to for stress relief, to numb pain and to rouse flagging bodies.

In wartime, medical surveillance, treatment and rehabilitation extended massively as the state recognised the value of maximising the efficiency of industrial labour. Manpower was in short supply and, therefore, needed to be maintained. This brought the state into conflict with these prevailing work-health cultures. Health education received a massive boost in wartime, with the state attempting to shape workers' attitudes and behaviour towards their bodies. This was particularly evident in the wartime workplace where the services of the Royal Society for the Prevention of Accidents (henceforth RoSPA) were deployed by the state in a sustained propaganda campaign to reduce risk-taking and promote healthy behaviour and 'safety-first' on the job. While targeting all workers, including inexperienced 'green' female dilutees, this campaign identified male workers long acculturated into unsafe, risky and unhealthy behaviour. The reason for this was clear: male workers monopolised the most hazardous jobs where fatalities were highest and accounted for around 90% of all workmen's compensation payments for industrial injuries, disease and fatalities (Fig. 6.1).

In these efforts to tackle 'carelessness' and macho risk-taking on the job the wartime state missed a trick. The campaign essentially blamed the victims for their injuries putting the onus on personal responsibility—'he risked an accident'; 'he didn't use eye protection – do you?'—rather than targeting management and work systems. Occupational health expert H.M. Vernon argued that British management failed to foster a strong safety culture noting that just 20% of companies with over a thousand employees in 1945 and less than 1% of smaller firms subscribed to the 'national safety first movement'.[14] This scepticism was shared by Mass Observation in their 1942 report, *People in Production*, in which management were castigated for their 'backward industrial science'.[15] The situation was better in more modern companies and worst in the regions dominated by the older heavy industries where management conservatism and complacency prevailed. In relation to Clydeside, for example, Thomas Ferguson, Professor of Public Health at the University of Glasgow and Medical Inspector of Factories (Glasgow), commented just after the war:

> The traditional heavy industry of Scotland – and especially of Clydeside –
> is apt to be Spartan in its outlook: employers and work-people alike have

Fig. 6.1 Second World War Ministry of Labour/RoSPA safety posters. (Imperial War Museum Archive.)

been bred in a hard school. It would be idle to pretend that Clydeside is accustomed to regard industrial health as a high priority.[16]

Another important manifestation of wartime interest in and control over workers' bodies was the extension of company doctors, welfare officers, nurses and medical clinics to all the larger workplaces, prompted by Bevin's Factories (Medical and Welfare Services) Order (1940). Occupational medicine provided another site for health education and helped to patch up workers affected by the rising incidence of industrial injuries and diseases in wartime. Such state-imposed company medicine had the most impact in the male-dominated industries where serious injury and occupational disease (such as pneumoconiosis) rates were highest, such as steel-making, heavy engineering, dock work, coal mining and shipbuilding. The new wartime Mines' Medical Service and the Docks' Medical Service provide striking examples. And this new layer of medical provision was aided by important advances in medical science and pharmacology. For example, the proliferation of x-ray technology in wartime enabled workers' bodies to be scrutinised in new ways, detecting tuberculosis and occupation-related respiratory ailments such as pneumoconiosis at earlier stages. For many working men this was double-edged, representing opportunities to maintain and extend working lives while also concomitantly constituting a new threat to their livelihoods. For example, tuberculous and pneumoconiotic workers were removed from employment for fear of epidemic cross-contamination and to minimise future workmen's compensation liabilities for companies.

Routine medical examinations—aping the military 'medical'—even spread to some of the largest wartime factories. In one such factory in Bridgend, Wales, for example, over 10,000 men were 'medically graded' in 1943 into three categories: 55% were graded 'A', deemed fit enough to have contact with potentially harmful chemicals (such as TNT); 22% were graded 'B', fit to work in other 'non-contact' departments; and 23% were graded 'C', as 'unfit', with disabilities such as vision defects, neurosis, heart problems, hernia, bronchitis, pneumoconiosis, rheumatism and arthritis.[17] Here bodies were directly measured according to their wartime productive potential. For male workers the resulting 'grade' provided an index of their masculinity, defining their breadwinning capacities.

The wartime health and fitness education campaign might be interpreted in a similar fashion as being manufactured to maintain and improve bodily capacity in the interests of war production. Certainly pharmaceutical, food and drink companies exploited the wartime message playing on tropes of keeping fit and maintaining masculine capacities in their wartime advertising.

At the same time, these adverts hinted at the vulnerability of bodies to infection, breakdown, burn-out, accidents and fatigue. 'Keeping at it' took its toll on workers' bodies. There was a growing recognition that stress was significant within the wartime reserved occupations as well as within the military. A special investigation into 'neuroses in industry' was established by the government research agency the Industrial Health Research Board in 1944. It reported that of 3000 workers in thirteen wartime engineering factories 8% had a form of disabling neurosis and 16% minor forms, with a quarter to a third of all illness absence caused by this.[18] Mental health was stigmatised, with stress and depression widely considered within working-class culture to be something that 'real men' did not experience. While clearly widespread across the civilian population in wartime, stress was rarely admitted in male workers' autobiographical accounts or articulated in oral testimonies. Clydeside war worker Willie Dewar commented: 'You never thought about stress then. You just carried on.'[19]

For civilian working men all this could be emasculating, eating away at their sense of self and independence while narrowing their initiative and diminishing their right to deploy their bodies (and neglect and abuse them) as they thought fit, without interference. Much of the tightened wartime surveillance and control over civilian bodies applied to all workers (men and women) but gender influenced how they were felt and perceived. This was because of the prevailing sexual division of labour and the meanings and values attached to industrial work (and especially heavy industrial work such as mining, steel and shipbuilding) as a site for the forging and sustenance of masculinity, including toughness, endurance and physicality.

Reconstructing the Body: Rebuilding Masculinities in the Wartime Workplace

The Second World War clearly challenged civilian working-class masculinities in profound ways. Concurrently, however, wartime developments enabled the strengthening of civilian masculinities, while working men were active agents in responding, mediating and shaping their own destinies. Fundamentally, the war provided men with jobs, security and enhanced capacity to provide for their families, reversing the deleterious and emasculating impacts of mass unemployment in the 1930s. This was felt in workers' bodies which again became fit and honed by repetitive physical labour processes (after years of unemployment and irregular, precarious work) and an improved diet, facilitated by rising real incomes and the wartime canteen movement. Workers' bodies were developed through the intensified wartime work regime in a not dissimilar way to how Emma Newlands argues soldiers' bodies were sculpted in wartime.[20] And in wartime male civilian workers were encouraged to stay healthy, safe and identify with fit strong muscular men.[21] An example would be the Ministry of Labour pamphlet *Fighting Fit in the Factory* (1941) (Fig. 6.2).

The damaging effects of the inter-war Depression on masculinity and on workers' bodies have been noted in research on Britain and the USA.[22] Marjorie Levine-Clark has commented that mass unemployment meant 'reliance on state welfare [which] marked them as failing to live up to the expectations of full masculine citizenship'.[23] The war changed this. War work quickly soaked up those unemployed (1.8 million in June 1938) creating virtual full employment by the end of 1941.[24] The war thus provided ample opportunities for the expression and fulfilment of provider masculinity with job security and empowerment, sustained increases in working hours and overtime, an intensification of work and exposure to more dangerous working (and living) conditions and improving wage rates. Significantly, according to Mass Observation in 1942, male workers were three times more likely than female workers to be working 'excessive' hours, defined as over ten hours a day.[25] Now re-energised worker-providers also had the added layer of respect that they were directly contributing to winning the war. While many young reserved workers yearned for the forces, their role in wartime production raised their importance and status and eroded the subordination and demoralisation which had been such a feature of working lives in the 1930s Depression in many areas of the country.

How was this articulated in oral testimonies and autobiographies? Stories ranged from the frustrated combatant craving to be in uniform and expressing a poignant sense of diminished masculinity to narratives where emasculation simply did not feature—and our interview cohort of fifty-six were exactly split down the middle in this respect. Commonly, in oral interviews men asserted their masculinity in 'hard graft' stories of their endurance of tough working conditions, working long hours in intensified, dangerous wartime work. D.C.M. Howe, an aircraft fitter at Vickers Aviation, recalled:

> Once we started then there were no days off at all. It was seven days a week for days and days on end ... But everyone really got down to it. It

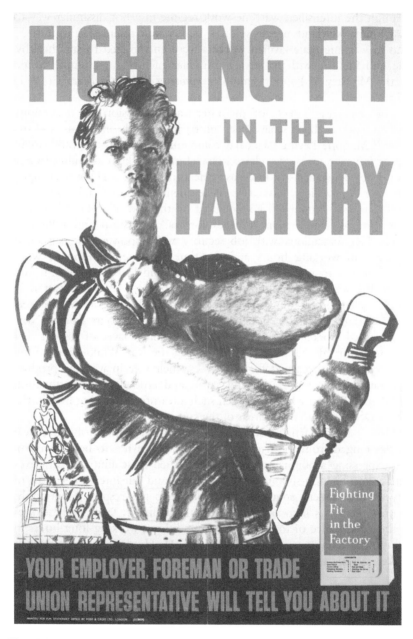

Fig. 6.2 Poster to accompany the *Fighting Fit in the Factory* pamphlet, 1941

was amazing the amount of work ... We used to churn out 24, 25 aircraft in one small place like that ... in a week.[26]

William Ryder, who worked at Woolwich Arsenal, recalled how keen men were for extra hours: 'I only had two Christmas Days off during the war ... We often started at six o'clock in the morning and sometimes it was six o'clock at night before you got away and one or two occasions we worked all night.'[27] In an interview conducted for the 'Voices from the Home Front' oral history project, shipyard worker Ted Boyle referred to the war as a 'nerve-wracking time',[28] while in an Imperial War Museum interview wartime coal miner Henry Barrett recollected: 'I've never seen work like it ... you shovelled coal. You shovelled coal as fast as possible ... It was mad down there.'[29] Some bodies gave up under the strain. In another 'Voices from the Home Front' interview Fred Clark, an aircraft wood machinist, recalled: 'I collapsed meself. 1941. Ulcerated throat and tonsils. Which the doctor said was the first sign of a nervous breakdown. It was the hours we was putting in ... We wasn't tired, we was just bloody walking dead!'[30] Aircraft factory worker Derek Sims recalled the numbing graft and fatigue of wartime: 'The long, the hours were ... oh they were, they were killers really. ... Yeah, it was, it was very heavy pressure.'[31] Sims recalled his father falling asleep at the dinner table from exhaustion and expressed his toughness and youthful masculine fortitude, by noting of the work conditions: 'we coped with them.' Evident in these personal testimonies are conscious attempts by narrators to define their masculinity by highlighting the pressures of wartime work and other 'duties' on their bodies, the sacrifices that had to be made and the tough conditions that had to be tolerated. They were telling us that hard graft was a manly responsibility and their contribution to the war. Masculinity was endorsed through such sacrifice.

Productive bodies tolerating long working hours and dangerous conditions commanded high wages. During the war male industrial workers earned considerably more than soldiers and while there was some wage levelling by gender and skill, at the end of the war wide margins persisted, with male workers still earning almost twice that of female workers.[32] This reversed the fortunes of the most vulnerable groups of male industrial employees during the 1930s recession. Coal miners, for example, rose up the wage league table after dropping back sharply in the 1930s. Thomas Carmichael, a wartime Merchant ship engineer, recalled his wages and war bonus: 'Oh, I was quids in, I was really in the money by that time.'[33] Shipyard worker Charles Lamb recalled with some pride buying his first wallet and being able to save £25 in it over a year during the war.[34] This created some resentment that workers were earning more than soldiers: 'That was a wee bit of a sore point with the Army people', Glasgow draughtsman Willie Dewar recalled.[35] John Thomas Murphy claimed in his 1942 autobiography *Victory Production* that 'it is impossible to move among the soldiers and sailors and airmen of all ranks without hearing scathing comments on the civilian population: on the munition workers who take home £10 to £15 a week.'[36] And wages rose fastest for those manual workers directly doing war-related work. One survey found manual workers' wages had risen by 71% whereas office and administrative staff salaries only rose by 10%.[37]

The regular and fat wage packet was the outward symbol of reconstructed civilian masculinity in wartime. Harry McGregor, a railway engineering worker, made repeated references to higher earnings: 'It was all about money ... I preferred to be in a reserved occupation, you know, because I think the wages were two shillings a day or something like that in the Army, you know. And I was earning more at Hyde Park.' He reinforced this preference with the comment: 'I think most of the Army thought, wished that they were in a reserved occupation.'[38] Similarly, wartime worker Jack Jones reflected in his autobiography:

> In many cases it was six, seven days a week of work. I suppose it could be argued that they were doing well financially out of it ... But there was no feeling that it would have been better in the Forces, or alternatively that people were shirking going in the Forces. Young men who were eligible went in, and those who were required to work in the factories, and it was a question of were required, it was essential work in the factories, had to work hard, and long hours. But it wasn't exactly a gift, not to go in the Forces.[39]

The testimonies of McGregor and Jones suggest a considerable degree of comfort in their reserved occupation status and male identities. There is little or no sense of emasculation on display here.

While many young reserved men felt that being in uniform was the only acceptable manly role in wartime, civilian masculinity was validated by reference to bodily attributes, experience and dexterities: skill; physical prowess; courage; and technical and scientific expertise. These were qualities that were much in demand by the intensified war economy and this in turn enhanced the economic and social value of such men. Without regular work in the Depression many workers' bodies had atrophied—or 'gone soft' as the novelist George Blake put it in *Shipbuilders* (1936). War work enabled muscles to be honed and workers to again be able to extract maximum capital out of their experience, physical strength and capacities and their socialisation into and ability to tolerate hazardous labour processes. Moreover, the wartime dilutees (replacement labour), male and female, required experienced workers to train them and this drew those 'unemployable' older men back into the workplace. Now these older men were *somebody* again, with war work providing a sense of identity, purpose, belonging and status. The same applied to the many formerly unemployed disabled male workers drawn back into the workplace as a consequence of wartime demands for labour.[40] As Julie Anderson's work has shown, the massive extension of rehabilitation treatment and facilities in wartime (including at the requisitioned Gleneagles Hotel in Scotland for miners) enabled the re-masculinisation of damaged, disabled and compromised bodies.[41] Concurrently, compensation systems and pensions for injury and death of civilians (in the workplace and by bombing) became equalised with the armed forces.[42] This economic validation facilitated the reconstruction of earning power as 'breadwinners', provided enhanced state benefits that replaced the wage for those disabled or widowed, and officially endorsed the idea of an equality of sacrifice in wartime between combatants and civilians.

The war also brought demands for technical skills and for supervision, management and leadership, with upward promotion common for working men from semi-skilled and skilled positions to those of charge-hand, foreman, superintendent and, in some cases, manager. With such upgrading, masculine status was enhanced. A deep sense of pride and achievement in being able to apply their skills, experience and physical capacities to useful war work was very evident across many oral testimonies. Charles Lamb, for example, commented: 'They needed shipbuilders, I mean, they, anybody I suppose could fire a rifle, but ... there wasnae any, everybody that could work in a shipyard.'[43] John Allen spoke passionately about the 'art' of shipbuilding,[44] while shipbuilding worker Alexander Davidson recalled: 'We took pride in our work, you know. And it had to be good. I mean, you couldn't be slovenly about something that men's lives depended on.'[45] V.S. Pritchett's official history of the shipyards, published in 1946, praises the wartime contribution of the shipbuilders and starkly represents the hegemonic masculinity of such workers.[46] In a similar vein, coal miner William Ramage recalled how he had worked a particularly difficult seam:

> I did that for a long time. I was good at it too. That, thirty feet took a bit o' shifting. There were some o' the lads that, out by, they wondered why, basically we were making more money than them, you know. One or, one or two o' them tried it, oh, they were lost. You needed the strength, the skill, the know-how ... It was tough, but it was very rewarding in the fact that we knew we were good at what we could do.[47]

Ramage's sense of pride in the job, his independence and confidence in his masculine prowess as a producer, is evident here. He also alludes to the competitive environment that coexisted with camaraderie within male working-class culture. Men strove to produce more than one another: to be the 'top dog'.

The bodily sacrifice of reserved men in coal mines, steel works and shipyards enabled civilian men to represent themselves as heroic 'hard men' making a pivotal contribution to the war effort. Bombing raids added to the risk for workers and enabled the construction of a narrative that emphasised that like soldiers they also faced up to danger and risk. Peter Henderson, President of the Scottish Trade Union Congress, said of miners in 1943: 'He too is a warrior facing danger every day of his life, his battle being fought under dangerous conditions. Hundreds are wounded daily and at least five are killed on each working day.'[48] The use of the terms 'warrior' and 'battle' linked the work of the miners to the war effort. And risks did rise substantially: work-related fatal accidents rose 28% and non-fatal accidents increased by more than 50% during the war.[49] The blackout made matters worse, degrading further the environmental pollution *within* factories (because windows were not to be opened) and raising accident risk levels, for example at the coal mine pit head and on the docks.[50] Shipyard worker Charles Lamb reflected: 'safety first itself was non-existent.'[51] Corners were cut and there was much tacit ignoring and subversion of health and safety rules and regulations during the war. Fred Millican, who was a reserved worker in Vickers arms factory in Newcastle, recalled: 'health and safety regulations, I would say were, if they existed we didn't know about them.'[52] In these stories reserved men were expressing a dominant high-risk male workplace culture, attempting to reassert their masculinity to be like combatants and perhaps to some extent compensating for any sense of emasculation felt through not being in uniform. Male industrial workers were socialised into high levels of risk and danger, and it became even more acceptable in wartime to mirror the risks taken by those in the armed forces. North British Locomotive apprentice Harry McGregor recalled that this was a taken-for-granted part of wartime working life: 'There were quite a few accidents. You know people got killed in there. And that was it ... You never thought anything about that really. Just worked away and that was it.'[53]

Interviewees frequently made reference to the dangerous nature of the work they did in wartime and the lack of safety provision. These danger and sacrifice narratives almost all included anecdotes about particular injuries sustained by themselves or colleagues. Alfred Thomas was transferred to Scotland to work in iron forging where he sustained a serious burn to the face. He recounted his story of hospitalisation and treatment, followed by an emasculating transfer to different work, where his face would not be affected by the heat, in which 'women were working mostly'. His narrative, like many others, referred to a different world where, in his memory, there were little or no safety measures in the workplace compared to the present day where health and safety had, as he put it, 'gone overboard'. He thereby affirmed his own manliness in these dangerous wartime work spaces.[54] Glasgow draughtsman Willie Dewar alluded to how workers would ignore protective gear such as helmets, gloves or goggles to avoid risking slurs against their manliness from workmates: 'Oh he's a "jessie", you know. A "jessie" was, well, like a woman, you know ... The majority of them [workers] that was sort of child's play to wear gloves, "oh no", or wear glasses, "no, no", but nowadays you're forced to do that.'[55] When Americans appeared in some shipyards later in the war they were pilloried for wearing hard helmets, heavy safety boots and gloves by hardened Clydeside workers. Shipyard worker Thomas Stewart recalled: 'you would scoff at them working with gloves ... daft!'[56] Peer pressure to 'man up' was significant here in a tough work culture that sneered at any refusal to take what were considered to be acceptable and normal risks on the job.[57]

In the most dangerous reserved occupations working men's bodies bore the scars of their work, and this too could be revered and a source of pride and identification as the embodiment of tough masculinity. Miners' bodies could be riddled with blue scars from injuries and cuts impregnated with coal dust. Some men showed with evident pride their wounds to the interviewer. Identifying one scar Ewart Rayner was quick to indicate: 'That didn't hurt, they just put three stitches in.'[58] Wartime Clyde shipbuilding worker John Allan commented: 'I've got marks on my body from working in the shipyard.'[59] His narrative focused on the dangers of the job, the toughness required and the lack of any significant safety provision: 'And you had no safety. They didn't supply you with gloves. They didn't supply you with goggles. They didn't supply you with helmets. Nothing.' Allan described in great detail the hazards of shipbuilding work in wartime, including an evocative account of working at heights and on staging and metal beams across the ship without safety harnesses. He recalled how socialised workers were to these dangers: 'There was a lot of things that happened in the shipyards but the men who worked in the shipyards didn't call it unusual … They knew the hazards were just part of the job.'[60] In expressing how this was 'just part of the job' Allan was referring to a power dynamic that was almost taken for granted: that management expected the men to accept a certain level of risk and bodily damage as a trade-off against relatively high wages. This production imperative coexisted with a work-health culture in which risk-taking was normalised and where it was assumed that men should naturally do the most dangerous work, as with the killing in the armed forces.[61] Men adapted to danger using their own accrued knowledge, intuition and experience to minimise the chances of bodily injury. In response to the question 'Was your work ever dangerous?' railwayman Jim Lister commented: 'Aye but like everything else, you were taught well. You had to watch.'[62] In the wartime workplace, however, these threats were inevitably heightened.

Industrial workers were also exposed to the risks of aerial bombardment, though relatively few workers (firemen and merchant seamen were the exception) appear to have been actually killed while on the job. Still, in the first three years or so of the war more male civilians were actually killed than male combatants. To maintain wartime production these dangers had to be withstood, manifest, as Helen Jones has shown, in the increasing practice of voluntarily choosing to continue working throughout air raids, relying on the factory rooftop 'spotters' to warn workers of any critical imminent risk to their particular workplaces.[63] Concerns over aircraft production led the government to encourage working during raids, with Churchill using the phrase 'front-line civilian' to valorise such behaviour through what Jones has called 'positive labelling'.[64] The persistent focus on air raids in oral testimonies represents a desire to draw upon well-worn tropes of wartime. However, as with the heightened risk of work-related accidents, injuries, breakdown, stress and disease, these evocative narratives of bomb damage, 'near misses' and the risk to life and limb of aerial bombing also served to discursively reconstruct masculinities which may have been threatened by reserved men's lesser status as non-combatants.

Occupational injury and disease rates also increased sharply for women workers during the war. However, the persisting sexual division of labour through the war meant that the risks were different in nature—something endorsed by a chauvinist workplace culture and legitimised by a patriarchal state which retained protective legislation that discriminated against women (as with the ban on employment underground). Female labour was predominately deployed in *subordinate* positions to men in the wartime workplace and the use of their bodies was *restricted* compared to men. In this respect, the superiority of men may well have been deepened by the controlling relationships they exerted over women in the workplace during wartime. Despite significant changes and transgressions, the traditional sexual division of labour remained largely intact during wartime even on the home front. While women took over many men's jobs across the economy there continued to be large swathes of work, including coal mining, iron and steel works, the railways, docks, heavy engineering, construction and much of shipbuilding, which remained almost totally monopolised by men and continued to be regarded as 'men's work' throughout the war. There continued to be a dangerous work 'taboo' which excluded women from the most hazardous and chronically unhealthy and dirty jobs—including coal mines—which were culturally deemed to be only suitable for men, even during the wartime emergency labour 'crisis'.

Working-class masculinity was also affirmed by reference in oral testimonies to their physical superiority over 'weaker' women and over other 'lesser' men with less capable bodies.[65] Blue-collar manual workers looked down on office workers as effeminate 'sissies'—these were 'pen-pushers' and 'gentlemen's trades', not doing a real 'man's work' and incapable of a hard day's physical graft.[66] And manual workers' status was enhanced in wartime by the greater value placed on physically making things. Thus blue-collar workers' wages rose faster than white-collar wages in wartime. Middle-class male dilutees had to earn trust and were widely considered as less able. Bevin boy Roy Deeley recalled: 'And any hard work some of them would sort of take it off you because we were a bit softer than they were. They were quite tough.'[67] Significantly,

William Ryder also expressed his 'hegemonic' masculinity by positioning himself in relation to what he regarded as more effeminate middle-class male dilutees, commenting: 'We had to knock them into shape.'[68] His narrative positioned Ryder as superior, nearer the top of the work hierarchy and affirmed his masculinity in contrast to women workers and other 'softer' white-collar employees who were considered less manly.

For working-class men, standing up for your rights in work—including facing up to the bosses—was another important marker of masculinity. This signalled toughness, independence and autonomy. Scottish coal miner and union official Alec Mills commented: 'If you were a weak man you would have did what the boss said.'[69] Talking about his father who was a foundry worker in Falkirk and 'very red' Tom Myles recalled: 'God help the boss that came and interfered with his work.'[70] Collective organisation was a powerful tool to maintain dignity at work and extend workers' rights. Historically, trade unions were capable of enabling breadwinner masculinity by negotiating higher wage rates and by keeping women out of skilled jobs, as Cynthia Cockburn's study of the printing trade and Sian Reynolds' account of Scottish bookbinders demonstrate.[71] Unions were strong proponents of the family wage and the ideal of the male breadwinner. Collective organisation—being 'part of the union'—critically bolstered working-class masculinity and industrial action, including striking, could be directly associated with manliness, while non-unionism ('scabs') was denigrated as effeminate.[72] Wartime circumstances reversed the inter-war collapse in trade unionism. The incidence of strikes, albeit usually short in duration, also rose in wartime, despite their illegality. UK union membership rose from a nadir of less than 4.5 million in 1933 to 8 million in 1945.[73] The British trade union movement in wartime continued to be dominated by men, a club run by men largely with male interests at its core, as evidenced by lukewarm support for ideas such as equal pay, abolition of the marriage bar and equal access to all jobs. For blue-collar workers, the revival of their trade unions and particularly the extension of collective bargaining to the shop floor in wartime (with the proliferation of shop stewards and the Joint Production Committees) were other important ways in which working-class masculinities were rebuilt after the ravages of the inter-war Depression. This provided the basis for the entrenchment of the male-dominated trade union movement into British economic and political life in the immediate post-war decades up to the 1970s.

Conclusion

In the hierarchy of wartime masculinities the soldier hero stood at the top while reserved men prevented from leaving their jobs inhabited a culturally subordinate or defensive masculinity. But this was negotiated and mediated in a fluid and dynamic fashion by male workers, while wartime circumstances provided the backcloth for the reforging of traditional breadwinner masculinities. How these civilian working men navigated and narrated this period in their lives when their manly status was under threat has been the subject of this chapter. In critically engaging with the emasculation thesis that dominates current thinking on male identities on the home front in wartime it is argued here that what has been overlooked is the extent to which the war facilitated the reconstruction of traditional breadwinner masculinity that had been so corroded by the Depression. Those who had directly experienced the precarious nature of work, vulnerability of labour markets, loss of employment, low wages (and related poverty), loss of power and autonomy (and the commensurate empowerment of the bosses) and the loss of dignity at work that this entailed were most likely to feel and express this sense of restored breadwinner masculinity in wartime. For reserved men the war brought job security, full employment, economic status, fat wage packets and the enhanced status associated with producing munitions, coal, steel, ships and other products that were vital to the war effort. A sense of pride in their bigger wage packets, their occupational skills and knowledge, physical and mental capacities, the ability to endure long, gruelling working hours and a 'speeded-up', more intense pace of work provided mechanisms for sustained and reforged masculinities. Crucially, the efforts of men in the workplace were also valorised by reference to the risks and dangers they faced in an intensified wartime work regime with higher rates of accidents, industrial disease and exposure to the risk of bombing.

A recurring way of expressing this in oral narratives was as patriotic 'grafters' willing to make sacrifices and expose their bodies to risks to support the war effort. They distanced themselves discursively from effeminate cowardly 'shirkers'. Reserved men's status as tough, resilient, indispensable 'skilled workers' and 'experienced labourers' provided some compensation for not being combatants. In their oral testimonies, recurring tropes were the heightened dangers and risks that they faced and a narrative of patriotic masculinity. A close association was articulated between their industrial work and the successful prosecution of the war effort. As wartime docker William McNaul recalled: 'Well I was doing my bit for the war effort. That's what we were doing.'[74] Reserved male industrial workers on the home front in wartime put their bodies on the line and in the process underlined their masculine capacities, demonstrating that, like combatants, they were 'real men'.

NOTES

1. S.O. Rose (2003), *Which Peoples War? National Identity and Citizenship in Wartime Britain, 1939–1945* (Oxford: Oxford University Press), p. 153; P. Summerfield (1998), *Reconstructing Women's Wartime Lives: Discourse and Subjectivity in Oral Histories of the Second World War* (Manchester: Manchester University Press), pp. 123, 149; C. Peniston-Bird (2003), 'Classifying the Body in the Second World War: British Men in and Out of Uniform', *Body & Society*, 9, pp. 31–48, here pp. 36, 39.
2. L. Robb (2015), *Men at Work: The Working Man in British Culture, 1939–1945* (Basingstoke: Palgrave).
3. See J. Pattinson, A. McIvor and L. Robb (2017), *Men in Reserve: British Civilian Masculinities in the Second World War* (Manchester: Manchester University Press). For a study of one important munitions-producing region, see also A. Chand (2016), *Clydeside Masculinities: Men in Reserved Occupations During the Second World War* (Edinburgh: Edinburgh University Press).
4. 'Hard man' characteristics in the context of the workplace included being able to tolerate tough, heavy physical work, take risks on the job and endure dangerous and hazardous labour processes and exposure to toxic materials. These conditions were typical of the 'heavy industries' that dominated the economy before the war. For a discussion, see R. Johnston and A. McIvor (2004), 'Dangerous Work, Hard Men and Broken Bodies: Masculinity in the Clydeside Heavy Industries c.1930–1970s', *Labour History Review*, 69:2, pp. 135–152.
5. R.W. Connell (1995), *Masculinities* (Princeton: Polity Press).
6. G. Mosse (1996), *The Image of Man: The Creation of Modern Masculinity* (New York: Oxford University Press); see also C. Wolkowitz (2006), *Bodies at Work* (London: Sage Publications).
7. G. Orwell (1937), *The Road to Wigan Pier* (London: Victor Gollancz), p. 21; W. Greenwood (1939), *How the Other Man Lives* (London: Labour Book Service), p. 32.

8. Mosse, *The Image of Man*, p. 24. See also I. Zweiniger-Bargielowska (2011), *Managing the Body: Beauty, Health, and Fitness in Britain 1880–1939* (Oxford: Oxford University Press).

9. Rose, *Which Peoples War?* Summerfield, *Reconstructing Women's Wartime Lives*; P. Summerfield and C. Peniston-Bird (2007), *Contesting Home Defence: Men, Women and the Home Guard in the Second World War* (Manchester: Manchester University Press).

10. Meyer, S. (2001), 'Work, Play and Power: Masculine Culture on the Automotive Shop Floor, 1930–1960', in R. Horowitz, (ed.), *Boys and their Toys? Masculinity, Technology and Class in America* (New York: Routledge), p. 17.

11. P. Howlett (1995), *Fighting with Figures: A Statistical Digest of the Second World War* (London: HMSO), p. 38.

12. A.G. Shaw (1944), *An Introduction to the Theory and Application of Motion Study* (London: HMSO), p. 36; P. Inman (1957), *Labour in the Munitions Industry* (London: HMSO), p. 430. Anne Shaw was a British expert in motion study who had pioneered its use at Metropolitan Vickers in Manchester before the war.

13. Johnston and McIvor, 'Dangerous Work, Hard Men', pp. 135–152. See also L. McCray Beier (2015), *For Their Own Good: The Transformation of English Working Class Health Culture, 1880–1970* (Columbus: Ohio State University Press).

14. H.M. Vernon (1945), 'Prevention of Accidents', *British Journal of Industrial Medicine*, 2:1, pp. 1–9, here p. 9.

15. Mass Observation (1942), *People in Production: An Enquiry into British War Production* (Harmondsworth: Penguin Books), pp. 126–127.

16. Cited in (1948), *British Journal of Industrial Medicine*, 5:1, here p. 184. For a wider discussion of management attitudes towards occupational health, see R. Johnston and A. McIvor (2008), 'Marginalising the Body at Work? Employers' Occupational Health Strategies and Occupational Medicine in Scotland c. 1930–1974', *Social History of Medicine*, 21:1, pp. 127–144.

17. J. P. Elias (1946), 'Medical Grading of the Industrial Worker', *British Journal of Industrial Medicine*, 3:1, pp. 11–14.

18. R.A. Fraser (1947), 'The Incidence of Neurosis Among Factory Workers', *Industrial Health Research Board Report*, No. 90 (London: HMSO).

19. Willie Dewar, interviewed by Arthur McIvor, 9 December 2008 (Scottish Oral History Centre Archive—hereafter SOHC—050/04).

20. E. Newlands (2014), *Civilians into Soldiers: War, the Body and British Army Recruits, 1939–1945* (Manchester: Manchester University Press).

21. V. Long (2010), *The Rise and Fall of the Healthy Factory: The Politics of Industrial Health in Britain, 1914–60* (Basingstoke: Palgrave), pp. 29–31.
22. A. Hughes (2004), 'Representations and Counter-Representations of Domestic Violence on Clydeside Between the Two World Wars', *Labour History Review*, 69:2, pp. 169–184; C. Jarvis (2004), *The Male Body at War* (DeKalb: Northern Illinois University Press).
23. M. Levine-Clark (2010), 'The Politics of Preference: Masculinity, Marital Status and Unemployment Relief in Post-First World War Britain', *Cultural and Social History*, 7:2, pp. 233–252, here p. 248.
24. Howlett, *Fighting with Figures*, p. 38.
25. Mass Observation, *People in Production*, pp. 160–161.
26. Imperial War Museum Sound Archive (hereafter IWM SA), 12882, D.C.M. Howe, reel 1, 1 May 1990.
27. IWM SA, 19662, William Edward Ryder, reel 1, 10 September 1999.
28. Ted Boyle, http://www.unionhistory.info/workerswar/voices.php. Accessed 15 November 2014.
29. IWM SA, 16733, Henry Barrett, reel 2, 2 July 1996.
30. Fred Clark, http://www.unionhistory.info/workerswar/voices.php. Accessed 15 November 2014.
31. Derek Sims, interviewed by Linsey Robb, 20 February 2013 (SOHC 050/12).
32. Parliamentary Papers (1942), *Pay and Allowances of the Armed Forces*, Cmd. 6385 (London: HMSO), pp. 2–3; *HC Deb 10 September 1942, vol 383 cc332–495;* Gazeley, I. (2007) 'Manual Work and Pay, 1900–70', in N. Crafts, I. Gazeley and A. Newell (eds), *Work and Pay in Twentieth-Century Britain* (Oxford: Oxford University Press), p. 69; P. Summerfield, (1986), 'The "Levelling of Class"', in H.L. Smith (ed.), *War and Social Change: British Society in the Second World War* (Manchester: Manchester University Press), pp. 182–183, 186; I. Gazeley (2006), 'The Levelling of Pay in Britain During the Second World War', *European Review of Economic History*, 2, pp. 175–204.
33. Thomas Carmichael, interviewed by Linsey Robb, 15 April 2013 (SOHC 050/35).
34. Charles Lamb, interviewed by Linsey Robb, 3 April 2013 (SOHC 050/27).
35. Dewar interview (SOHC 050/04); see also Ronald Tonge, interviewed by Linsey Robb 28 March 2013 (SOHC 050/24).
36. J.T. Murphy (1942), *Victory Production! A Personal Account of Seventeen Months Spent as a Worker in an Engineering and an Aircraft Factory* (London: John Lane), p. 138.
37. Mass Observation, *People in Production*, p. 171.

38. Ibid.
39. Jack Jones, http://www.unionhistory.info/workerswar/voices.php. Accessed 15 November 2014.
40. S. Humphries and P. Gordon (1992), *Out of Sight: Experience of Disability, 1900–50* (Plymouth: Northcote House Publishers), p. 132.
41. J. Anderson (2011), *War, Disability and Rehabilitation: 'Soul of a Nation'* (Manchester: Manchester University Press).
42. E. Newlands (2011), 'Civilians into Soldiers: The Male Military Body in the Second World War', PhD thesis, University of Strathclyde, pp. 204–208. See also P.W.J. Bartrip (1987), *Workmen's Compensation in the Twentieth Century* (Aldershot: Avebury), pp. 178, 185–198.
43. Charles Lamb, interviewed by Linsey Robb, 3 April 2013 (SOHC 050/27).
44. John Allan, interviewed by Linsey Robb, 7 November 2011 (SOHC 050/09).
45. Alexander Davidson, interviewed by Linsey Robb, 10 April 2013 (SOHC 050/32).
46. V.S. Pritchett (1946), *Build the Ships: The Official Story of the Shipyards in Wartime* (London: HMSO).
47. William Ramage, interviewed by Linsey Robb, 29 April 2013 (SOHC 050/43).
48. Scottish Trade Union Congress (1943), *Annual Report*, p. 80.
49. *Annual Report of the Chief Inspector of Factories* (1945), Cmd. 6992 (London: HMSO), p. 6; H.A. Waldron (1997), 'Occupational Health during the Second World War: Hope Deferred or Hope Abandoned', *Medical History*, 41, pp. 197–212; R. Johnston and A. McIvor (2005), 'The War at Work: Occupational Health and Safety in Scottish Industry, 1939–1945', *Journal of Scottish Historical Studies*, 24:2, pp. 113–136.
50. Tommy Morton interview, in I. MacDougall (ed.) (2001), *Voices of Leith Dockers* (Edinburgh: Mercat Press), p. 110; Scottish Mines Inspectors (1945), *Annual Report* (London: HMSO), pp. 57–58.
51. Lamb interview (SOHC 050/27).
52. Fred Millican, interviewed by Linsey Robb, 26 March 2013 (SOHC 050/20).
53. Harry McGregor, interviewed by Arthur McIvor, 13 July 2009 (SOHC 050/05).
54. Alfred Thomas, interviewed by Linsey Robb, 3 May 2013 (SOHC 050/45).
55. Dewar interview (SOHC 050/04).
56. Interview with Thomas Stewart, 10 June 1996, *2000 Glasgow Lives Project* (Glasgow Museums Oral History Collection).

57. See Johnston and McIvor, 'Dangerous Work, Hard Men', p. 143; Chand, *Masculinities on Clydeside*, pp. 44–46

58. Ewart Rayner, interviewed by Linsey Robb, 22 March 2013 (SOHC 050/18).

59. Allan, interview (SOHC 050/09).

60. Ibid.

61. D. Walker (2011), '"Danger was something you were brought up wi": Workers' Narratives on Occupational Health and Safety in the Workplace', *Scottish Labour History*, 46, pp. 54–70.

62. Jim Lister, interviewed by Linsey Robb, 19 April 2013 (SOHC 050/38).

63. H. Jones (2006), *British Civilians in the Front Line: Air Raids, Productivity and Wartime Culture, 1939–1945* (Manchester: Manchester University Press), pp. 59–60, 197.

64. Ibid., p. 197.

65. See, for example, Richard Fitzpatrick, interviewed by David Walker, 13 August 2004 (SOHC 022/01); IWM SA, 19662, William Edward Ryder, reel 1, 10 September 1999.

66. Allan, interview (SOHC 050/09); R. Spedding (1988), *Shildon Wagon Works: A Working Man's Life* (Durham: Durham County Library), p. 47.

67. IWM SA, 20055, Roy Deeley, reel 1, 26 January 2000.

68. IWM SA, 19662, Ryder.

69. Alec Mills, interviewed by Arthur McIvor and Ronnie Johnston, 19 June 2000 (SOHC 017/C1).

70. Tom Myles, interviewed by Wendy Ugolini, 6 November 2008 (SOHC 050/02).

71. C. Cockburn (1983), *Brothers* (London: Pluto); S. Reynolds (1989), *Britannica's Typesetters* (Edinburgh: Edinburgh University Press).

72. J. Jones (1986), *Union Man: An Autobiography* (London: Collins), p. 17.

73. A. McIvor (2001), *A History of Work in Britain, 1880–1950* (Basingstoke: Palgrave), p. 201.

74. William McNaul, interviewed by Linsey Robb, 27 March 2013 (SOHC 050/22).

Acknowledgements For an extended discussion of the issues aired here, see J. Pattinson, A. McIvor and L. Robb (2017), *Men in Reserve: British Civilian Masculinities in the Second World War* (Manchester: Manchester University Press), especially Chaps. 4 and 5. I am grateful to the editors of this volume and to external readers for their comments on earlier drafts of this work, including Emma Newlands, Wendy Ugolini, Geoff Field and Tim Strangleman.

CHAPTER 7

'Bright Chaps for Hush-Hush Jobs': Masculinity, Class and Civilians in Uniform at Bletchley Park

Chris Smith

Bletchley Park, the headquarters of Britain's cryptanalysis bureau during the Second World War, has become an increasingly significant landmark in the British cultural memory of the war. Senior Bletchley figures have been the subject of biographies, newspaper coverage, popular histories, television documentaries and, in the case of the now famous Alan Turing, even major motion pictures. The result is that the image typically presented of the agency is highly particular—an institution characterised by eccentric geniuses, who muddled their way to victory—the 2014 film, *The Imitation Game*, being a prime example.[1] As Christopher Moran notes, the establishment's 'gifted practitioners have become a shorthand term for community, triumph over adversity, even the idea of Britishness itself'.[2] Indeed, this was a view shared by intelligence officials themselves.[3] The art of cipher-cracking was regarded as an intellectual puzzle that required a lateral approach. In popular renditions of the Bletchley

C. Smith (✉)
Coventry University, Coventry, UK
e-mail: ac5356@coventry.ac.uk

© The Author(s) 2018
L. Robb and J. Pattinson (eds.), *Men, Masculinities and Male Culture in the Second World War*, Genders and Sexualities in History,
https://doi.org/ 10.1057/978-1-349-95290-8_7

145

Park story, the best cryptanalysts and analysts were scholars, prominently specialists in languages and mathematics, crossword experts, chess players and others with trained minds, and principally male.

As both popular and academic historians have shown, this is a misleading narrative. First, Bletchley Park was merely the headquarters and largest of several stations and offices of the Government Code and Cypher School (GC&CS). The focus on Bletchley Park alone has been a distorting factor which has sidelined the contributions of those agency workers employed in satellite stations and partner organisations—not least the Y Service, which was tasked with intercepting and triangulating the origins of wireless traffic. Secondly, GC&CS employed over 10,000 individuals by December 1944, approximately three-quarters of whom were women and the experiences of female staff have increasingly attracted scholarly interest in recent years.[4] Thirdly, historians, particularly of science and technology, have persuasively challenged the idea that the agency succeeded because of the efforts of a few key intellectual figures. Instead they have pointed towards the development of managerial and industrial processes in cryptanalysis and information management in building GC&CS's success.[5]

Significant though all of these contributions have been in building a more complete understanding of this vitally important wartime intelligence enterprise, little attention has been given to the processes which led to the emergence of the popular, and indeed internal wartime, view that Bletchley Park succeeded because of the efforts of a corps of ingenious eccentrics. This was because those individuals engaged at the sharp end of wartime cryptanalysis and intelligence analysis were convinced that brains trumped a sophisticated grounding in the nuances of practical military matters. As the eminent historian and wartime intelligence officer (later Sir) F. Harry Hinsley noted, while summarising the skills required in the production of naval intelligence, 'an academic exercise which, like the elucidation of a Latin text or the wrestling of deductions from the Doomsday Book, called more for an immersion in detail than for experience at sea'.[6] In order to understand the basis for this view, qualified though it has been by historians such as Jon Agar,[7] it is necessary to turn to the wider cultural influences, particularly that of dominant wartime ideals of masculinity and those of Britain's intelligence community, on the development of the agency's internal wartime culture. This culture, as this chapter will argue, was heavily coloured by internal notions of masculinity and the ideal man for the job of intelligence work.

From its origins in the First World War, GC&CS developed its own peculiar hierarchy of masculinity which did indeed highlight many of the features which have so captured the popular imagination—which was both derived from wider British understandings of masculine behaviour and yet apart from it. Masculinity in wartime Britain, as Sonya Rose has argued, emphasised heroic military manliness, though tempered in opposition to the brutal aspects of Nazi masculinity.[8] Specifically middle-class configurations of manliness were built around ideas of patriotism, service and gentlemanly chivalry, but not necessarily intellectualism. The ideal man at Bletchley, however, was rather different. He was, first and foremost, a gentleman scholar to whom traditional notions of formal rank were only peripherally important. Wartime military masculinity, with its reverence for uniform, drill and violent displays of masculinity, was also subordinated, despite a wartime influx of regular military personnel into the agency.

Importantly, some of Bletchley's men were, for administrative ease or owing to recruitment strategies, nominally members of the armed forces. However, the distinction between civilian and service personnel is both complex and misleading. Most of those men in uniform were not career military men, but 'civilians in uniform', rarely expected to conform to military etiquette—something the organisation itself was reluctant to enforce. Notwithstanding their presence at Bletchley Park as uniformed personnel, the internal culture of GC&CS, despite its military function, was hybrid: part military and part civilian. The tropes of masculinity, associated with servicemen in wider British wartime culture, rarely applied to these individuals in full—many of whom were distinctly intellectual and thoroughly middle class.

This chapter will primarily draw upon GC&CS's administrative records and veteran accounts to cast light on the variety of work, wartime experiences and the construction of masculinities within this highly unusual institution. First, it will explore the development of the professional British intelligence community from the late Victorian and Edwardian periods and consider how the agency, founded in 1919, located itself in this world. Secondly, it will explore recruitment processes and the type of man (and occasionally woman) it sought for its most celebrated roles—cryptanalysts who broke ciphers, and linguists who translated and analysed intelligence. Thirdly, it will explore challenges to these notions, as wartime pressures forced increased diversity in recruitment strategies and policies, which brought in a wider variety of men and women into this secret world to perform a range of different roles. That said, as a result of limited interest from historians and relatively sparse archival evidence related to those workers occupying lower grade positions, the central subjects of this chapter are those men recruited as cryptanalysts and intelligence officers. Ultimately, the chapter shows that Bletchley Park occupied a liminal space between overt forms of military service and civilian contributions to the war effort on the home front and that this facilitated the development of an internal hegemonic masculinity unique to the organisation.

'THESE MEN KNEW THE TYPE REQUIRED': MASCULINITY AND ESPIONAGE, 1909–39

GC&CS was formed on 1 November 1919, the third and final of Britain's major intelligence agencies. The other two, the Secret Intelligence Service (SIS, better known as MI6) and the Security Service (also known as MI5), had been founded a decade earlier in 1909. It was in this ten-year period that British intelligence efforts were centralised, institutionalised and professionalised.

Late Victorian and Edwardian notions of masculine virtue, particularly as they pertained to the gentlemanly classes, formed the ideal for early recruitment of agents and intelligence officers. Such an individual, among other characteristics, was well bred, socially connected, patriotic, militaristic and a proficient sportsman. He was also an amateur and dilettante, distinct from the working and lower middle-class professional, capable of skilfully turning his hand towards a wide range of interests and pursuits.[9] By the beginning of the twentieth century, the British intelligence community was built around highly developed social networks which, as John Fisher notes, were bound together by social class, family ties, education and, on occasion, military service.[10] Espionage was not seen as a vocation conducted by professionals, but a form of dangerous service which the right sort of patriotic gentleman simply adopted. As the British agent George Alexander Hill noted in his memoirs: 'A spy carries his life in his hands. His existence is one of hazard, joyous or the contrary. Spies in the British service have commonly taken up their dangerous duty out of sheer love of adventure.'[11] Moreover, it was a privileged upbringing which provided the best preparation and Hill was dismissive of formal professional instruction. He noted: 'If I had gone to a special school for years, studied espionage as a profession, I could not have had a better training than life gave me in my early days.'[12] This was not entirely snobbery and his upbringing certainly came in handy—Hill had been educated by French and German governesses and, as a result, had a mastery of a variety of languages from an early age.[13]

Unsurprisingly, then, from the outset MI5 and MI6, formed together as the Secret Service Bureau in 1909, had a particular type of man in mind when it came to recruitment. An agent required a stiff upper lip; he needed to be calm in the face of danger and crisis; he needed to be socially well connected; though intelligence and academic achievement were certainly not frowned upon, ability on the playing field was important; military or police experience was prized; and he needed to be a gentleman. These were traits which showed remarkable continuity and endured for years. As John Cairncross, a veteran of two British intelligence services (and also a Soviet mole) in the 1940s noted, in a letter to the novelist Graham Greene in 1991: '[t]he MI5 outfit has always struck me as an upper class specifically English outfit.'[14]

When GC&CS was formed in 1919, it shared significant cultural DNA with the wider intelligence community and many of the same idealised masculine traits were equally prized by the new institution. By 1939 with around three-quarters of scholarships awarded to public school products, Oxford and Cambridge were still unquestionably the most socially exclusive of Britain's universities, and they constituted the primary source of the agency's recruitment.[15] GC&CS's association with Cambridge dated from the First World War. Prior to the formation of the organisation, Britain's military cryptanalytic work had been performed by bureaus in the Admiralty (Room 40) and the War Office (MI1b). Significantly, Room 40 was founded by the scientist Sir James Alfred Ewing. Ewing had been appointed Professor of Mechanics and Applied Mathematics at Cambridge in 1890 where he remained until taking up his Admiralty post in 1903. When the First World War required the rapid construction of a first-rate cryptanalytic service, Ewing utilised his contacts at Cambridge to find bright young men with an aptitude for languages.[16]

GC&CS's central mission, according to its first head, Commander Alastair Denniston writing in 1944, was twofold. First, it was overtly tasked with ensuring the security of the communications traffic of the British state. The second and covert responsibility was to intercept and analyse the traffic of foreign powers.[17] The rise of the Soviet Union ensured that the activities of the Kremlin were at the forefront of the cryptanalysts' attentions.[18] Meanwhile, the fall of Germany from great power status, the sense of complacency this security brought with it, and the economic turmoil of the inter-war period, ensured that GC&CS was initially awarded only limited funds and resources and suffered during wider government retrenchment in 1921.[19] The result was a small team, with relatively few new arrivals until the late 1930s. By that time it had become increasingly clear that, under Adolf Hitler, Germany was resurgent, militarily aggressive and posed a clear threat to British interests. As such, Britain's cryptanalysis service was founded with only fifty-three employees, half of whom were women employed in clerical and secretarial roles, and even after a substantial recruitment drive in the run-up to the Second World War, the agency still only began the conflict with approximately 200 staff members.[20]

The core of the workforce, the upper echelons in particular, were individuals who had been involved in cryptanalysis and intelligence since the First World War. As such, their work in cryptanalysis predated GC&CS itself. These were individuals like Commander Alastair Denniston, the head of the organisation, who had latterly been the chief of the Admiralty's cryptanalytic section during the First World War. Senior members of his team included his deputy a career naval officer, Commander Edward Travis; his senior cryptanalyst and noted Cambridge classicist Dillwyn Knox; and chief administrator Nigel de Grey (who cracked the infamous 1917 Zimmerman telegram).[21] These three men were veterans of Room 40 during the First World War and proven cryptanalysts. Similarly, senior figures, who had served in MI1b, such as John Tiltman, had come to occupy senior positions within the new intelligence institution and remained in place until the Second World War.[22] Some of their colleagues from the Great War had, however, returned to their lives in academia where they were able to act as talent spotters in the event of another war. 'These men', according to Denniston, 'knew the type required'.[23]

This channel of recruitment became the standard during the inter-war period and select university officials were asked to draw up short, exclusive lists of the right 'type' of 'man', who might be willing to serve his country. In 1932 Denniston contacted Mr C.E.D. Peters of Oxford

University, asking him to look out for potential recruits, and added: 'In the last war you may remember that 40 O[ld]. B[uilding]. was the Admiralty Cryptographic Bureau and this Bureau was recruited almost entirely from the Universities.'[24] In 1935, as tensions between Italy and Britain were growing over the question of Abyssinia, Denniston wrote to Peters once again.

> In the past years you have been of very great assistance to us in producing candidates for our unusual work. Therefore I am writing to tell you that in the event of Anglo-Italian relations becoming somewhat strained I might have to apply to you to obtain trustworthy men with a thorough knowledge of Italian for translation and intelligence work.[25]

A few days later, Denniston followed up his letter with a further note, stating: 'During the war of 1914–18 a good many dons in residence who thought they could be spared did offer for this type of work.'[26]

By 1938 this system had further evolved and taster training courses were delivered at Oxbridge colleges. The graduates of those courses acted, once they had been accepted into the organisation, as further conduits for recruitment of academics and students.[27] One of the most successful of these recruits-turned-recruiter was Gordon Welchman. A mathematician at Sidney Sussex, Cambridge, Welchman began earmarking his own students, several of whom, including the famous cryptanalysts Joan Clarke and John Herivel, would eventually join him at Bletchley Park.[28] The result of all of this was that cryptanalysis, translation and interpretation duties was primarily conducted by bright young men (and a few women), drawn from Britain's elite universities.

Graduates from other universities do not appear to have been much considered at all during the inter-war years; certainly correspondence between Denniston and the universities was primarily limited to Oxford and Cambridge throughout the 1930s.[29] On occasion, Denniston did write to contacts at the University of London. However, as he confided to a Foreign Office colleague in 1938, he was reluctant to 'inform London University of the vacancies as it is always difficult to get in touch with them for these positions of a delicate nature, and at the last interview they supplied three or four candidates whose qualifications were quite unsatisfactory'.[30] Similarly, in the same letter, Denniston made it clear that female candidates were, by and large, to be avoided. He had not contacted the women's Oxbridge colleges for one post because

GC&CS already had a good internal female candidate—one female applicant was evidently more than sufficient.

So, besides being well educated, what type of man were the recruiters looking for? First, he was required to be bright. The preferred candidates not only had to be Oxbridge graduates, but particular emphasis was placed on attracting those with first-class degrees—considered a guarantor of sufficient powers of intellect. Although GC&CS was increasingly turning towards mathematics, the precise academic expertise mattered less and it continued to place a great deal of stock in the tried-and-tested belief that the literary disciplines produced quality officers. As Denniston would note, 'an individual with a taste for modern languages would be a suitable man for us. It is true that a man with a mathematical mind is probably the most suitable, but we have several distinguished classicists who are among our most able members.'[31] Secondly, the man had to be both young and of strong character. Individuals prone to 'nerve weakness', men who lacked the quintessential British 'stiff upper lip' of popular imagination, were disqualified from consideration.[32] Similarly, older men were also out of the running; one applicant in 1937, aged 33, was deemed 'too old'.[33] Though experience showed that young men were deemed more likely to crack under the strain of the work, older individuals were thought more problematic. They were deemed to be too rigid and insufficiently capable of learning the new skills required for the role.[34] Thirdly, as noted above, connections and a nod from an individual already inside the growing network of contacts, either as a trusted recruiter or as a practitioner, was important. In addition to ensuring that candidates were of sufficient aptitude, recruitment based on elite education was also a mechanism to acquiring 'trustworthy men'.[35] Possession of the right school and university tie was an indicator that the recipient had been inculcated in gentlemanly values and, as a result, was worthy of trust.

'NOT BEING AT THE FRONT WAS SOMEHOW DISHONOURABLE': HEGEMONIC MASCULINITY AND WARTIME BLETCHLEY PARK

These practices developed over the course of GC&CS's history and continued into the Second World War. When describing the precise nature of the wartime recruitment process, Peter Calvocoressi, a senior Bletchley Park officer and later respected jurist, historian and publisher, revealed in 1980 that the institution was heavily informed by upper middle-class cultural practices, environments and attitudes towards social class. Recruiters 'made forays into [public] schools and colleges, boardrooms and clubs. They put questions that were veiled and yet understood. They could not say precisely what they were looking for, but between friends and over a glass of sherry enough would be conveyed: bright chaps for hush-hush jobs.' Of course, at least initially, the 'old-girls' network was less prized.[36] Calvocoressi, like the recruiters, reflected the belief that self-discipline, public service and duty were all instilled into members of the upper middle classes through education and upbringing.[37] Members of that world could surely be trusted. Indeed, even in 1980, Calvocoressi still argued that it was this class factor which ensured the maintenance of the secrecy surrounding Bletchley Park until 1974.[38] A similar attitude was taken when it came to the appointment of some managers, when, on occasion, the academics occupying such positions proved unequal to the task. In such instances, GC&CS turned to the world of business. For instance, Sir Eric Jones, who would become the Director General of the Government Communications Headquarters (Britain's post-war cryptanalysis organisation) from 1952 to 1960, had been an executive at a textile factory before the war. Following a period of service in the Air Ministry, he was appointed into a middle management role at Bletchley Park precisely because of his abilities as a manager.[39]

Though there were vastly increased demands for well-educated young men in wartime, (such men were sought after by a whole host of agencies, industries and military services, not least the other intelligence agencies), GC&CS's recruit policies for cryptanalysts and translators remained largely unchanged. When trawling for three temporary senior assistants, a senior civil service rank remunerated with a generous £600 per annum, to translate Italian decrypts, a set of specific qualifications were outlined. Applicants required 'First-class Italian and first-class intelligence. Candidates are required for positions of responsibility and for work which requires leadership, accuracy and speed.' No doubt given the seniority of the position and the required leadership element, the recruiters were instructed to look for 'men (if possible)', but only those aged between twenty-five and forty; the young remained favoured.[40]

Clearly then, certain assumptions surrounding the characteristics which made a good cryptanalyst and intelligence officer had become ingrained. Moreover, they had crystallised into a specific hegemonic masculinity unique to Bletchley Park. The ideal young man was a patriotic gentleman, trustworthy, from a 'good' family, well educated, and, above all, very bright. Those individuals who did not fit this mould were viewed as a potential liability, not just to the success of the work, but to themselves. One veteran, Paul Fetterlein, in an interview with Lindsay Baker for the Imperial War Museum, recalled rumours of individuals, unable to cope with the strain of the work, taking their own lives.

> People took it very, very seriously and I know in the newspapers today they say all about the great successes people had and so on and how important that was. But they don't mention those who were failures at it, and there were some people who took it very badly. In fact there were two or three suicides; people who tried to do a code and, you know, and you sort of work week, after week, after week and nothing happened, it can be very depressing. And as I said, there were some people who couldn't take it and committed suicide. […] They felt that they had failed England in its hour of need.[41]

Interestingly, Fetterlein was explicit in noting that he had never actually known any such individual personally and nor were such matters discussed at Bletchley Park itself. Instead, the rumours circulated in various fashionable London intellectual circles frequented by Bletchley Park's staff during their time off.

While dominant middle-class masculinity of Bletchley Park revolved around scholarly gentlemanliness, wider British hegemonic masculinity placed greater importance and emphasis on other masculine traits. Masculinity was increasingly associated with military service and the soldier hero. Those men out of uniform were, according to Sonya Rose, forced to identify and stress the 'heroic features of their masculinity' in other ways and 'drew upon both a language of military battle and a language of working-class manhood'.[42] From GC&CS's point of view, this created some problems when it came to recruitment. If the performative aspects of wartime British masculinity privileged military heroism, then a government desk job, with little explicit relevance to the war effort clearly could lack appeal. To get around the problem of unwilling, but well-qualified, potential recruits, recruitment officials in the Ministry of Labour and National Service were instructed to compel candidates of high quality to attend interviews 'under Defence Regulation 80b if necessary'. Moreover, recruiters were further instructed that 'no submission should be withheld because a candidate does not wish to be considered, provided the qualifications are suitable'.[43]

Another unfortunate side effect was that a number of men found that their masculinity and manliness were open to public question and they, in turn, were subjected to humiliation. These kinds of public shaming of men who did not conform to the characteristics of hegemonic masculinity on display in wartime Britain were, in some respects, reminiscent of the campaigns launched against civilian men during the First World War, though difficult to quantify in terms of scale.[44] More recent research based on oral history testimony has, however, suggested that rather than enduring external pressure from within their communities to join the armed services, British men on the home front during the Second World War were more likely to subject themselves to internalised pressures. This manifested itself in the form of feelings of inadequacy that such men placed on themselves because they felt that they should be doing 'more' to fight for King and Country.[45] One solution for such men, who were prevented from entering military service, was to at least create the appearance of military service and to join the Home Guard. Complete with a near identical uniform to that of regular army personnel (the identifying signifier of Home Guard status being easily removed and reattached as required),[46] civilian men were able to demonstrate what Connell and Messerschmidt describe as 'complicit masculinity'.[47] That is, they enjoyed the 'benefits of patriarchy without enacting a strong version of masculine dominance', which in wartime Britain emphasised active military service. For the middle-class, academically minded cryptanalysts and codebreakers of Bletchley Park, this was difficult if not impossible to achieve. Many of them, despite being of military age, were not in uniform and though they were engaged in work of clear national importance to the war effort, it was secret in nature. Even though alternative options, such as the Home Guard were available,[48] for some they were not enough. The language and mediums for expressing military masculinity, in describing their work to friends and family outside of work circles, were unavailable.

At Bletchley Park, some men faced overt external pressure to leave the relative safety of the home front while others subjected themselves to internal pressure. In terms of the former, Gordon Welchman, the head of a major Bletchley Park section, recounted in his memoir, a case in which a young man under his command 'received a scathing letter from his old headmaster accusing him of being a disgrace to his school'. Yet, as

Welchman explained, internal and external pressures went hand in hand: there was an 'inevitable feeling that not being at the front was somehow dishonourable'. Despite their 'exhausting' and vital job, young men at Bletchley Park 'longed to play an active part in the fighting'.[49] Such individuals, not only had to face their own sense of unease, but also had to contend with the local community where their presence had not gone unnoticed. One local resident, in a published collection of oral history interview excerpts, remembered pondering whether the new arrivals to the town were 'skiving'.[50] Bletchley staff were also clearly and acutely aware of local suspicion, as was recorded in a poem entitled Bumph Palace: 'For six long years we have been there/subject to local scorn and stare.'[51]

In a notable example, Donald Michie, a veteran and later a pioneering figure in the field of artificial intelligence, recalled his own excruciating humiliation in a briefing filled with young women of the Women's Auxiliary Air Force (WAAF) in which he sat 'like an ugly duckling'. The WAAFs, he recalled, 'felt only contempt for an apparently young male in civilian attire. Some of them had lost boyfriends in the RAF, and many had boyfriends still alive but in daily peril.'[52] The painful experience, which he described as a 'white feather' incident, but also appears to be in equal part the internal pressure of imagining what the WAAFs were thinking about him, clearly played on his mind and, some time later, those feelings of inadequacy were externally reinforced by his father. Naturally, Michie had been unable to inform his family what he was doing and all they knew was that he was involved in nondescript war work. So, when, at the St George's Golf Club, his father had been asked how his son was contributing to the war effort 'his mind was unavoidably blank' and, in turn, asked Michie whether he had 'considered active service'. Having been humiliated twice, first by a group of young women and then by his father, Michie asked for a transfer to the North African desert, for which his superior (Colonel Pritchard) gave him a dressing-down.

> 'I have to instruct you to return to duty. You see, Mr Michie, we have a war on our hands. Inconvenient, but unfortunately true. Unless you have further questions, you are free to return at once to your section.' Pause. 'And by the way, I do not expect you to raise such matters again.' Pause. 'Either with me or with anyone else.' Longer pause. 'As for your father, I do not anticipate that he will raise them either.'

On that matter, it transpired that Pritchard was right, as Michie learned years later: his hitherto disappointed father was 'paid a visit' by a military official.[53] The issue of security was, understandably, key. Not only were the men of Bletchley Park, as Pritchard noted, in many cases making their best possible contribution to the war effort, but even if it were desirable for them to change role to one of active military service, that was impossible.[54] In many cases, they simply knew too much and their risk of capture by the enemy was too great. They were stuck at Bletchley whether they liked it or not.

'Galling to Regulars': Competing Masculinities

One area in which the general labour shortage provoked by the Second World War did force change in GC&CS's recruitment practices, which had in other respects been remarkably resilient, was its approach to university recruitment. While a primacy continued to be placed on Oxbridge, Nigel de Grey noted sadly that: 'As national recruiting became more methodical this system tended to clash with the proper authorities. There were also diminishing returns as men and women joined the Services.' The net had to be widened once national recruitment policies became more 'methodical'.[55] Though de Grey was not specific on the precise timing of this change, it is a reasonable assumption that he was alluding to the further extension of conscription under the National Service Act (No 2) in December 1941. As a result, recruiters began trawling other universities, the armed forces and the civil service for suitable talent.[56] This, however, came with it its own problems as new arrivals brought challenge to the dominant image of masculinity within the agency—particularly regular service personnel.

Though GC&CS had been formed around men who had served in the First World War, many of them as military officers, during the interwar period and the organisation's mobilisation during the late 1930s, it had become decidedly civilian in character. As de Grey noted in 1949, 'Direct contact with Universities, secondary schools, etc. In general this method produced not only the original 60 high-grade people but also considerable numbers afterwards.'[57] Yet, by June 1942, some 37% of GC&CS's personnel were in military uniform, a figure which would continue to rise over the course of the war.[58] The gender composition also radically changed as women were increasingly employed to conduct auxiliary functions, typically in machine operation and clerical work.[59]

However, very few of these (eventually thousands of) women were employed in cryptanalysis and translation—those were, of course, the 'men's jobs'. Instead, they were typically placed into these forms of auxiliary 'women's work'. In this respect, Bletchley Park clearly conformed to Peggy Inman's observation (and that of many others since) that comparatively few women were allowed to undertake 'male' jobs, despite popular notions to the contrary.[60] In GC&CS, the far greater challenge to gender and the dominant internal configuration of masculinity came from the arrival of other men.

The influx of military personnel first created tensions, particularly surrounding the question of pay. The nub of the problem was that civil servants were largely less well remunerated than their counterparts in the military services. The result was that men conducting identical work could receive radically different pay. In addition, it was also frustrating for regular officers, who had earned their rank and pay, that temporary officers, individuals parachuted into uniform and into a relatively high rank, were equally well remunerated.[61] The issue of equal pay for equal work continued to plague senior managers throughout the war and was never satisfactorily resolved.[62]

Besides creating administrative problems, the increasingly military character of the agency brought with it cultural conflicts which revolved around the introduction of new, competing masculine ideals, to Bletchley Park. One of the central features of the organisation was that, despite being quasi-military since its conception, it did not for the most part observe military traditions. This issue, which included limited adherence to uniform etiquette, came to a head when an Admiral visited Bletchley and, unable to spot any members of the Women's Royal Naval Service, returned to London thoroughly disgruntled by the lack of discipline on display.[63] This issue of uniform, in the literal sense, also arose in other areas of business, not least mess arrangements. At the outset of the war, it had been usual for GC&CS's military officers to wear their uniforms as and when they pleased and for enlisted men in the ranks to wear them perpetually.[64] Indeed, the donning of uniform by military officers had been actively discouraged because, as noted above, they did the same work as civilians and it was assumed that the construction of artificial differences might result in friction. When a new cafeteria open to all ranks was proposed, the issue of officers being able to eschew uniform, as agency tradition had determined, came to a head. While those in the ranks would be expected to wear their uniforms, officers would not, which provoked 'grounds for resentment'. Ultimately it was proposed that 'it would be good policy' to ensure that military personnel wear their uniform 'the whole time'. The basis for that recommendation was:

> It has been stated on many occasions that discipline is not very ridged here, particularly among the Service personnel. I think that is a perfectly correct statement, but we have some odd officers here to say the least of it, many of whom do not behave as officers and therefore cannot fairly expect to be treated as such.[65]

Of course, given that GC&CS emerged from the Admiralty and War Office and had strong connections to each of the Whitehall military service ministries, men in uniform had always been present. However, wartime mobilisation and conscription also ensured that, at times, it was preferable for bureaucratic purposes to formally place an individual into uniform only to immediately then second them to GC&CS.[66] One problem was that enlisted men were also recruited into cryptanalysis and translation work, making the differences in formal seniority and pay particularly acute. The solution was extraordinarily rapid promotion. Asa Briggs,[67] for example, who joined the army directly from Cambridge University in 1941 as a private soldier and seconded to GC&CS in 1942, was swiftly promoted to the rank of Regimental Sergeant Major—a member of the highest group of non-commissioned officers. In 1945, after he had left Bletchley Park, he described himself being treated as a 'real RSM', highlighting the significant distinction between what the rank meant at Bletchley and its very considerable importance in the regular armed forces.[68]

As the example of the visiting Admiral demonstrates, the acquisition of regular military men, who held very different ideas regarding how officers and enlisted men and women should behave to that of the civilians and soldiers in uniform, created tensions. As de Grey explained in 1949, the 'very low standard of "military" behaviour in a civil institution [was] galling to regulars'.[69] The most pronounced examples of this occurred not within the walls of Bletchley Park itself, but rather just outside them. The rapid expansion of the agency, which numbered around 8000 at Bletchley Park alone by December 1944, ensured that local billets had swiftly been exhausted. The response to this problem had been the construction of two purpose-build military accommodation camps on the immediate outskirts of the facility. These were operated by the army and RAF respectively, staffed by regular military personnel uninitiated into the secret work conducted within the walls of the Park, and run under closely observed military rules and rituals.

This clash between the ill-disciplined behaviour of the civilians in uniform who worked for GC&CS and what Paul Fussell memorably described as military 'chickenshit' ('behavior that makes military life worse than it need be: petty harassment of the weak by the strong; open scrimmage for power and authority and prestige; sadism thinly disguised as necessary discipline; a constant "paying off of old scores"; and insistence on the letter rather than the spirit of the ordinances') was pronounced. To make matters worse, among the key victims of 'chickenshit' were 'the artist, the "so-called intellectual," the sneerer at athletics, the "smart ass", the "stuck up," the foreigner – anyone conceived to be "not our crowd."'[70] Certainly, the arrival of regular military discipline soon saw Bletchley staff confronted with 'chickenshit'. In his memoir, James Thirsk, another non-commissioned officer at Bletchley Park, presented the army camp commander, Colonel Fillingham, as a 'formidable' and 'awe-inspiring' figure. Fillingham is reported to have delighted in berating his ill-disciplined troops for various minor infractions and introduced the dreaded 'PT' [Physical Training].[71] Similarly, Asa Briggs fell foul of a camp lieutenant because of a failure to correctly fold the blankets on his bedding. The lieutenant might have later come to regret his military pedantry when he later applied to Briggs' Oxford college.[72]

There were, of course, many hundreds of other men working for GC&CS whose work and contribution to the success of the vast cryptanalytic exercise have, by and large, left little archival trace. Such individuals represent yet another strand of masculinity within the agency, typically drawn from the lower strata of Britain's social class system. These were the mechanics, security staff, gardeners, clerks, technicians and so on. For instance, the fabled machines constructed to aid the deciphering of Axis messages, to collate collected intelligence and communications equipment designed to transport this product to government ministries and across the world to distant military commands, were primarily maintained by men—typically non-commissioned officers from the armed forces.

In all, there were just under 250 such mechanics employed by the agency by September 1944.[73] Yet the archives provide little detail regarding the selection process for these men or the kinds of recruit they acquired. The most obvious conclusion to draw from this is that they were simply seconded. Certainly, this was the case when it came to the approximately 4000 women from the armed forces stationed at Bletchley and its satellite (usually termed 'out stations') facilities. Many of these women were assigned to work at Bletchley Park because, following their basic training, they declared themselves willing to work on 'special duties'. The process for men, particularly those performing technical work, was rather different.

Among the clearest accounts of the selection procedure, by the former RAF electrical engineer Ken McConnell, indicates that the process was far from simple. McConnell had been trained before the war as an electrical engineer, which was classified a reserved occupation, precluding him from conscription. However, following the Dunkirk evacuation, he was permitted to volunteer for the RAF and, having been accepted, he spent two years plying his trade on aircraft. He was then selected to perform secret work and sat an arduous exam.[74] In a short account submitted to the BBC People's War archive, Denis Whelan recalled that most of the crews which maintained specialised cryptanalytic machines were made up of men from the Royal Engineers. As a civil service telephone engineer seconded to the Foreign Office, Whelan's job was to build devices to test those cryptanalytic machines. However, because the machines were temperamental, he and a colleague were assigned as on-call engineers regularly visiting Bletchley Park and its various out stations testing machine faults. Whelan made little reference to his passage into secret work, but did recall that it involved an interview.[75] Finally, Mr H.L. Swatton, another General Post Office engineer, before being transferred to Bletchley Park, was not only interviewed but subjected to a hands-on test of his technical skill with a variety of equipment.[76]

Even from these few examples, it is clear that the men in the 'lower' orders of the organisation were typically highly skilled in their technical fields, but that their route to Bletchley Park involved a fairly rigorous interviewing process which, in some cases even involved a practical element. The fairly easy transition into secret work, which, in the case of at least some cryptanalysts, involved a sounding out over drinks, did not apply to lower graded male staff. Of course, they did not mix in the same circles, they did not possess the appropriate school tie and had not attended the 'right' university—they were not 'gentlemen'.

CONCLUSION

Over the course of its existence GC&CS developed a unique, internal configuration of masculinity which drew from a variety of sources. These included wider British middle and aristocratic gentlemanly society, the common-room culture imported from Britain's universities and the archetype of the gentleman spy from the wider intelligence community. In particular, the war saw the development of a distinct type of employee: the soldier in uniform, as individuals from a civilian and often scholarly background were placed into military attire for the duration of the conflict. Over time, however, the men stationed at Bletchley Park, in high-status, intellectually demanding roles such as cryptanalysis and translation, were supplemented by men sourced from the regular armed forces. The majority of these men, particularly those out of military uniform, were clearly distinct from, and were expected to conform to, a different template of masculinity to those outlined by historians such as Sonya Rose in wider British society. Of course, these men were not appointed for their martial ability or trained for such a role. They were, however, required to have a distinctly middle-class background complete with an elite education, most typically with university training. This not only ensured that candidates were of a high intellectual calibre—a necessity for many of the agency's jobs—but also created the illusion that because they were 'gentlemen' their discretion and honour were beyond question. This exclusivity was, of course, not always possible particularly in the case of lower tier male staff; skilled 'professionals' like technicians were, instead, heavily vetted and subjected to intense interviews and tests prior to appointment.

GC&CS was not always, however, a melting pot of masculinity. Instead, competing ideas took root at different times and the influx of new groups of men disturbed any sense of equilibrium. For instance, the arrival of regular military personnel into a largely civilian organisation led to consternation from both the regulars disturbed by the lack of discipline and the decidedly unmilitary denizens of Bletchley Park suddenly faced with the prospect of uniforms, drill and PT. The fact that many of these individuals were out of uniform, or perceived to be engaged in outwardly unheroic work also presented problems as men, on occasion, felt and were perceived to be failing their masculine military duty at a time of war. Meanwhile, further down the hierarchical rungs, typically obscured in the archives and overshadowed in popular discourse regarding the establishment, were hundreds of men from different socio-economic backgrounds—the 'professional' class— who travelled a markedly different route to arrive at Bletchley Park.

In short, the masculine characteristics desired by GC&CS included those of the professor-turned-codebreaker and hard-headed intelligence professional. The ideal cryptanalyst and translator was an intellectual, but he was also cool-headed and in possession of a stiff upper lip; he was a gentleman amateur but also willing to tolerate management in an increasingly professional environment. Popular emphasis on Turing-like caricatures understates the complex matrix of masculine characteristics valued by the agency and the variety of roles it required filling, but it does reflect how the institution viewed its staff and the qualities it valued. As one visiting intelligence officer, Ewen Montagu, recalled being told by a colleague at Bletchley Park, 'an acrostic brain is better at this game'.[77]

NOTES

1. *The Imitation Game* (2014), Dir. Morten Tyldum. The Weinstein Company, Film.
2. C. Moran (2013), *Classified: Secrecy and the State in Modern Britain* (Cambridge: Cambridge University Press), p. 256.
3. This image was primarily fostered by memoirists in the 1970s and 1980s. For examples, see F.W. Winterbotham (1974), *The Ultra Secret: The Inside Story of Operation Ultra, Bletchley Park and Enigma* (London: Orion); P. Calvocoressi (1980), *Top Secret Ultra* (London: Cassell).
4. A. Burman (2013), 'Gendering decryption – decrypting gender: The gender discourse of labour at Bletchley Park 1939–1945', unpublished MA dissertation, Uppsala University; J. Abbate (2012), *Recoding Gender: Women's Changing Participation in Computing* (Cambridge, MA: MIT Press), pp. 11–39; C. Smith (2015), *The Hidden History of Bletchley Park: a Social and Organisational History* (Basingstoke: Palgrave Macmillan); T. Dunlop (2015), *The Bletchley Girls: War, Secrecy, Love and Loss: the Women of Bletchley Park tell their story* (London: Hodder and Stoughton); M. Smith (2015), *The Debs of Bletchley Park and Other Stories* (London: Aurum Press).
5. J. Agar (2013), *The Government Machine: A Revolutionary History of the Computer* (Cambridge, MA: MIT Press), pp. 203–209.
6. F.H. Hinsley (2001), 'BP, Admiralty, and Naval Enigma', in F. H. Hinsley and A. Stripp (eds), *Codebreakers: The Inside Story of Bletchley Park* (Oxford: Oxford University Press), p. 78.

7. Agar, *The Government Machine*.
8. S. Rose (2004), 'Temperate Heroes: Concepts of Masculinity in Second World War Britain', in S. Dudink, K. Hagemann and J. Tosh (eds), *Masculinities in Politics and War: Gendering Modern History* (Manchester: Manchester University Press), pp. 177–195.
9. For a wider discussion of gentlemanly characteristics, see P. Mason (1993), *The English Gentleman: The Rise and Fall of an Ideal* (London: Pimlico).
10. J. Fisher (2002), *Gentleman Spies: Intelligence Agents in the British Empire and Beyond* (Stroud: Sutton), p. 12.
11. G.A. Hill (1932), *Go Spy the Land: Being the Adventures of IK8 of the British Secret Service* (London: Cassell), p. 5.
12. Hill, *Go Spy the Land*, p. 7.
13. M. Kitchen (2004), 'Hill, George Alexander (1892–1968), intelligence officer', *Oxford Dictionary of National Biography*: http://www. oxforddnb.com/index/67/101067487/. Accessed 22 December 2016.
14. John J. Burns Library, Boston College, Massachusetts, MS1995-03, Box 13, Folder 35, John Cairncross, 'Additiona [*sic*] note for Graham', undated [likely 5 March 1991].
15. For Oxbridge's social exclusivity, see R. McKibbin (2000), *Classes and Cultures: England, 1918–1951* (Oxford: Oxford University Press), pp. 248–249. For GC&CS's recruitment policies, see Smith, *The Hidden History of Bletchley Park*, pp. 41–50.
16. C. Andrew (1986), *Secret Service: The Making of the British Intelligence Community* (Sevenoaks: Scepter), p. 150.
17. A. G. Denniston [1944] (1986), 'The Government Code & Cypher School Between the Wars', in C. Andrew (ed.), *Codebreakers and Signals Intelligence* (London: Frank Cass), p. 49. This document first appeared in print in *Intelligence and National Security*, 1:1, pp. 48–70.
18. For details regarding GC&CS's inter-war period activities, see M. Smith (2001), 'GC&CS and the First Cold War', in M. Smith and R. Erskine (eds), *Action This Day* (London: Bantam), pp. 15–40.
19. Denniston, 'The Government Code & Cypher School Between the Wars', p. 49.
20. Smith, *The Hidden History of Bletchley Park*, pp. 17–18.
21. A telegram sent by Arthur Zimmermann, the Secretary of State for Foreign Affairs of the German Empire, attempted to encourage Mexico to invade the USA. This was intercepted and read by British cryptanalysts and shared with Washington.
22. Tiltman replaced Knox as the agency's chief cryptanalyst after the latter's death in 1944. Smith, *The Hidden History of Bletchley Park*, p. 36.

23. Denniston, 'The Government Code & Cypher School Between the Wars', p. 52.
24. The National Archives (hereafter TNA), Kew, HW 72/9, A.G. Denniston to C.E.D. Peters, 26 April 1935.
25. TNA, HW 72/9, A.G. Denniston to C.E.D. Peters, 4 October 1935.
26. TNA, HW 72/9, A.G. Denniston to C.E.D. Peters, 7 October 1935.
27. Denniston, 'The Government Code & Cypher School Between the Wars', p. 52.
28. A. Briggs (2011), *Secret Days: Code-Breaking in Bletchley Park* (London: Front Line), p. 43.
29. TNA, HW 72/9, *passim*.
30. TNA, HW 72/9, A.G. Denniston to T.J. Wilson, 16 May 1938.
31. TNA, HW 72/9, A.G. Denniston to E.A. Cresswell, 25 February 1938.
32. TNA, HW 72/9, A.G. Denniston to O.V. Guy, 27 June 1932.
33. TNA, HW 72/9, A.G. Denniston to E.A. Cresswell, 1 January 1937.
34. TNA, HW 50/50, Memorandum by Nigel de Grey, 17 August 1949, p. 7.
35. TNA, HW 72/9, A.G. Denniston to C.E.D. Peters, 4 October 1935.
36. P. Calvocoressi (2011), *Top Secret Ultra* (Cleobury Mortimer: M & M Baldwin), p. 20.
37. S. Gunn and R. Bell (2003), *Middle Classes: Their Rise and Sprawl* (London: Phoenix), p. 100.
38. Calvocoressi, *Top Secret Ultra*, pp. 23–24.
39. Smith, *The Hidden History of Bletchley Park*, pp. 31–32.
40. TNA, HW 64/63, 3 Senior Assistants job specification, 19 August 1942.
41. Imperial War Museum, Sound Archive, Paul Fetterlein interviewed by Lindsay Baker, 23436, reel 5.
42. S. Rose (2004), *Which People's War?: National Identity and Citizenship in Wartime Britain, 1939–1945* (Oxford: Oxford University Press), p. 195.
43. TNA, HW 64/73, A. W. Kearn [Ministry of Labour and National Service], Vacancies in the Foreign Office, 29 April 1943.
44. Rose, *Which People's War?*, p. 179.
45. J. Pattinson, A. McIvor and L. Robb (2016), *Men in Reserve: British Civilian Masculinity in the Second World War* (Manchester: Manchester University Press), ch. 3 *passim*.
46. P. Summerfield and C. Peniston-Bird (2007), *Contesting Home Defence: Men, Women and the Home Guard in the Second World War* (Manchester: Manchester University Press), p. 225.
47. R. W. Connell and J. Messerschmidt (2005), 'Hegemonic Masculinity: Rethinking the Concept', *Gender and Society*, 19:6, p. 832.
48. Smith, *The Hidden History of Bletchley Park*, p. 145.

49. G. Welchman (2014), *The Hut Six Story: Breaking the Enigma Codes* (Cleobury Mortimer: M & M Baldwin), p. 86.

50. G. Blane (1998), 'Outside the Gates', in R. Cook (ed.), *Bletchley Voices: Recollections of Local People* (Stroud: Chalford Oral History), p. 95.

51. [Baroness] Bobby Hooper quoted in M. Smith (1998), *Station X: The Code Breakers of Bletchley Park* (London: Channel Four Books), p. i.

52. D. Michie (2006), 'Codebreaking and Colossus', in B.J. Copeland (ed.), *Colossus: The Secrets of Bletchley Park's Code-breaking Computers* (Oxford: Oxford University Press), p. 224.

53. Michie, 'Codebreaking and Colossus', p. 233.

54. Welchman, *The Hut Six Story*, p. 86.

55. TNA, HW 50/50, Memorandum by Nigel de Grey, 17 August 1949, p. 4.

56. TNA, HW 64/73, [unknown author], M.115, 6 April 1943; TNA, HW 50/50, Memorandum by Nigel de Grey, 17 August 1949, pp. 4–6.

57. TNA, HW 50/50, Memorandum by Nigel de Grey, 17 August 1949, p. 4.

58. TNA, HW 64/70, [Untitled document listing Military/Civilian staff figures and related issues], 23 June 1942.

59. For a statistical breakdown of GC&CS's staff, see K. Johnson and J. Gallehawk (2007), *Figuring it out at Bletchley Park: 1939–1945* (Redditch: BookTowerPublishing), pp. 61–65.

60. P. Inman (1957), *Labour in the Munitions Industries* (London: HMSO), p. 53. See also: P. Summerfield (1984), *Women Workers in the Second World War: Production and Patriarchy in Conflict* (Manchester: Manchester University Press), ch. 7; H.L. Smith (1986), 'The Effect of the War on the Status of Women', in H.L. Smith (ed.), *War and Social Change: British Society in the Second World War* (Manchester: Manchester University Press), pp. 208–229.

61. TNA, HW 64/67, Pay for Cryptographers, 13 August 1941.

62. Smith, *The Hidden History of Bletchley Park*, pp. 65–66.

63. Smith, *The Debs of Bletchley Park*, p. 90.

64. Asa Briggs, a non-commissioned officer recalled in his memoir, however, that uniform was never a requirement within the walls of Bletchley Park. Briggs, *Secret Days*, p. 107.

65. TNA, HW 64/70, [Untitled document listing Military/Civilian staff figures and related issues], 23 June 1942.

66. Welchman, *Hut Six Story*, pp. 190–192

67. After the war Briggs went on to be a highly distinguished historian and in 1976 was made a life peer.

68. Briggs, *Secret Days*, p. 140.

69. TNA, HW 50/50, Memorandum by Nigel de Grey, 17 August 1949, p. 5.
70. P. Fussell (1990), *Wartime: Understanding and Behavior in the Second World War* (Oxford: Oxford University Press), p. 80.
71. J. Thirsk (2008), *Bletchley Park: An Inmate's Story* (Bromley: Galago), pp. 79–81; Briggs, *Secret Days*, p. 102. Note, however, Briggs became a favourite of the colonel and was spared much discomfort.
72. Briggs, *Secret Days*, p. 106.
73. Johnson and Gallehawk, *Figuring it Out*, p. 93.
74. K. McConnell, 'My Secret War', *BBC WW2 People's Archives*, a6844106 http://www.bbc.co.uk/history/ww2peopleswar/stories/06/a6844106. shtml. Accessed 22 October 2016.
75. D. Whelan, 'Denis Whelan – His Association with Bletchley Park', *BBC WW2 People's Archives*, A3019592, http://www.bbc.co.uk/history/ ww2peopleswar/stories/92/a3019592.shtml. Accessed 22 October 2016.
76. Bletchley Park Trust Archive, Other People's Stories, vol. 3, Mr H.L. Swatton, Personal notes and interview transcript, 16 April 2001.
77. E. Montagu (1979), *Beyond Top Secret U* (London: Corgi), p. 45.

CHAPTER 8

'The Cushy Number': Civilian Men in British Post-war Representations of the Second World War

Linsey Robb

In 2010 the BBC children's history programme *Horrible Histories* included a song, sung as an upbeat pop number, extolling the virtues of women's contributions to the Second World War:

> We're the girlies from the thirties
> Wash the dishes, scrub the floor
> When all of a sudden our hubbies went to war
> Did you think we'd shrink in England's needy hour
> You what? Course not.'Cause we've got Girl Power
> Our men are fighting World War Two
> But we're not gonna boo-hoo-hoo
> It's our World War Two, too, girls
> Plenty we can do girls
> We're the World War Two Girls.
> Our war begins right here.[1]

L. Robb (✉)
Northumbria University, Newcastle Upon Tyne, UK
e-mail: linsey.robb@northumbria.ac.uk

© The Author(s) 2018
L. Robb and J. Pattinson (eds.), *Men, Masculinities and Male Culture in the Second World War*, Genders and Sexualities in History,
https://doi.org/ 10.1057/978-1-349-95290-8_8

169

The song goes on to explain that women were working in factories and the fields 'while our men fight far away'. In doing so this comedy pop song encapsulates the predominant image of Britain's Second World War experience. Britain's war is popularly conceptualised as a war in which men put on military uniforms and were replaced en masse by female dilutees. Such an image was prevalent throughout the war, and is now perpetually reinforced by Britain's ongoing cultural preoccupation with the Second World War which permeates film, television, radio and literature.[2] These representations are central to modern understandings of the period and, largely as a consequence of this, the British 'collective memory' of the war almost entirely omits civilian men. Indeed, this dominant image ignores the multiple roles male civilians played during the war. It is oft forgotten that even at the peak of armed forces employment there were twice as many men in civilian occupations as in uniform.[3] This included millions of men of fighting age in reserved occupations, those deemed to be irreplaceably necessary on the home front by the state in occupations as varied as docker, farm worker and miner, among innumerable others. These men were, therefore, forbidden from entering the armed forces. Moreover, there were 60,000 men who declared conscientious objection in Britain during the Second World War, a significant increase on the 16,000 who declared as such during the First World War. In addition, there were many who simply fell outside the remit of military service, due to either age or disability. Therefore, the roles played by men on the home front were diffuse. However, despite increasing interest in civilian male masculinity the postwar depictions of men on the home front remain under-researched.[4] This chapter, therefore, explores the various ways civilian men have been represented in film and on television in the years since the war in order to place these forgotten men back into Britain's wartime story.

THE FRUSTRATED HERO

Since 1945 British culture has been inundated with tales of the Second World War both in print and on screen. In many ways these have differed from wartime cultural depictions. The celebrated image promulgated in wartime was of a 'people's war' which promoted the vital role of both the home front and the military. However, those films, for example, made during the 'war boom' of the 1950s, such as *The Cruel Sea* (Charles Frend 1953), *The Dam Busters* (Michael Anderson 1955) and

The Battle of the River Plate (Michael Powell and Emeric Pressburger 1956), told heroic tales of bravery which often centred on upper-class officers in the services. They certainly did not emphasise civilian men's roles on the home front.[5] However, the popular film *Dunkirk* (Leslie Norman 1958), which was the second highest grossing film of 1958, differs from this usual pattern.[6] The film depicts the infamous events in Dunkirk in June 1940 by interweaving two stories. One story arc focused on a group of British Expeditionary Force soldiers stranded in France while the parallel story focused on a band of civilians who are persuaded to use their 'small boats' to aid the rescue. The main focus of the civilian group is John Holden, played by Richard Attenborough, owner of a small factory. Holden is, rather unusually, explicitly stated to be in a reserved occupation. His civilian status, however, is thoroughly criticised. His friend, journalist Charles Foreman, accuses him of exploiting the war for profit exclaiming 'a new baby, 200 gross of buckles, unlimited petrol and all the whisky you want. You're sitting pretty aren't you Holden? Yes it is a lovely war.' When Holden protests that 'the army's got to have buckles doesn't it?' Foreman retorts 'Especially if it's caught with its pants down. Still someone's got to make'em. Let's thank our lucky stars we're not wearing'em eh?' The obvious implication of this exchange is that Holden is a coward and not contributing to the war effort. Indeed, he is manufacturing buckles, a peripheral item of low importance which serves to highlight his trivial civilian status. Foreman underscores this in a later speech to his wife when he declares:

> Holden makes me sick, he's a like a lot more in this country. Is this supposed to be a war effort? ... This debate in the house, where's it got us? Chamberlain settled in as much as ever, patting us on the head and saying that everything's going to be all right so that little squirts like Holden can sit back on their sub-contracts and make more money than he ever did in peace time.

As such the film makes clear its disdain for civilian men by suggesting such men were profiteering. The film continually asserts that military action is the only acceptable role for the wartime man. Holden is redeemed not by a validation of his necessary civilian service but by entering the battlefield. Holden, with Charles Foreman, takes his own boat to France to join in the rescue of stranded British servicemen. Although Foreman is killed by aircraft fire Holden survives the attacks, ultimately saving several British soldiers. When Holden returns to Britain alongside the rescued servicemen, he is mistaken for a soldier. His prideful smile, enjoying the error, is telling. The closing voiceover declared 'no longer were there fighting men and civilians, there were only people. A nation made whole.' Such statements replicate the wartime sentiment of 'all in it together'. However, the film itself clearly deviates from this message. Civilian status was openly shown to be contemptible and it is only by paralleling actions more commonly associated with the military that Holden redeemed himself from his shameful civilian status.

While the 1950s was the golden age of the war film by the 1970s they had severely declined in popularity. However, in many cases the representation of the war shifted from the big screen to the small with a large number of television dramas and sitcoms set during the war being shown in this period. Subject matter was diffuse but there was often an overt focus on the home front, something which had been omitted in the war film genre which were more often than not militaristic in focus. Older audiences especially, according to Michael Paris, retained an interest in the war and they were treated to such programmes as *Dad's Army*, first shown between 1968 and 1977, *Secret Army*, broadcast between 1977 and 1979, *Colditz*, on television between 1972 and 1974, and innumerable others.[7] However, the 'paradigmatic example' of Second World War drama, argues James Chapman, was *A Family at War*. This extremely popular series ran for a total of 52 episodes from 1970 until 1972. The show focused on the predominantly home front experiences of one Liverpudlian family, the Ashtons, as they weather bombing, deaths, marriages and the strictures of rationing.[8] In *Family at War* civilian status, especially for young men, was presented as a burden. Characters facing the prospect of reserved status, for example, were generally depicted as eager to escape to the military. Central cast member Tony Briggs—a cousin of the Ashtons—is angered when his father suggests he would be reserved in the family printing business.[9] Tony is increasingly burdened by his civilian status and his familial relationships bolster his desire for military service. All three sons in the Ashton family, Tony's cousins, are on the front line: eldest son David is an RAF pilot, middle son Philip is a soldier and even sixteen-year-old Robert is facing the enemy as he traverses the seas as a wireless operator in the Merchant Navy. Tony is ashamed to be around his family, especially his aunt whose sons are all in danger.[10] Indeed, he has a heated exchange with his father, Sefton, around the issue of, as he perceives it, his minority civilian status:

Tony: My aunt has two sons and a son-in-law called up not to men-
         tion Robert training for the Merchant Navy.
Sefton: What's that got to do with anything?
Tony: Has it escaped your notice I'm of military age?
Sefton: That's enough of that nonsense.

The conversation shifts abruptly after this but eventually Tony apolo-
gises to his father and further admits his guilt at being out of uniform
declaring: 'I'm sorry for that. I really can't face aunt Jean.'[11] However,
Sefton's pleas for his son to remain a civilian are in vain. Ultimately, off
screen and between episodes, Tony enlists in the navy.

Moreover, these are not unique events in *Family at War*. Daughter of
the main Ashton family, Freda, has a romantic relationship with neigh-
bour Peter who is reserved as a draughtsman. Like Tony before him
he expresses the pressures he feels to be in uniform openly and angrily.
For example, the following conversation takes place between Peter and
Freda's brother Philip:

Peter: I don't know if she'd [his mother] cope if I was away too.
Philip: You're a draughtsman, it's a reserved occupation.
Peter: I meant if I volunteered.
Philip: Why should you want to?
Peter: It's not that I want to. I like my job. I think I can go a long way if
         I stick at it.
Philip: Does anyone say you ought to?
Peter: They don't say it exactly. Well not straight out.
Philip: Well there you are then.
Peter: But I know a lot of them resent it. And their families. I can see them
         looking at me. 'He's alright but my boy's had to go. He's got it
         cushy.'
Philip: The only reason you haven't been called up is because you're
         more use where you are.[12]

In reality many of those in reserved occupations reported similar experiences. Indeed, the pressure to enlist was usually an internalised desire to
be in uniform and fighting on the front lines. External pressures to serve
were rare.[13] This is acknowledged by Philip later in the episode when
he tells Peter's mother: 'He might be miserable if he stays. All his age
group are gone or going. I don't think you understand the pressure.'[14]

Moreover, it is obvious that Peter is preoccupied with the outward markers of military service, most notably a uniform, rather than considering the necessity of highly skilled technical work in fighting and winning a protracted total war. Philip tries, again, to convince Peter to stay in his reserved occupation telling him:

> Philip: Peter, this is a war of technologies. You're needed where you are. There's any amount like me.
> Peter: I'll wear a label round me neck—'technologist'—then everyone will salute.[15]

Indeed, Peter's ire reaches its peak when he finds Freda kissing an Australian pilot, an act which causes Peter to rail angrily at Freda declaring: 'Women are all the same nowadays. Like some ancient tribe. Stick a bit of war paint on him and you can't help yourselves. No decency. Why don't you do like last time and start giving out white feathers.'[16] While triggered by Freda's betrayal, Peter's remarks reflect as much his internalised fears of emasculation as they do Freda's actions. Indeed, Peter's attitude reflects both wartime and post-war sensibilities in which military service outranked civilian service, regardless of its import to the war. Moreover, despite Philip's efforts Peter, like Tony before him, disregards his reserved status and enlists in the navy. However, before he can take up his new role he is killed performing Civil Defence duties during an air raid. In including this plot turn the writers and producers of the show could arguably have been highlighting the dangers all civilians faced and attempting to create a parity of sacrifice between civilians and those in the armed forces. However, given that Peter's love interest Freda spends much of the next episodes guiltily obsessing over Peter's death it is equally, if not more, likely his demise was included to further increase the melodrama in this soap opera of a show.

THE VOLUNTARY CIVILIAN

Despite the overwhelming depiction that civilian men were eager to escape for a life in the military, there were glimpses of those who displayed comfort in their civilian status. Freda's eventual husband Ian Mackenzie in *Family at War* faces no slurs on his masculinity nor ever intimates any desire to be in uniform. However, he is a doctor, a profession that carries a status that transcends wartime, and as such the necessity of his profession to civilian, and military, life is evident. Moreover, in an episode titled 'Hope against Hope' (1970), RAF pilot David's wife, Sheila, meets Colin, a machine tool designer, on a train. Rather unusually he tells Sheila happily about his civilian status:

> I'm in the royal civilians. The powers that be think I'm more use doing my own job. I'm Colin with the cushy number. Friends in the army and that ... Don't jump to conclusions but I like being Colin with the cushy number. It beats being shot at. Don't think me selfish but I'm just not a king and country man ... There was a bloke at work who was convinced people stared at him. Thinking he was a conscientious objector or a consumptive or something. So for the last few months he's been walking round with a limp so people will imagine he's a war hero or something. Can you imagine that?[17]

Once again *Family at War* accurately depicts the mainly internalised pressure civilian men felt to be in uniform. Colin is unusual in this respect as he is presented as immune to this pressure. Yet he is not an unambiguous character. His main storyline is as a potential suitor to Sheila, the wife of David, the RAF pilot. Their obvious romantic attraction is never consummated and their relationship remains chaste. However, his open pursuit of a married woman turns Colin into a morally dubious character, even when contrasted against David's numerous wartime affairs. While Colin is routinely and robustly rebuffed his romantic intentions for another man's wife undermine his positive discussions of his reserved status. Moreover, such a depiction represents one of the persistent wartime fears military men expressed during the Second World War. While stationed far from home, either in British barracks or in foreign theatres of war, men in uniform repeatedly expressed concern that their wives, girlfriends and sweethearts would be the sexual and romantic targets of civilian men on the home front. Indeed, Sally Sokoloff asserts that between 1943 and 1944 (coinciding with the arrival of thousands of American soldiers) Britain experienced a 'veritable epidemic of worry about the fidelity of wives and sweethearts'.[18] Moreover, this theme formed the central plot of the John Mills film *Waterloo Road* (Sidney Gilliat 1945) in which Mills plays a soldier who goes AWOL to protect his wife from the advances of a villainous spiv. *Family at War*, therefore, carries this key wartime worry into the post-war period where, yet again, the civilian man is persistently represented as deviant.

This correlation between civilian status and dubious moral character is oft-repeated in a *Family at War*. Eldest sister Margaret forms a sexual relationship with a conscientious objector, Michael Armstrong. The affair takes place shortly after the erroneously presumed death of her husband in Dunkirk and is condemned by many of her family. While this condemnation centres largely on her recent bereavement it is exacerbated by their illegitimate child, ultimately miscarried, and non-marital cohabitation. His conscientious objection also proves to be a bone of contention with Margaret's family. Again, it is the civilian man who is presented as a sexual deviant. As Sonya Rose states, of the war itself, 'Frequently conscientious objectors were publicly shamed by being labelled "sissies", "pansies", and other terms denoting effeminacy and that their sexuality was suspect.'[19] Clearly such emasculating notions persisted into the postwar period. Moreover, Michael's conscientious objection, however, is less than certain as he explains to Margaret:

> I was a clerk before this lot started. When they found out I was a CO they put me on army pay. It wasn't the money I minded. It wasn't the anonymous letter, who can tell where they came from anyway. What I did mind was losing my friends, most of them, or maybe they lost me. You're never altogether free from embarrassment. There's or yours. You're never sure quite how it happens but you just seem to drift away or they do … And quite a few people with my beliefs changed them … Bertrand Russell, Joad [philosophers] … if they're right I'm wrong.[20]

It must be noted, however, that conscientious objectors are noticeably absent from the tales told about the Second World War. Indeed, *Family at War* is an extremely rare example of this extended inclusion. Yet there were vastly more conscientious objectors in Britain during the Second World War than in the First World War. However, conscientious objection is more popularly connected with the earlier war. The 'conchie' is a perennial figure in depictions of the Great War. Such pointed omissions and inclusions largely reflect popular conceptions and understandings of each war. The First World War is now widely condemned as an unnecessary waste of life, a war where lions were led by donkeys to their deaths. As such the figure of the conscientious objector reflects the modern audience's understandings of warfare and provides a mouthpiece for the views which will resonate with contemporary viewers. In sharp contrast the Second World War is popularly conceived of as a 'just' or 'good' war, a war where bolshie little Britain stood up to an evil dictator. The figure of the conscientious objector does not sit comfortably within this framework and, as such, is absent from contemporary popular culture.

Instead civilian men who do appear are often implicitly or explicitly shown to be morally inferior. Most notably, the character of the 'spiv' is a recurrent character in both dramas and sitcoms set during the Second World War. Perhaps most famous, in a British context, is *Dad's Army*'s Walker (James Beck). It is strongly implied that Walker is avoiding military service as he is clearly of military age and apparently physically fit. In one episode, 'The Loneliness of the Long Distance Walker' broadcast in 1969, his 'allergy to corned beef' is declared as the reason for his civilian status, the obvious implication of which is that Walker is shirking. Similarly, in the 1982 series *We'll Meet Again* (produced by London Weekend Television for ITV) the character of Sid Davis, an obvious and open spiv, is arrested not for trading black market goods but for avoiding his conscription. Again, the association of civilian status with criminality is clear as is the recurrent idea that the only way to be a civilian was to evade service. This motif continues to the present day. BBC drama series *Land Girls* (broadcast between 2009 and 2011) about the wartime lives of several members of the Women's Land Army features several morally dubious civilian male characters. The concept of reserved occupations is never alluded to and men out of uniform are either dodging conscription or medically unfit. One farm worker, for example, has a 'special exemption' because of his flat feet. The same worker later tries, in an episode titled 'The War in The Fields', to sexually assault Iris, one of the titular land girls. Similarly, another of the land girls, Connie, is coerced by a spiv who follows her from London into defrauding the rural community in which she is based. This again cements the connection between civilian status and low moral character.

THE DISAPPEARING CIVILIAN MAN

There are few contemporary representations of the war which legitimise the presence of civilian male characters. Indeed, despite the vast numbers of civilian men who remained on the British home front they are often conspicuously absent from modern cultural depictions, a phenomenon which becomes more marked as the distance from the war increases.

Penny Summerfield notes of Britain's cultural relationship with the Second World War that:

> 'Remembering' the Second World War even if one did not live through it, or did so only as a child, has certainly been characteristic of those living in Britain since 1945, but it is not a simple matter of each generation being locked in understandings that were on offer when they were young. On the contrary, responses to texts alter during the life course as imaginative engagement with the past mutates, conditioned by changing personal political and cultural contexts.[21]

Indeed, a central example of how modern Britons understand the Second World War is 1990s time-travel sitcom *Goodnight Sweetheart*, broadcast between 1993 and 1999. The show depicts an ordinary modern man, a television repairman, with the strange ability to journey back to wartime London. In the early series the wartime scenes are set mainly in the heavily industrialised East End. However, the Royal Oak Pub, the central wartime location, is frequented almost solely by older men. Civilian men of working age are entirely omitted. The programme's single reference to the area's industrial contribution to the war effort comes with a brief allusion to female factory workers and their bawdy behaviour in the pub.[22] This increasingly rare depiction of civilian men perhaps reflects a generational shift in the production of British media. From the 1980s, when the decline becomes most obvious, writers and producers would have increasingly had little first-hand memories of the war. As such modern depictions of the war rely more and more heavily on obvious tropes of the conflict. This in turn has arguably further simplified popular conceptions of the war itself. The civilian man has become the victim of this process, losing out to the much more cinematically appealing stories of military men, with their tales of bravery and derring-do, and women entering new professions which are more televisually and cinematically appealing than men, for example, staying in their existing civilian jobs.

Indeed, in contemporary depictions wartime masculinity is often presented as singularly militaristic. Graham Dawson's assertion that 'military virtues such as aggression, strength, courage and endurance have repeatedly been defined as the natural and inherent qualities of manhood, whose apogee is attainable only in battle' certainly holds true of modern depictions of the Second World War.[23] For example, in the opening episode of 2015 series *Home Fires*, a show centred on a rural branch of the Women's Institute, military service is declared a natural desire for young men. During a discussion between butcher Bryn Brindson, played by Daniel Ryan, and his wife Miriam played by Claire Price, regarding their son's eagerness to enlist, Bryn declares: 'young men are drawn to war like moths to flame, it's their chance to prove themselves.' Miriam retorts sharply 'or be blown to pieces trying', to which the butcher replies 'from a bullet or regret, there's more than one way to die ... it's not a choice, not for most.'[24] In this cosy female-led Sunday night drama there is an overt emphasis on the overwhelming desire men, all men, felt to be in uniform. While there is, unusually, one conscientious objector within the show he is presented as an aberration and is duly mocked by his fellow villagers, for example by having his bike tarred and feathered. However, the other male villagers nearly all long to enlist. At the beginning of one episode a farmer, Stanley, confesses to the vicar, despite the vicar's assurances that farming is a reserved occupation, that 'I can't sit on my tractor while we go the same way as the Czechs and the Poles. I'm more use over there.'[25] Even the vicar himself describes a longing to be in the military, telling his wife 'there are boys from Great Paxford who will soon find themselves calling out for their mothers in fear or pain but their mother's won't be able to help them in their hour of need. I can ... It's where I believe my duty lies ... I truly believe that is how I can best serve God being there alongside them.'[26] Quite obviously modern depictions of the war insist a powerful longing for military service was a near universal experience, a depiction which is simply not representative of actual male experience during the war.[27] Moreover, any deviation from this leaves characters in such depictions open to, sometimes vicious, attack. In 1996 the BBC broadcast a mini-series titled *No Bananas*, the title itself a reference to the infamous lack of foreign fruit in Britain during the war. The series predominantly focused on a soldier Harry Slater's conflicted feelings about two love interests. Harry enlists early in the war and is injured at Dunkirk, an experience which forces him to question his desire for military service. He admits to his father that he is considering declaring himself a conscientious objector, a prospect which appals his father. His father declares: 'You can't do this to me ... It'd be the end of [my life]. Bad enough Tom spivving, but at least he does something for the people. What does a bloody "conchie" do? Nothing!'[28] This open derision of civilian status is a common trope. In *Goodnight Sweetheart* there is a persistent undertone of mockery of the central character for his lack of uniform. In one early episode Gary's fictional wife 'Marilyn Monroe', in actuality Gary's young grandmother whose address he is using without her knowledge, is thought to be cheating on him with a submariner (in reality Gary's eventual grandfather). Eric, Gary's love interest's father, snipes: 'She's taken up with a submariner. A fighting man. A real man. Not some pansy who writes love songs and pretends to be a spy.'[29] In a later episode, Gary attempts to bank a large quantity of pound notes, forged in the present day, and as a cover story he tells the bank manager he made the money as a songwriter. The manager is unimpressed and chides Gary, asking him: 'Instead of enlisting to fight the enemies of the king? Hardly the act of a patriot if I may say so.'[30] These are just two examples of the constant challenges Gary faces in the course of the show. There are frequent assumptions he is a spy as well as regular slurs on his masculinity. As Pattinson, McIvor and Robb have shown, in reality such slurs were extremely rare.[31] Such portrayals then seem to be somewhat of a modern invention. However, wartime imagery has constantly been reimagined to make new points not only about the war itself but about contemporary society. Indeed, Paula Hamilton argues:

> In the new millennium, we are in a strange temporal and demographic transition. War memories are becoming a largely intergenerational phenomenon, removed from the direct eyewitnesses, as meanings shift ever more radically in relation to current circumstances, assuming different shapes in our generational imaginations.[32]

As such, *Goodnight Sweetheart* arguably uses the war to explore the currently perceived 'crisis in masculinity'. For example, in the opening episode, 'Rites of Passage' (1993), Gary laments the loss of military life and the industrialised skills which his forefathers had enjoyed, stating:

> The trouble with women is they know how to make men feel like little boys. It'd be different if I'd ever had to kill anything. What we men lack in society today is a rite of passage. Our fathers did national service, their fathers fought in the war; experiences which marked their shift into manhood ... Of course you've got your apprenticeship system. When my granddad did his five years as a cooper ... they marked his entry into manhood by coating him in brewers' malt, rolling him down five flights of factory steps and into the Thames. Its moment ripe with symbolism, that.[33]

This statement is telling in several ways. First, it laments the rise in female power, a theme which becomes central to the show as it progresses. Secondly, Gary's speech also bemoans the loss of two central masculine identities, industrial skill and warfare. By the mid-1990s the idea of a 'crisis in masculinity' had taken root in the popular imagination. Stephen Whitehead notes:

> A discourse of masculinity in crisis has emerged to some prominence. That is, across many societies, most notably but not only in the Western world, the idea that men are facing some nihilistic future, degraded, threatened and marginalized by a combination of women's 'successful' liberation and wider social and economic transformations has become a highly potent, almost common-sense, if at times contested, understanding of men at this point in history.[34]

It is possible that Laurence Marks and Maurice Gran, writers of *Goodnight Sweetheart*, were attempting to lampoon such a retrograde notion. Indeed, Gary's rousing opening speech about his grandfather's workplace initiation is undercut when he wryly admits that: 'Alright, he was so badly injured he wasn't able to ply his new trade but the principle ...' [35] This suggests the audience were meant to find Gary's insistence on nostalgia for a past 'when men were men' somewhat risible.

The sitcom, however, does not go on to explore this theme. Throughout the programme's six series, especially in the latter three where the storylines become increasingly preposterous, Gary gets the opportunity to act out several clichéd masculine fantasies. In addition to his constant pretence of being a spy Gary becomes involved in many adventures which would not seem out of place in a *Boy's Own* adventure. Such a focus may reflect the enduring popularity of fictionalised accounts of the Second World War aimed at young boys, which represent the war as an escapade as seen, for example, in the classic story *The Kingdom by the Sea* by Robert Westall.[36] Adventure is ever-present in *Goodnight Sweetheart*. For example, in the episode titled 'Come Fly With Me' (1997), on the night before his bigamous wedding to Phoebe, he is drunkenly convinced to aid a Canadian airman on a bombing mission. Subsequently, he is forced to ditch into the sea and spends the night afloat in the Channel. In addition, in a later episode, '... But We Think You Have to Go' (1998), he is recruited for a secret spy mission in France where he is aided by the French resistance and ultimately captured by the Gestapo before he makes his escape. Finally, and perhaps most ludicrously of all, in the final episode, 'Accentuate the Positive' (1999), he saves Clement Attlee from a would-be assassin, thus ensuring Britain's 1945 Labour government and the inception of the welfare state. These constant escapades contrast sharply with his life in the present day, where his marriage seems permanently dysfunctional and his unsatisfactory work as a television repairman, and then as the owner of an unsuccessful Second World War memorabilia shop, is constantly ridiculed by his wife and best friend. Maurice Gran, one of the writers of *Goodnight Sweetheart*, admits that: 'In the past he's a hero, and in the present he's a nobody.'[37] Gary's wartime self is cast as the provider for Phoebe. Despite running a pub, and later a nightclub, she is reliant on Gary for money and rationed goods. Gary generally accompanies his arrival in the past with the presentation of gifts from the present. Moreover, the wartime changes to gender roles are unusually underplayed in the series with little reference being made to women's war work. The wartime character of Phoebe is continually contrasted with Gary's present-day wife Yvonne, who from the outset is an ambitious businesswoman and by the end of the sixth series is a self-made multimillionaire. Moreover, Gary's relationship with Yvonne is, from the start, less recognisably affectionate than his love affair with Phoebe. Both women are constructed as stereotypes of temporally specific examples of femininity. Yvonne is the power-suited sarcastic modern women seeking to 'have it all', while Phoebe is concerned with propriety and image, wearing classic 1940s clothes and baulking at the idea of Gary cooking or doing housework. This juxtaposition is brought to a head in one of the closing episodes of the final series when Gary is forced to choose between his present and past wives. He opts for Phoebe because 'she needs him more' than independent, capable Yvonne.[38] As such, the programme could be seen as nostalgia for a time when gender roles were more rigid. Civilian male roles do not fit well into this nostalgic, and heroic, view of the past. While in his opening speech Gary laments the loss of the apprentice system the show as a whole celebrates wartime adventure and derring-do. However, as during the war, this may reflect the fact that for those in many civilian roles there is no obvious story arc.[39] For men entering the military, women embarking on new occupations and even children being evacuated to the countryside there is a clear storyline and a journey on which to take the characters—chronicling new experiences, new skills acquired, new friendships made. For civilian men who remained employed in their pre-war, often low-key, jobs the stories that can be told are not nearly as transformative nor as exciting. Consequently, they are rarely seen on page or screen.

THE EMASCULATED CIVILIAN

The very few male civilian characters which are depicted on the British home front are almost universally unfit for service. This is the case, for example, in *Foyle's War*, a detective drama set in Hastings, Sussex broadcast by the BBC since 2002. The two male leads who investigate these crimes are evidently outside the remit of the military. Detective Chief Superintendent Christopher Foyle is a man in his fifties who had served in the First World War. In addition, in the early episodes of the series he persistently attempts to get out of his local police role into the War Office, a request which is repeatedly denied. Moreover, Foyle's Sergeant, Paul Milner, is invalided out of the army in the first episode, 'The German Woman' (2002), having lost his leg during the Norwegian campaign. Indeed, like Milner, medical disqualification is the most commonly depicted reason for being out of uniform. For example, in the 1995 Angela Huth novel *Land Girls*, and its 1998 film adaptation, farm worker Joe has asthma, changed to a heart condition in the film version, which curtails his military ambitions. The contrast between the healthy young 'mobile women' sent to work on his father's farm and his inertia caused by his ill-health is obvious.[40] However, land girl Stella attempts to persuade him that 'someone's got to organize the massive job of feeding the country. Hallows Farm is making the sort of contribution you shouldn't under-value.' This, however, does little to change Joe's mind:

Times like this [at a military dance] it hits you. Being one of the very few not in uniform. You feel such a rotten shirker ... The day I failed my medical was the worst day of my life. Never forget it: this icy room with that poster on the wall – you know the one, *Your Country Needs You.* This cocky little doctor. Afraid your country doesn't need you, my lad, he said. You can't expect to fight the enemy if you're fighting for your own breath. Stands to reason. I told him – I told him I was much better than I had been as a child – growing out of the asthma fast. But nothing would change his stubborn little mind ... My ambition was to join the HAC [Honourable Artillery Company]. You're wise and you're right. But I can't help the guilt, the shame. I'd rather be fighting.[41]

Despite being a civilian Joe is still clearly an attractive partner: in both versions of the story he forms a romantic relationship with each of the land girls in turn. The enduring popularity of stories set on the home front, and especially romance stories, renders it unsurprising that writers include civilian male characters as a permanent presence. Yet the focus on men deemed medically unfit, rather than more obviously masculine pro-tagonists, is more of a puzzle. In some ways it is likely this focus reflects the increasingly simplistic view of the war which dominates modern British culture, a simplistic conceptualisation which has almost erased the many vital contributions civilian men made to the war effort from the public imagination. Instead the British home front is popularly conceived as the terrain of only women and children. However, it also reflects the idea that, as seen in *Dunkirk* and *Family of War*, not accepting civilian status was seen as normal and even desirable behaviour. The implication was often that civilian status could be avoided and therefore should be avoided. In contrast, men deemed medically unfit simply could not be expected to enlist. As such while they may be pitied they are certainly not shirkers, arguably the greater crime in modern understandings of the Second World War.

There is also a persistent trope of civilian men being presented as ridiculous. The most obvious example of this is *Dad's Army*, a peren-nial television favourite ever since it first began broadcasting in 1968. The show was scripted by Jimmy Perry and David Croft, both of whom had actually served in the Home Guard. The show centres on a pre-dominantly elderly band of Home Guard volunteers as they pursue their missions with humorous consequences. The younger members of the platoon are inherently comical—for example, Private Frank Pike (Ian Lavender) too young for military enlistment but also a coddled idiot. In many ways *Dad's Army* presents the typical perceptions of British men during the Second World War. The show reveals that men were out of military uniform because they were either too young, too old or actively avoiding service. The show's co-creator, Jimmy Perry, stated that, in reality, the age make-up of the Home Guard was much younger than that presented in the programme, but they purposefully chose to present an aged band of volunteers to ramp up the comedic value.[42] The civilian man as clown is widely seen in representations of the Second World War. It is prominently seen in 1990s sitcom *Goodnight Sweetheart*. Regular character Reg Deadman is presented as both an unskilled policeman and a general simpleton. In one episode, Gary asks Reg: 'would you call me debonair?' Reg's retort to this is: 'What do you want to go changing your name for?'[43] Similarly, 1970s comedy series *Backs to the Land* (broadcast between 1977 and 1978) depicts three urbane young land girls as they adjust to life in rural Norfolk. Reflecting common representations the farmer is the main comedic figure. He is constantly outwitted by his female charges and is presented as somewhat simple, often ending up physically humiliated and covered in manure. For example, in the opening episode he declares that his sons should never have gone to the army as they were in 'reversed occupations'.[44] This trope persists in more recent representations. The BBC drama series *Land Girls*, not to be confused with the novel and film of the same name, was broadcast between 2009 and 2011. The show is melodramatic, often presenting heightened emotional storylines. However, the main civilian male character presented, farmer Frederick Finch played by comic actor Mark Benton, is often the focus of ridicule. As in *Backs to the Land*, he is the farmer on which a group of young land girls are billeted. From his first appearance on screen he is clearly intended as a comic figure. The wistful romantic music which had been playing ceases as he walks into the scene and he attempts to wheedle one of the land girls into delivering some black market pork chops while insisting they are not black market. He is undermined by young evacuee Martin who innocently insists 'they are black market, he told me they was'. In response Farmer Finch says 'and you remember I did the zippy mouth thing', accompanied by an exaggerated mime of zipping his mouth and throwing away the key, undoubtedly intended to have a humorous effect. It is clear that this representation of the civilian man as fundamentally comedic is persistent.[45] Yet such a portrayal essentially emasculates those men and certainly contrasts poorly with the heroic reverence still bestowed upon the fighting man.

CONCLUSION

In conclusion, the civilian man has been much maligned in post-war culture. The often-necessary roles played by millions of civilian men have been effectively written out of Britain's wartime story despite their centrality to both victory and survival. On the rare occasion a reserved man is shown, their situation is shown to be one to be avoided at all costs. Instead, it is often emphasised that a military uniform was the only acceptable way to be a man in this period. Those out of uniform are left open to jibes and scorn, often shown to be army-dodging crooks and would-be wife stealers rather than vital cogs in pursuing a course of total warfare. Moreover, the civilian man is often a focus of ridicule, the butt of the joke and, therefore, far from a masculine figure.

NOTES

1. First broadcast in Series 2, Episode 4 of *Horrible Histories* on 3 June 2010.
2. For further information on wartime representations, see L. Robb (2015), *Men at Work: The Working Man in British Culture, 1939–1945* (Basingstoke: Palgrave Macmillan).
3. P. Howlett (1951), *Fighting with Figures: A Statistical Digest of the Second World War* (London: HMSO), p. 8.
4. See, for example, P. Summerfield and C. Peniston-Bird (2003), 'The Home Guard in Britain in the Second World War: Uncertain Masculinities?' in P.R. Higate (ed.), *Military Masculinities: Identity and the State* (London: Praeger), pp. 57–69; P. Summerfield and C. Peniston-Bird (2007), *Contesting Home Defence: Men, Women and the Home Guard in the Second World War* (Manchester: Manchester University Press); S.O. Rose (2003), *Which Peoples War? National Identity and Citizenship in Wartime Britain, 1939–1945* (Oxford: Oxford University Press).
5. P. Summerfield (2009), 'Public Memory or Public Amnesia? British Women of the Second World War in Popular Films of the 1950s and 1960s.' *Journal of British Studies*, 48:4, pp. 935–957.
6. P. Summerfield (2010), 'Dunkirk and the Popular Memory of Britain at War, 1940–58'. *Journal of Contemporary History*, 45:4, pp. 788–811, here p. 807.
7. M. Paris (2007), 'Introduction: Film, Television, and the Second World War—The First Fifty Years', in M. Paris, *Repicturing the Second World War: Representations in Film and Television* (Basingstoke: Palgrave Macmillan), p. 7.
8. J. Chapman (2007), 'Re-presenting war: British television drama-documentary and the Second World War', *European Journal of Cultural Studies*, 10:1, pp. 13–33, here p. 13.
9. Lines from 'Lines of Battle', *Family at War*, first broadcast 28 April 1970.
10. Lines from 'The Breach in the Dyke', *Family at War*, first broadcast 19 May 1970.
11. Ibid.
12. Lines from 'If it's got your Number on it', *Family at War*, first broadcast 28 July 1970.

13. J. Pattinson, A. McIvor and L. Robb (2017), *Men in Reserve: British Civilian Masculinities in the Second World War* (Manchester: Manchester University Press), p. 99.

14. Lines from 'If it's got your Number on it', *Family at War*, first broadcast 28 July 1970.

15. Ibid.

16. Ibid.

17. Lines from 'Hope against Hope', *Family at War*, first broadcast 16 December 1970.

18. Sally Sokoloff (1999), '"How are they at home?": Community, State and Servicemen's Wives in England, 1939–45', *Women's History Review*, 8:1, pp. 27–52, here p. 38.

19. Rose, *Which Peoples War?*, p. 175.

20. Lines from 'Hope against Hope', *Family at War*, first broadcast 16 December 1970. The philosopher Bertrand Russell amended his long-held stance on pacifism during the Second World War, conceding that war may, on occasion, be the lesser of two evils. Similarly, C.E.M. Joad, popular wartime philosopher remembered for his role in the popular BBC radio show *The Brains Trust*, rescinded his previously held pacifist beliefs after the Spanish Civil War.

21. P. Summerfield, '"The long ago war looms large in my life": Men, Women and the Cultural Memory of the Second World War, a Mass-Observation study', in L. Noakes and J. Pattinson (2013), *British Cultural Memory and the Second World War* (London: Bloomsbury), pp. 39–40.

22. Lines from 'It's a sin to tell a lie' *Goodnight Sweetheart*, first broadcast 15 January 1996.

23. G. Dawson (1994), *Soldier Heroes: British Adventure, Empire and the Imaginings of Masculinity* (London: Routledge), p. 1

24. Lines from Episode 1.1, *Home Fires*, first broadcast 3 May 2015.

25. Lines from Episode 1.3, *Home Fires*, first broadcast 17 May 2015.

26. Ibid.

27. See, for example, Pattinson, McIvor and Robb, *Men in Reserve*.

28. P. Cave (1996), *No Bananas* (London: BBC Books), pp. 183–184.

29. Lines from 'I get along without you very well', *Goodnight Sweetheart*, first broadcast 16 December 1993.

30. Lines from 'Don't get around much anymore', *Goodnight Sweetheart*, first broadcast 20 February 1995.

31. Pattinson, McIvor and Robb, *Men in Reserve*, p. 124.

32. P. Hamilton (2010), 'A Long War: Public and the Popular Memory', in S. Radstone and B. Schwarz (eds), *Memory: Histories, Theories, Debates* (New York: Fordham University Press), p. 301.

33. Lines from 'Rites of Passage', *Goodnight Sweetheart*, first broadcast 18 November 1993.
34. S. Whitehead (2002), *Men and Masculinities* (Cambridge: Malden), p. 51.
35. Lines from 'Rites of Passage', *Goodnight Sweetheart*, first broadcast 18 November 1993.
36. R. Westall (1983), *The Kingdom by the Sea* (London: Mammoth).
37. T. Masters (2013), 'Goodnight Sweetheart: Musical future for time travel sitcom', BBC News, 17 November: http://www.bbc.co.uk/news/entertainment-arts-24808201. Accessed 1 July 2014.
38. Lines from 'Just in time', *Goodnight Sweetheart*, first broadcast 20 May 1999.
39. Robb, *Men at Work*, p. 70.
40. W. Webster, (2007), '"Rose-tinted Blighty": Gender and Genre in Land Girls', in Michael Paris (ed.), *Repicturing the Second World War: Representations in Film and Television* (Basingstoke: Palgrave), pp. 19–20.
41. Angela Huth (2012), *Land Girls* (London: Constable), pp. 171–172.
42. Summerfield and Peniston-Bird, *Contesting Home Defence*, p. 183.
43. Lines from 'How long has this been going on', *Goodnight Sweetheart*, first broadcast 15 April 1997.
44. Lines from 'A Miss is as good as a Male', *Backs to the Land*, first broadcast 15 April 1977.
45. Lines from 'Childhood's End', *Land Girls*, first broadcast 7 September 2009.

CHAPTER 9

Commemorating Invisible Men: Reserved Occupations in Bronze and Stone

Corinna Peniston-Bird

This chapter explores the emphases and omissions in the commemoration of British men on the home front in the Second World War in the context of the hierarchies of war and remembrance. The research is based on analysis of war and post-war memorials (viewed in situ where possible), and related prose sources, cross-referenced against the War Memorials Register (WMR), which contains the details of over 68,000 memorials in the UK.[1] The methodology sets the materiality of the memorials, their form, message and location, within the historical theorisation of the construction of the People's War, and the impact of the war on gender identities.[2] This combination is fundamental. As Nuala Johnson argues: 'The materiality of a particular site of memory sometimes masks the material social relations undergirding its production by focusing the eye on its aesthetic representation independent of the sometimes less visible ideas (social, economic, cultural power relations) that underpin the final product.'[3] It is equally important to think of the silences and their implications. Historical attention to civilian

C. Peniston-Bird (✉)
Department of History, Lancaster University, Lancaster, UK
e-mail: c.m.peniston-bird@lancaster.ac.uk

© The Author(s) 2018
L. Robb and J. Pattinson (eds.), *Men, Masculinities and Male Culture in the Second World War*, Genders and Sexualities in History,
https://doi.org/ 10.1057/978-1-349-95290-8_9

189

masculinities in wartime has grown, with a particular focus on the relationship to military masculinities, public representations and how men (and women) experienced or perceived the civilian male identity.[4] Here the goal is to interrogate why the civilian male in a reserved occupation has struggled to find a place in the popular imagination and commemoration. The men who worked and survived on the home front constitute a highly diverse group, challenging to commemorative practices not least because of the multiplicity of roles encompassed. They also challenge existing models of the impact of war on constructions of gender and their nigh invisibility in sculptural commemoration suggests the challenges of representing a 'fuzzy', not 'fixed' gender boundary.[5]

The issue of the commemoration of the Second World War remains topical. Since the turn of the twenty-first century, a spate of new memorials has been commissioned, from animals in war to Bomber Command. These memorials were not conceived as a focus for collective mourning and historians have offered various reasons for their continued proliferation. Jay Winter suggests, for example, that 'the memory boom of the late twentieth century is a reflection of a complex matrix of war damage, political activity, claims for entitlement, scientific research, philosophical reflection, and art'.[6] More critically focused on Britain, the architectural historian Gavin Stamp has called it 'a pathetic attempt at national self-justification by a former imperial power in decline, looking back to World War II both nostalgically and assertively as our last independent heroic movement'.[7] There also appears to be a domino effect as more contributors to the war effort find representation. Of particular significance is the National Memorial Arboretum (NMA) in Alrewas, Staffordshire (founded in 1997; opened 2001) where over 330 memorials are located.[8] Since its inception, its commemorative function has become increasingly military (although it officially commemorates 'military associations, charitable organisations, emergency services, fraternity groups and individuals').[9] As an increasing number of wartime roles and organisations found representation there, from the Burma Railway memorial to the Royal Air Force Barrage Balloons Memorial, omission has been viewed as increasingly significant. Thus, for example, in 2014, a memorial was erected to the Women's Land Army and Women's Timber Corps (Denise Dutton (sculptor), 2014), supplementing the existing Scottish memorials (Malcolm Robertson (sculptor), Queen Elizabeth Forest Park near Aberfoyle, 2007); (Peter Naylor (sculptor), Clochan 2012). A figurative memorial to the Auxiliary Territorial Service (ATS) (Andy De Comyn (sculptor)) was unveiled in 2006, not least in response to the contentious lack of embodiment in the memorial to The Women of World War II unveiled the previous year (John Mills (sculptor), Whitehall, London, 2005; see the section 'Hierarchies of service' below). The location also offers an alternative space to the symbolism and dominance of the capital.

Wherever the memorials are located, in many of the recent projects, education as motivation is also of stated significance to the instigators, conscious that current and future generations will no longer have any living memories of the period. For example, in the case of the Battle of Britain memorial (Donald Insall Associates (architects) Paul Day (sculptor), Victoria Embankment, London, 2005), discussed in the section 'Hierarchies of service' below, the founder of the Battle of Britain Historical Society, Bill Bond, was inspired by a conversation he overheard in 1995 in the sergeants' mess at RAF Caltershore when two senior RAF non-commissioned officers (NCOs) shared their ignorance: 'What was this Battle of Britain all about then?' 'I've no idea; something to do with the War, I think.'[10] Bond also cited a poll which suggested that 4 per cent of the British population believe the Battle of Britain was fought 'with bow and arrows' and condemned an educational system that 'has let us down'.

The new memorials reflect the widening definition of what constitutes a suitable subject for a war memorial and what is worthy of remembering, continuing the evolution from the commemoration of 'great men' to mass death, to mass service. In 2007, for example, the Department of Constitutional Affairs advised that:

> Any physical object erected or dedicated to commemorate those killed as a result of armed conflict should be regarded as a war memorial. War memorials to those who served and returned alive as well as civilian casualties and animals should also be included.[11]

Service is defined here as military; civilian commemoration is reserved for the dead. That exclusivity has not reflected recent practice, however. The most complex category of representation today is service on the home front, a complexity fostered by the shift in emphasis in remembering the war as both global and domestic. As Janet Watson argues:

> In the 1980s, the key commemorative participants were the veterans. In the 1990s, however, the Second World War became increasingly everyone's war, no matter what they had done between 1939 and 1945, or

indeed if they had even been alive then. As the glory of the war broadened to including seemingly everyone, however, it became harder and harder to see those who were still excluded.[12]

As the rhetoric of the People's War, in which the British fought the war 'all in it together', solidified in commemorative activities, an increasing number of sub-groups of the British collective war effort have sought or found public recognition, from broad categories to highly specific groups. In 2004 the Animals in War Memorial was unveiled in London (David Backhouse (sculptor); Hyde Park, London, 2004) followed a year later by the memorial to the Women of World War II (John Mills (sculptor); Whitehall, London, 2005), both emphasising service.[13] More specific roles have also found representation, for example, in the erection of memorials to the 'Lumberjills' (members of the Women's Timber Corps) and Land Girls listed above and with the most recent addition of 'Pull don't Push' (Ray Lonsdale (Sculptor), Dalby Forest, 2015); Women of Steel (Martin Jennings (sculptor), Barker's Pool Sheffield City Centre, 2016); and the Bevin Boys (Harry Parkes (Design), National Memorial Arboretum, Staffordshire, 2013); all have been described as memorials, not monuments, and explicitly commemorate—celebrate—service, not death.

Despite these trends, there is a group which remains under-represented, especially given their statistical predominance in the war effort. While civilian women lead in the list above, civilian males are often invisible in the commemoration of the collective war effort. The Schedule of Reserved Occupations reserved men from military service on the basis of their roles and their age, as young as eighteen if their skills were deemed of greater value on the home front. The goal was to prevent skilled personnel from being conscripted into the services, and the list encompassed a wide range of jobs: engineering in particular, but also men in textile and clothing, in the boot and shoe trades, printers, pottery workers, journalists, civil servants and more.[14] In 1945, for example, a peak of 4.5 million men were serving in the Forces but over 10 million were working on the home front. Depending on the year, the ratio with service men vacillated between around 1:2.5 and 1:4, similar to the tooth-to-tail ratio (combat-to-non-combat roles) within the military, which was 1:4 in 1939.[15] The further the occupation was from paralleling the characteristics of military service, the less likely it is that the role is remembered: Bevin Boys, young men conscripted into mining rather than the forces between 1943 and 1948 to address the coal shortage, were at least conscripted, and into a singularly masculine—and dangerous—profession.[16]

During the war, both ends of the male age spectrum were represented as desperate to do their bit, although such depictions can be read as either reflection or exhortation.[17] However, popular perception frequently suspected the civilian of military age (18–41, rising to 51 over the course of the war, but applying particularly to those men at the younger end) of disability or corruption. Omission and suspicion of the civilian male remains a feature in the commemoration of the Second World War, complicated in the first instance by the serviceman as epitomising male service, and the home front as a female domain. For example, in St Michael's Church in Little Ilford, an oak plaque proclaims:

1939 1945 / TO THE GLORY OF GOD / TO THE HONOURED MEMORY / OF THE MEN AND WOMEN OF / LITTLE ILFORD WHO GAVE / THEIR LIVES IN THE FIGHT / FOR FREEDOM AND TO THE / WOMENFOLK AT HOME / WHO BY THEIR GREAT COURAGE / AND DEVOTION TO DUTY / GAVE US OUR LIBERTY.[18]

The home front is gendered here as exclusively female, an emphasis also found in figurative memorialisation, sometimes alongside the inclusion of infants to emphasise vulnerability and care for the future, such as in the Liverpool Blitz Memorial (Tom Murphy (sculptor), St Nicholas Church, Pier Head, Liverpool, 2000). The missing body of the civilian male stands in marked contrast to the contemporary corporeal reiteration of the warrior hero, that is, for example, the memorial to Bomber Command (Liam O' Connor (architect); Philip Jackson (sculptor), Green Park, London, 2012).

There are gender-neutral memorials to service on the home front, for example, in the evocative grounds of St Michael's Cathedral in Coventry, a city akin to London regarding its identification with aerial bombardment. The large horizontal circular stone plaque reads: 'In gratitude to God and to commend to future generations the self-sacrifice of all those who served on the home front in the Second World War' (2000). Similarly, in 2006 Burton-on-Trent sponsored a memorial at the National Memorial Arboretum, which also avoided any gender specificity: 'A tribute to those who worked on the home front to support the war effort.' (Fig. 9.1).

Both of these memorials are stone adorned with prose: they suggest solid significance, but not embodiment. Neither can be decoded at a

Fig. 9.1 The memorial to the Home Front, National Memorial Arboretum, Staffordshire (Author's copyright)

distance, nor without text. They do not render more visible civilian male service in the narrative of the war; indeed, the emphasis on 'support' emphasises military service at the apex of the hierarchy, and the role of support is traditionally aligned with women. 'Self-sacrifice' is equally loaded a term; this is not the self-sacrifice of the fallen soldier akin to that of Christ dying so that others may be saved, but the self-sacrifice of enduring with stoicism the challenges of the war at home: in the war itself, the idea of sacrifice on the home front often also sought to contain women's temporary adoption of unconventional gender roles.

The Civilian Male in Wartime

In the Second World War, the military male securely occupied the apex of the wartime hierarchy of service, while the civilian male's position was more fluid, qualified by age, occupation and geographical location—and within the home, his familial status. Propaganda posters sought to claim parity of service with such slogans as 'The Attack Begins in the Factory' or 'They also Serve', or by paralleling industrial machinery with the technologies of war.[19] Long working hours, poor working conditions and a double burden of employment and civil defence duties suggest that the parity of sacrifice was not merely morale-boosting grandiloquence. The historical consensus, however, is that the rhetoric of parity was seldom wholly sincere, nor convincing.[20] In both poster series, for example, while the captions suggest codependence, the images exclusively depict the combat zone: the civilian male is invisible in all but rhetoric. There are no feature films focusing on men in industry to parallel *Millions Like Us* (directed by Sidney Gilliat and Frank Launder, 1943), which celebrated the novelty of women in factory service, although there were Ministry of Information shorts for targeted audiences.[21] Not all civilian occupations could so easily be glorified as weapons of war either, as was recognised in a letter written to the editor of *The Times* in 1941 by an employee of a furniture manufacturer, who described what he called 'Work Without Praise'.

> There is a vast but almost unrecognised army of men and women who are doing much the same work as they did in peacetime. They are employed in workshops and small factories making mattresses for hospitals, chairs and tables for barracks, brooms and dishcloths for canteens, and cleaning Civil Defence uniforms and wardens' blankets. For them there are no royal visits, no E.N.S.A. concerts, no encouraging telegrams from the minister. They are uncertain of their position in the Schedule of Reserved Occupations. Their work is probably not 'protected.' They are giving of their best, but often wonder whether they should move to a more 'essential' job.[22]

The civilian male of military age was and remained difficult to mobilise as symbolic of a national commitment to the war effort. This is not merely a consequence of the mundane nature of some of their roles. A further factor is periodisation: the duration of the occupation was less likely than military service to coincide with the war years—because men might already be in those roles, and they did not necessarily leave them at the war's end. An obvious example would be agricultural workers, who were reserved at twenty-one, and, in practice, were unlikely to be called up in any event. As Linsey Robb notes, Kenneth Clark, head of the War Artist Advisory Committee, commented that: 'The trouble about war pictures of agriculture is that they are rather hard to distinguish from peace pictures'—a problem which would favour the representation of the wartime Land Girl over the male agricultural worker, even though male workers outnumbered the former by three to one.[23]

There is one interesting wartime exception to the omission of the representation of the civilian male in image: the memorial to Sydney David Cosgrove Smith and ninety others killed through enemy action on 25 September 1940 at the Bristol Aeroplane Company in South Gloucestershire (Fig. 9.2).

The Bristol Aeroplane Company was located in Filton opposite the church, which now houses the memorial. The factory had been targeted after German intelligence had identified it was poorly defended: a bombing raid left 72 dead and 166 injured in the factory alone. A further 19 died later of their injuries. Outside the factory, 58 people were killed and a further 154 seriously injured.[24] The memorial takes the form of a reredos, an ornamental church screen, which depicts two workers kneeling at the foot of a cross, with the factory and the church, which was used as a mortuary, in the background (James Ashman, a parishioner (designer), South Gloucestershire, 1942). Their supplicant posture positions them as either victim or mourner. The reredos was presented by William G. Verdon Smith, the Managing Director of the Bristol Tramways and Carriage Co., Ltd which became the Bristol Aeroplane Company (BAC). His relative Colonel Sydney Smith served on the Board, and his son Sydney David Cosgrove Smith died at the age of twenty-two on his way to hospital (Fig. 9.3).

This is a fine example of a community-based memorial, by inception, design and location. The rolled-up sleeves and overalls clearly emphasise the working identities of the supplicants, emphasised by the factory and crane behind them. It also suggests the differentiation between national and local representations, an observation borne out by further analysis of memorials to civilian men. As a memorial to loss of life, however, it does not challenge the hierarchies of commemoration.

Service and Death

A distinction was drawn between military service, death in service and death in civilian occupation. The former occupations of serving personnel had been recognised in work-sited memorials in the First World War, and continued in and after the Second. These reflect both mourning and community. The Dowlais Factory ICI memorial (Pant, Mid Glamorgan,

Fig. 9.2 Close-up of the screen. The text boxes read: 'To the Glory of God and in faithful memory of Sydney David Cosgrove Smith and ninety others of the Bristol Aeroplane Company.' Right hand side: 'These all died in the works from enemy action on September the twenty fifth 1940. This screen was designed and made by workers of the Company' (Courtesy of Reverend Robert Conway, Assistant Priest, St Peter's Filton)

n.d.), for example, was erected 'in grateful memory of the men from Dowlais Factory who fell in the Second World War', and we find a similar memorial to the employees of the Royal Ordnance Factory (Irvine, Strathclyde, n.d.); and the Ministry of Agriculture in Westminster, among many others.[25] Subtle shifts of emphasis from battle to home front are apparent after the Second World War in comparisons to inscriptions from the First World War—for example, at J Lyons and Co, in Hammersmith (formerly Tea Factory, Greenford), where the inscription first read: 'Erected by J Lyons and Company Ltd in memory of the staff who fell in the Great War' (1922). It was addended: 'and in memory of the men and women who fell defending the home front' (1947,

Fig. 9.3 The reredos. After the church was enlarged in 1962 the reredos was located in the St George's Room. Since its restoration in 2009, it has been placed in the baptistry in the main body of the church (Courtesy of Chris Gooding, PCC Secretary, St Peter's Church, Filton, Bristol)

rededicated 2002).[26] The C. Shippam Ltd Factory in Chichester (n.d.) has a bronze memorial to both world wars, 'in grateful remembrance / of the members of the staff / who made the / supreme sacrifice / and of over one hundred others who answered their country's call and happily survived.'[27] The latter reflects the greater probability of survival in the Second World War, which gave impetus to the listing of service, not death, to express a local commitment to the war effort.

Air raids challenged the dominance of military service in the commemoration of war, however, as death was no longer predominantly the preserve of military service personnel. Community memorials may remember civilian identities by gender and age, as on the pillar in Southampton that is 'dedicated / to the men, women / and children of / Southampton who lost / their lives during the / Second World War'.[28] Their juxtaposition reflects lack of agency ('lost' not 'gave', the latter more common terminology for the dead of the forces), and the monument itself is overshadowed by the cenotaph beside it, the respective scale suggesting degree of honour.[29] Memorials to the victims of air raids targeting industry were more likely to include occupational identities as relevant to their death. The Mining Engineering Company (MECO) memorial (Worcester) commemorates when the workers were targeted by one German bomber on 3 October 1940 as they came out for their lunch break. Seven employees were killed and a female employee lost her sight in the air raid. Doris Tindall is mentioned 'in sympathy' alongside the colleagues who lost their lives.[30] Similar memorials can be found at Rolls Royce (Crewe, where 17 were killed), Vickers Aircraft Factory (Weybridge, Surrey), the Marconi Works and Cunliffe Owen Aircraft Ltd (Hampshire), among others.[31]

These memorials most often take the form of a plaque which has the advantage that it may require only wall space (although some are mounted on surfaces custom-built for the purpose) and is not prohibitively expensive. The lettering may be supplemented by the emblem of the company or a prop relevant to the occupation, such as an aircraft propeller, the latter drawing on the status of the symbols of combat.[32] The meaning is also derived from the location: in Westminster City Hall there is a circular black plaque of prose which commemorates Westminster's councillors and officers alongside the civil and emergency services 'for their actions during World War II' (Westminster, 1995).[33] The London location as the seat of government and the heart of the Blitz offers a context of sobriety, emphasised also by the date of unveiling, to coincide with the VE Day celebrations. Indeed, the WMR shows a surge in rededications of war memorials in the 1990s as well as new memorials.[34]

Civilian workers who died in industrial accidents rather than as a consequence of enemy action were less likely to be commemorated as victims of war. The memorial to the men of Kells, in Whitehaven, Cumbria, does not include the names of William Steele and Richard Ashburne who died in an accident at the Royal Ordinance Factory, Drigg on 25 July 1941, nor that of a soldier who died while off duty.[35] In contrast, Thomas Martin Cooke (crane driver) and Christopher Fieldhouse (apprentice fitter) are commemorated on a bronze plaque mounted on a crane base for losing their lives 'when on duty as firewatchers on the platform of the crane formerly occupying this site. Wrecked and brought down by enemy/air attack on the night of 7th—8th May 1941.'[36] This memorial was rededicated in 2010 and moved from the shipyard to the Barrow Dock Museum. These examples suggest the shifts in commemorative emphases introduced by the nature of the war: civilians are remembered as victims in air attacks or when losing their lives serving in civil or home defence; service is commemorated to underpin collective identities in occupational and regional localities but is more likely when service has an overt association with the war effort. There are also two distinct time periods for memorialisation: the war and its immediate aftermath, and then a renewed impetus from the 1990s, exhibited in rededications, rediscoveries and, indeed, the establishment of the National Inventory of War Memorials in 1989 (the predecessor of the WMR). These memorials collectively suggest the importance of industrial labour to the war effort and the dangers of the home front, but they do not extend to the representation of civilian service more broadly and the significance of reserved occupations for men at war.

HIERARCHIES OF SERVICE

Analysis of memorials unveiled from the fortieth anniversary of the war onwards suggests that these reflect the wartime hierarchy of service which was defined by three spectra—proximity to death and danger, proximity to action, and overt and obvious connection to the war effort—criteria which derive from, and continue to favour, service personnel. The hierarchy of death is evident, for example, in the debates of a committee formed in 1939, tasked to consider whether 'His Majesty should now be advised to extend the Royal Message of Condolence to cover the relatives of persons killed in enemy action'. They acknowledged that civil defence organisations would be 'liable to the same risk of death as the personnel of the three fighting services'; and that multiple categories of civilians 'may all be regarded as in the front line and the ordinary man or woman in the street may lose their lives by enemy action'. However, they concluded that the Royal Message of Condolence would be devalued if extended to any but relatives of the Forces or the Merchant Navy. Various solutions were suggested, ranging from the Minister of Health expressing the deep sympathy of His Majesty's government to the Home Secretary expressing 'their Majesties' sympathy' on Home Office-headed paper (as opposed to Buckingham Palace notepaper). The fear, however, was that 'a message sent by a Minister will not be sufficiently appreciated'.[37] Such bureaucratic debates confirm military service at the apex of the hierarchy and are suggestive of its durability as a contributing factor to the absence of the civilian male in commemorative practices.

The boundary between military and civilian identities was not rigid, however, given the mobilisation of the male population under conscription into a 'civilian army' and the dual service at home in uniformed civil and or home defence alongside occupation. Members of civil defence such as Air Raid Precautions were embodied in propaganda posters, and these are paralleled in post-war commemoration, as is the Merchant Navy: both are represented in sculpture and stained glass, for example. Grimsby Town Hall has a victory window which depicts the badges of the fighting and non-fighting forces 'to honour and record the service of men and women of Grimsby' (Harry Grylls (designer) Grimsby, 1949).[38] The all-inclusive nature of the dedication, however, belies the challenges of symbolising service which had neither uniform nor badge and it is no coincidence that one element of the campaign for remembrance has been the retrospective granting of honours (Bevin Boys Veterans Badge, 2008; Arctic Star for members of the British Armed Forces and the Merchant Navy on Arctic convoys, 2012; at council level, commemorative medallion Women of Steel, Sheffield, 2016).[39] The nature of reserved occupations did not necessarily lend itself to a group identity and thus to representation as a collective, nor were all civilian occupations as visually distinct as those of firefighter or merchant seaman. This is a challenge not only in figurative sculpture, but in public rituals also; when the Bevin Boys joined the Remembrance parade in 1998, for example, they sported modern white helmets to mark them as miners. Firefighters and the Home Guard had the benefit of being in uniform, although the former defy the periodisation of the war.[40] This contributed to the repurposing of their memorial. In 1991 a bronze memorial entitled 'Blitz' was dedicated to the men and women of the UK Fire Service 'who had made the ultimate sacrifice in the defence of the realm in World War II'. Sculpted by John Mills, the memorial depicts an officer and two firefighters responding to a fire. The instigators, the Firefighters Memorial Charitable Trust, emphasised the depiction: 'Rarely do you see such a work of art with three life-sized bronze figures actively engaged in their professional duties.'[41] Its location is also significant: it stands to the south of St Paul's Cathedral, drawing on the latter's significance as a symbol of British resilience to the Blitz. In 2003, however, it was rededicated as the National Firefighters Memorial to include all firefighters killed in the line of duty (John Mills (Sculptor), Carter Lane Gardens, London, 1991, rededicated 2003).[42]

Befitting the narrative of Britain as the 'Island Nation' that 'rules the waves', the Merchant Navy has been represented at multiple sites including London, Cardiff, Liverpool, Staffordshire, Harwich, Edinburgh and Plymouth, among others. It too inhabits a liminal space between the Forces and civilian occupations.[43] The Tower Hill memorial (London) was erected after the First World War (Edwin Lutyens (designer); William Reid-Dick (sculptor), London, 1928) and extended after the Second (Edward Maufe (designer); Charles Wheeler (sculptor), 1955) with a memorial depicting staunch masculinity. The posture parallels that of the depiction of the soldier (Fig. 9.4), for example, on the London and North Western Railway War Memorial (Reginald Wynn Owen (architect), Ambrose Neale (sculptor), Euston Station, London 1921) and the monumentality of his coat suggests both his battle against the elements and a uniform by paralleling representations of the soldier's greatcoat, for example, by Charles Jagger on the Royal Artillery Memorial (Fig. 9.4).[44]

Catherine Moriarty has explored the impact of the absence of the body of the military male—abroad, and, at worst, with no known grave—in the commemorative practices after the First World War and, specifically, figurative sculpture which 'replaced the many absent, fragmented corpses which were, at this time, still being salvaged from the battlefields, reinterred and, if possible identified'.[45] In the case of the Merchant Navy, whose bodies were often lost at sea and who have 'no known grave', this monument too acts as substitute corporeality.

Juliette Pattinson, Arthur McIvor and Linsey Robb suggest that the predominant characteristic of the memorials to civilians is that they commemorate extraordinary service. We find women who defied the gender norms of their day, such as those of the Special Operations Executive, and men, such as Alan Turing, both by his brain and his sexuality.[46]

Fig. 9.4 Charles Wheeler's representation of a Merchant Seaman (Author's copyright)

The secondary literature on men in reserved occupations has tended to focus on working-class masculinities, and the specific roles of firemen, miners, agricultural workers, the Merchant Navy and members of the Home Guard (who encompassed men of varied occupations).[47] The statistics, however, list the four largest civilian occupations of the middle of the war (1942) as metals, engineering, vehicles and shipbuilding; the distributive trades; national and local government; and transport and shipping (followed by 'miscellaneous services'). Although these figures do not distinguish by gender of the employee, and industry dominates, this suggests that reserved white-collar occupations are worthy of greater attention.[48] Many such occupations lack any glamour; men in, say, retail and the civil service were neither undercover nor distinctly visible, nor were they likely to assume a right to recognition and form a collective such as the Bevin Boys Association. A further contributing factor is another legacy of the war: the expansion of 'red tape' in national and local government was hardly popular. *Love Story* (directed by Leslie Arliss, 1944) offers a rare cultural representation of a military-aged civilian male in a feature film, albeit only briefly. The somewhat 'namby-pamby' unnamed young man of the Ministry (which one is also not disclosed, which permits him to stand for any and all) is firmly put in his place by an older, down-to-earth Yorkshire man, Tom Tanner (played by Tom Walls), who calls him a 'bottleneck' and implies what he can do with his precious forms. Bureaucrats, grocers and teachers have proved challenging to integrate in the narrative of the People's War, despite the incorporation of the mundane in the latter.

Although sculptural memorials after the First World War represented only a small percentage of the total, they are common in retrospective memorialisation of the Second perhaps because they permit both symbolism and narrative to educate the unfamiliar.[49] The memorial which engages most in the diversity of wartime occupations is the memorial 'The Women of World War II'. Its design reflects the unique and contentious decision to commemorate women on the home front and in the auxiliary forces side by side: seventeen roles in total (John Mills (sculptor), Whitehall, London, 2005). In the resultant battle over the memorial's design, members of the auxiliary forces, or those in civilian roles, competed as to who had experienced the greater suffering, worst working conditions and had had less fun, and thus exhibited the greatest dedication to the war effort. It is challenging to identify a forum where such a competition could be articulated for male roles, and the exclusively male combat role militates against quite the same paralleling of service possible for women all cast in supporting roles. Objections to the memorial by female veterans suggested it would be more appropriate to commemorate civilian women alongside civilian men, rather than alongside women of the forces. In January 2001, the vice president of the Bevin Boys Association, Warwick H. Taylor, made the fruitless suggestion that 'in all fairness' Bevin Boys should be 'equally named on such a memorial' which could be dedicated to 'the Men and Women of World War II'.[50]

This memorial might suggest a potential shift in the commemoration of men: the proliferation of representations of diverse roles each demanding acknowledgement for *their* place in the People's War. Yet there is no comparable memorial to men. Unlike in the case of women, the gender category of male does not function as an umbrella term under which all war service, whether military or civilian, can be represented. There is, however, one memorial which represents male civilian service alongside military male service, within a stark hierarchy: Paul Day's memorial to the Battle of Britain.

The site chosen on the Victoria Embankment was the smoke outlet for the team locomotives on the District Line of the underground built by the renowned engineer Joseph Bazalgette—a shed-sized horizontal erection that was essentially a chimney. The memorial commemorates the Allied aircrew that fought in the battle, educating the public on the number of different nations involved in the battle for the skies, but it 'was also felt that the men and women of the ground crew, radar system, aircraft production, rescue services and indeed all other participants (practically the whole country) should be honoured too'.[51] In addition to lists of dead crew, there are thus two relief panels. The first commemorates Fighter Command, including the Blitz on London and civil defence workers desperately working in the rubble, as well as a domestic interior. The second panel was to offer 'the wider experience of the Nation as a whole at war'. Paul Day described its concentration:

> on the home front, the people who worked outside of Fighter Command ... Notably there is the observer corps, the civilians who were actually sitting in bunkers ... then there's the factory work. I've chosen to broaden my vision of the battle to be inclusive, in some ways to be an educational tool, this wasn't the apotheosis of the young men of the RAF ... the country had to be welded together for us to believe it was possible to withstand the might of Germany.[52]

Day was adamant, however, that pilots had to be at the centre of this monument on both sides—'Their lives are at its heart'[53]—reinforcing the conventional hierarchy of service. In terms of depictions of gender roles, there is one female pilot (well camouflaged), Women's Royal Naval Service (WRNS or, more commonly, Wren) plotters, factory girls and housewives; the males include pilots and ground crew, gunners on anti-aircraft batteries and helmeted civil defence workers battling the consequences of air raids. The second frieze begins with a public air raid shelter. It is populated predominantly by women and children of both sexes, but there is a man in a cloth cap at the front, presumably an observer outside the shelter perusing the skies; the domestic interior also includes a middle-aged man also gazing up above as his wife, perhaps, pours the tea.[54] The factory is exclusively female, combat is exclusively male, and the civilian males depicted are either too young or bordering on being too old to be eligible for military service, perpetrating the invisibility of conscription-aged men on the home front.

GENDER IN WAR: THEORY AND PRACTICE

The existing models of the gender order in wartime can be illuminating, but do not fully explain why and how civilian men are—or are not—commemorated. Polarisation theory places men and women in relation: at one end, the militarised male goes to war, to defend domestic femininity at the other.[55] Penny Summerfield's 'gender contract' describes a similar relationship between the sexes, in which 'men were pledged to fight for women, who undertook to maintain home and family. These were the patriotic wartime roles of the two sexes.'[56] However polarisation and the gender contract could not survive the exigencies of war, and in particular, the increased demand for labour. Margaret and Patrice Higonnet introduced the iconic metaphor of the double helix to describe why, despite their potential, neither world war led to significant change in the distance between the sexes, in male dominance and female subservience:

> The female strand on the helix is opposed to the male strand, and position on the female strand is subordinate to position on the male strand. The image of the double helix allows us to see that, although the roles of men and women vary greatly from culture to culture, their relationship is in some sense constant.[57]

In the First World War, this hierarchy was stated clearly, for example, on the poster which described a member of the Queen Mary Army Auxiliary Corps as 'the girl behind the man behind the gun'.[58]

Today, we can see both these models represented on Day's memorial: the opposite ends of the spectrum represented in the heroism of the pilots and the domesticity of the tea-pouring mother; the double helix suggested by the distinction maintained between the male combatant and even uniformed female service: only the male pilot can break out of the physical confines of the structure. However, civilian men's position in the gender order is more ambiguous: members of the Women's Auxiliary Airforce (WAAFs) in the plotting room are clearly lower in the hierarchy than the combat pilots, but where do they stand, for example, in comparison to the male civil defence workers? Their presence suggests a need for a third model of gender in war, one which allows for fuzzy boundaries, the centre of the gender spectrum where masculinities and femininities overlapped. This overlap should not merely be understood as transgression (with women encroaching on male roles), but as the area where civilian and military—and male and female—roles were less obviously distinct, sharing proximity to the war effort, similar living conditions, and risk to life or limb.

It is this ambiguous status in the fuzzy gender boundaries of war that explains the nigh invisibility of the young civilian male at war: only by his absence can the gender order appear stable. As Linsey Robb argues, in wartime representations industrial workers were at best depicted as 'the men behind the man behind the gun'; but this was a position hitherto reserved for 'the girl'.[59] The dearth of figurative representation on war memorials speaks to his elusive masculinity, rendered ambiguous by his uneasy relationship to the hegemonic masculine role in war, and by the gendering of the home front as a feminine space. It is also suggestive of a hierarchy of civilian roles that sits uncomfortably within the rhetoric of being 'all in it together', but which militates against a common collective identity in which all contributions really were or are deemed of equal value. In representations of women, the breadth of roles adopted are acknowledged, but their potential to disrupt hierarchies of service is limited when they are reduced to the collective of a gender identity and located firmly as peculiarities of the war. This is particularly apparent on the monument to The Women of World War II which represents women through their gendered clothing from which the body is also absent. The wartime rhetoric which emphasised how exceptional these roles were and that expressed gratitude for the sacrifice women had made in denying their true female natures for the duration—and the duration only—has proved remarkably resilient in a society otherwise happy to present the conflict as a war of transfiguration or at least reconfiguration—of class, for example. However, the men who challenged the gender contract most by *not* adopting a military identity, nor even a uniform, are marginalised in commemorative practices—not only memorials but in other forms of cultural representation, such as television. Their roles are insufficiently distinct from those undertaken in peacetime, or in war by women, and therefore undermine the hierarchies of service which underpin the gender order.

Civilian men's inconsistent access to memorialisation echoes contemporary suspicions of their commitment to the war effort. The continuities in these men's professional lives militates against their inclusion in a post-war narrative predicated on change, both in terms of the disruption wrought to individual lives but also on a collective, national, level. The periodisation of the profession may instead reflect Britain's decline as an industrial nation. Continuity does little to promote contemporary militarism or voluntarism, embedded in British commemorative practices, albeit those pertaining to men. Most civilians did not have a sense of entitlement to public recognition through their occupations. Nor did all occupations lend themselves to a group identity and thus to self-perception or representation as a collective. Their gender is significant also because there is no generic civilian category for male service. This contrasts with the representation of the range of women's occupations in war: the civilian woman symbolised by turban, pinny or breeches, or the figure of the nurse, who in the original imagining of The Women of World War II was intended to stand for all civilian women alongside three women of the auxiliary services. The wartime visual signifiers of male civilian identities—trouser braces, for example, or a pipe—have not translated into a vocabulary of remembrance, not least because they do not imply obvious activity.[60] Above all, it is the construction of women as providing support for military men that problematises men in similar support roles undistinguished by gender or role. Because of their capacity to disrupt conventional narratives of service, of masculinity and of the gender order, the majority thus remain largely invisible.

NOTES

1. The Register can be consulted at: http://www.iwm.org.uk/memorials/search. Accessed 23 May 2017. The Register includes memorials to members of the armed forces, civilians and animals from all wars and to those who died in service.

2. G. Abousnnouga, and D. Machin (2011), 'Visual Discourses of the Role of Women in War Commemoration: A Multimodal Analysis of British War Monuments', *Journal of Language and Politics*, 10:3, pp. 322–346; J. Davies (1992), 'War Memorials', *The Sociological Review*, 40, pp. 112–128; A. Hood (2009), 'Material Culture: the Object' in S. Barber and C. Peniston-Bird (eds.), *History Beyond the Text: A Student's Guide to Approaching Alternative Sources* (London and New York: Routledge), pp. 175–197. See below for gender theorists.

3. N. Johnson (2002), 'Mapping Monuments: The Shaping of Public Space and Cultural Identities', *Visual Communication*, 1:3, pp. 293–298, here p. 296.

4. See, for example, J. Pattinson, A. McIvor and L. Robb (2017), *Men in Reserve: British Civilian Masculinities in the Second World War* (Manchester: Manchester University Press); L. Robb (2015), *Men at Work: The Working Man in British Culture, 1939–1945* (Basingstoke: Palgrave Macmillan) & (2014), '"The Front Line"': Firefighting in British Culture, 1939–1945', *Contemporary British History*, 29:2, pp. 179–198.

5. The roles of 'amber' on a traffic light is an accessible way of imagining this category. 'Fuzzy logic', 'fuzzy boundaries' and 'vagueness' have been applied in a wide variety of contexts from computer science to biology to educational theory. I first found its application to gender in I. Visser (2002), 'Prototypes of Gender: Conceptions of Feminine and Masculine', *Women's Studies International Forum*, 25:5, pp. 529–539.

6. J. Winter (2006), *Remembering War: The Great War between Memory and History in the Twentieth Century* (New Haven, CT: Yale University Press), p. 45.

7. G. Stamp (2010), 'The Planned World War II Memorial to the Dead of RAF Bomber Command', *Apollo*, mvi, 80. My thanks to Adrian Churchman for drawing my attention to this.

8. For a listing, see the National Memorial Arboretum's (NMA) website: http://www.thenma.org.uk/whats-here/memorial-listing/. Accessed 22 May 2017.

9. Cited from the NMA website: http://www.thenma.org.uk/whats-here/about-the-memorials/. Accessed 20 April 2017.

10. Bill Bond in Stephen Saunders (Director/Producer) (2008), *A Day to Remember*, ASA Productions, Film.

11. War Memorials in England and Wales, Guidance for Custodians, Burials Team, DCA, March 2007: http://webarchive.nationalarchives.gov.uk/+/http:/www.dca.gov.uk/corbur/war-memorial-guidance.pdf. Accessed 26 April 2017.

12. Janet Watson (2014), 'Total War and Total Anniversary: The Material Culture of Second World War Commemoration in Britain', in L. Noakes and J. Pattinson (eds.), *British Cultural Memory and the Second World War* (London: Bloomsbury), p. 176. The excluded to which Watson refers are those who fought under the Imperial flag, particularly if not white. She describes these men too as 'invisible'.

13. C. Peniston-Bird (2012), 'War and Peace in the Cloakroom: The Controversy over the Memorial to the Women of World War II', in S. Gibson and S. Mollan (eds.), *Representations of Peace and Conflict* (Basingstoke: Palgrave Macmillan); Peniston-Bird (2013), 'The People's War in Personal Testimony and Bronze: Sorority and the Memorial to The Women of World War II', in Noakes and Pattinson (eds.), *British Cultural Memory*, pp. 67–87.

14. Schedule of Reserved Occupations (Provisional) (1939) (London: HMSO).

15. War Cabinet, release from the Armed Forces of Key Men in Industry. Note by the Minister for Co-Ordination of Defence. 4 October, 1939. (W.M. (39) 37th) The National Archives (TNA), CAB 67/1/20. This is not to argue there was no hierarchy of military service personnel within that category. Julian Maclaran-Ross, a writer conscripted into the army, observed that in Wrens' eyes, for example, 'RAF officers rated tops, being classified in turn by rank and number of decorations, naval officers came second and Brown Jobs a long long way behind.' J. Maclaren-Ross (1965), *Memoirs of the Forties* (London: Cardinal), p. 104.

16. T. Hickman (2008), *Called Up, Sent Down: The Bevin Boys' War* (Stroud: History Press). They served alongside volunteers, and older and reserved miners.

17. For a contemporary representation, see, for example, J. Lee (1942), 'Smiling Through: Key Man / "T'aint no use. Everytime I tries to join anything, they tells me that Oldest Inhabitant be Reserved Occupation"', *Evening News*, 24 February, British Cartoon Archive (BCA), JL2045. For discussion of the pressures on men and the relationship to physical fitness, see C. M. Peniston-Bird (2003), 'Classifying the Body in the Second World War: British Men In and Out of Uniform', *Body and Society*, 9:4, pp. 31–48.

18. War Memorials Register (hereafter WMR), Imperial War Museum, Reference number: 56324. The register can be found at http://www. iwm.org.uk/memorials/search. Accessed 7 March 2017.

19. Both series can be seen in the catalogue of the Imperial War Museum: for Roy Anthony Nockolds, 'The Attack begins in the Factory', see, for example, ART IWM PST 14359; for Fred Taylor's series 'They also Serve', see, for example, ART IWM PST 3427.

20. See Pattinson, McIvor and Robb, *Men in Reserve*; Robb, *Men at Work*; P. Summerfield and C. M. Peniston-Bird (2007), *Contesting Home Defence: Men, Women and the Home Guard in the Second World War* (Manchester: Manchester University Press).

21. See C. M. Peniston-Bird (2018), 'Were Fires Started? Exploring Gender in British Cinema of the Second World War', in S. Edwards, F. Sayer and M. Dolski (eds.), *Histories on Screen: The Past and Present in Anglo-American Cinema and Television* (London: Bloomsbury Academic).

22. Ralph C. Sunley of Atcraft Works, Alperton, Middlesex, 'Work Without Praise', *The Times*, 23 August 1941, p. 5.

23. Robb, *Men at Work*, pp. 30, 19.

24. An account of the raid can be found in the Aviation Archive, 'Air Raid at Filton 25th September 1940': http://www.aviationarchive.org.uk/stories/pages.php?enum=GE126&pnum=0&maxp=8. Accessed 7 August 2016. The reredos is also mentioned in M. Halsum (n. d.), *Filton Parish Church: A History and Guide* (Bristol: UEW Bristol Printing and Stationery Services) and W.L. Harris (1981), *Filton Gloucestershire: Some Account of the Village and Parish* (W.L. & L.N. Harris). I am deeply indebted to Bob Conway and Chris Gooding, PCC Secretary, St Peter's Church, Filton, Bristol who both responded in a detail beyond the call of duty to my enquiries.

25. WMR 6779, 11503, 57727, 34414.

26. WMR 11822.

27. WMR 16934.

28. WMR 21779.

29. WMR lists over 10,000 hits for the description 'gave their lives', as opposed to 1,609 for 'lost their lives'. The latter is also found in commemorations of military deaths, but it is interesting to consider further in which contexts and with what sense of victimhood. See, for example, WMR 66093.

30. WMR 65629.

31. WMR 57677, 64416, 22217, 21619.

32. See, for example, the memorial in Cheshire at Bentley Motors plc which consists of a three-bladed propeller with dedicatory plaques on each blade, placed on a circular board with wooden surround. At the centre

of the blades is a decorative laurel wreath enclosing a dove. It commemorates 'our / colleagues who lost / their lives [at 3.09 pm on Sunday / 29th December / 1940/] whilst working / in the factory to / support the war / effort'. WMR 57677.

33. This is noted above, but see also WMR 11352.

34. WMR 21627.

35. WMR 66871.

36. WMR 4150.

37. TNA, RG26/20, Civilian deaths due to war operations. I am most indebted to Jayne Morgan, MA, for sharing this reference with me.

38. WMR 51878.

39. These include the badges of the Royal Observer Corps, National Fire Service, Civil Defence, Red Cross, Women's Land Army, St John Ambulance Brigade and the Special Constabulary and Borough Police, Mines Disposal Unit, Civil Defence, the Women's Voluntary Service, as well as the services. WMR 51878.

40. For the Home Guard, see, for example, the 'new church', Holy Cross, Ferrymead Gardens, Greenford Magna, Middlesex, erected in 1939–1940. A paving stone within informs that the lanterns by the south doors perpetuate the memory of the Greenford Home Guard (1940–1945). (Although the Home Guard was disbanded in 1944.) See also the Home Guard Memorial (Corbyn Head, Torquay, 2000) which serves a triple function to commemorate service, all Home Guards who died performing their duties and specifically those who died in a local incident. The juxtaposition warns against trivialising the force.

41. 'The Worshipful Company of Firefighters': http://www.firefighterscompany.org/charities/charities-supported/firefighters-memoriable.html. Accessed 7 March 2017.

42. Ibid.

43. See, for example, the Merchant Seafarers' War Memorial, Cardiff Bay Wales (Brian Fell (sculptor), Cardiff Bay, Wales, 1997). The memorial to the Merchant Navy Convoy (2003) commemorates over 46,000 British merchant seafarers and fishermen lost in all conflicts of the twentieth century. Planted at the NMA, it originally took the shape of 2,535 trees representing the British vessels lost: https://monkbarns.wordpress.com/tag/merchant-navy-convoy/. Accessed 7 August 2016.

44. Royal Artillery Memorial (Charles Jagger (sculptor) and Lionel Pearson (architect), Hyde Park Corner, London, 1925); C. Moriarty (2004), 'Remnants of Patriotism: the Commemorative Representation of the Greatcoat after the First World War', *Oxford Art Journal*, 27:3, pp. 291–309.

45. C. Moriarty (1995), 'The Absent Dead and Figurative First World War Memorials', *Transactions of the Ancient Monuments Society*, 39, pp. 7–40.
46. Special Operations Executive (plaque, Westminster Abbey, London, 1996); (Bust depicting Violette Szabo, Karen Newman (sculptor), Albert Embankment, London, 2009). See also Alan Mathieson Turing (Glyn Hughes (sculptor), Sackville Park, Manchester, 2001).
47. Summerfield and Peniston-Bird, *Contesting Home Defence*; A. Mak (2017), 'Conspicuous Consumption in Wartime? Welsh Mining Communities and Women in Munition Factories', in C. Peniston-Bird and E. Vickers (eds.), *Gender and the Second World War: Lessons of War* (London: Palgrave).
48. P. Howlett (1995), *Fighting with Figures: A Statistical Digest of the Second World War* (London: Central Statistical Office), p. 38, Table 3.3 'Distribution of total manpower'.
49. According to Adrian Gregory, in total only 2.2% of British war memorials were sculptural. A. Gregory (2008), *The Last Great War: British Society and the First World War* (Cambridge: Cambridge University Press), p. 258.
50. This is documented in the files of the memorial charity, 1 Jan 01 YG/4*700; Planning. Files in possession of the author.
51. Cited on the Battle of Britain Historical Society: https://bbm.org.uk/airmen/bobhistsoc.htm. Accessed 8 March 2017.
52. Paul Day on *A Day to Remember*.
53. Paul Day, description of monument scenes by the sculptor: https://bbm.org.uk/airmen/prog-scenes.htm. Accessed 7 March 2017.
54. Contemporary images would suggest this is inaccurate; see, for example, the image of Hawker Hurricanes in assembly shops Brooklands, Brooklands Museum archive courtesy of BAE Systems on Exploring Surrey's Past: http://www.exploringsurreyspast.org.uk/themes/subjects/military/battle_of_britain/airfield/hawker_hurricanes_in_assembly_shops_brooklands_small-jpg/. Accessed 14 March 2007; or Elsie Dalton Hewland (1940–1947), 'Assembling a Hawker Hurricane', Manchester City Galleries: https://artuk.org/discover/artworks/assembling-a-hawker-hurricane-205190. Accessed 14 March 2007.
55. J.B. Elshtain (1987), *Women and War* (Brighton: Harvester); J. Bourke (1996), *Dismembering the Male: Men's Bodies, Britain and the Great War* (London: Reaktion Books), pp. 12–13.
56. P. Summerfield (1997), *'My Dress for an Army Uniform': Gender Instabilities in the Two World Wars* (Lancaster: University of Lancaster).
57. M.R. and P.L.R. Higonnet (1987), 'The Double Helix', in M. Randolph Higonnet et al. (eds), *Behind the Lines: Gender and the Two World Wars* (London: Yale University Press), pp. 31–47, here p. 34.

58. The image can be viewed, for example, at the National Army Museum, accession number NAM. 1989-06-78-1: https://collection.nam.ac.uk/detail.php?acc=1989-06-78-1. Accessed 28 February 2017.

59. Robb, *Men at Work*, p. 58.

60. See, for example, J. Lee (1940), 'Smiling Through: New Poor / "Excuse me, but may I fill my pipe?"', *Evening News*, 22 October, BCA JL1773; Lee (1941), 'Smiling Through: Public Menace / "Avoid him like the plague. That's not a saxophone in that case … it's his borrowing pipe."' *Evening News*, 24 June. BCA JL2976; J. Lee (1942), 'Smiling Through: Tension: 'Oh, any kind of belt. Just one to tighten. Actually, of course, I wear braces.' *Evening News*, 11 March. BCA JL2057. See also Peter Fraser's famous poster 'Dig on for Victory', for example, on TNA website: http://www.nationalarchives.gov.uk/wp-content/uploads/2014/03/inf-3-96.jpg. Accessed 28 February 2017.

Acknowledgements This chapter is dedicated to Catherine Eaglestone for her unstinting support.

Erratum to: Fantasies of the 'Soldier Hero', Frustrations of the Jedburghs

Juliette Pattinson

Erratum to:
Chapter 2   in: L. Robb and J. Pattinson (eds.), *Men, Masculinities and Male Culture in the Second World War,* **Genders and Sexualities in History, https://doi.org/10.1057/978-1-349-95290-8_2**

In the original version of the book, the PhD thesis by J Morley [2] referenced as 34 in Chapter 2 was inadvertently omitted from the section entitled "Make me a Soldier, Lord … Make Me a Man': Growing up in the Shadow of War". The author [1] would like to apologise for this accidental omission.

(1) J Pattinson
(2) J Morley

The online version of the original chapter can be found under
https://doi.org/10.1057/978-1-349-95290-8_2

E1
L. Robb and J. Pattinson (eds.), *Men, Masculinities and Male Culture in the Second World War,* Genders and Sexualities in History,
https://doi.org/ 10.1057/978-1-349-95290-8_10

INDEX

© The Editor(s) (if applicable) and The Author(s) 2018
L. Robb and J. Pattinson (eds.), *Men, Masculinities and Male Culture in the Second World War*, Genders and Sexualities in History, https://doi.org/ 10.1057/978-1-349-95290-8

0203230714

CPI Antony Rowe
Eastbourne, UK
August 26, 2019